# 法庭口译
## 案例解析

A Casebook of Court Interpreting

主　　编：赵军峰

执行主编：张鲁平

编　　者：赵军峰　张鲁平　罗雯琪

　　　　　王　超　管　雯　胡晓凡

主　　审：张新红

中国政法大学出版社

2023·北京

**图书在版编目（ＣＩＰ）数据**

法庭口译案例解析/赵军峰主编. —北京：中国政法大学出版社，2023.7

ISBN 978-7-5764-1037-2

Ⅰ.①法… Ⅱ.①赵… Ⅲ.①法庭－英语－口译 Ⅳ.①D9

中国国家版本馆 CIP 数据核字(2023)第 146868 号

-----------------------------------------------------------------------------------------------

| 出 版 者 | 中国政法大学出版社 |
|---|---|
| 地　　址 | 北京市海淀区西土城路 25 号 |
| 邮寄地址 | 北京 100088 信箱 8034 分箱　邮编 100088 |
| 网　　址 | http://www.cuplpress.com (网络实名：中国政法大学出版社) |
| 电　　话 | 010-58908586(编辑部) 58908334(邮购部) |
| 编辑邮箱 | zhengfadch@126.com |
| 承　　印 | 固安华明印业有限公司 |
| 开　　本 | 720mm×960mm　　1/16 |
| 印　　张 | 20 |
| 字　　数 | 350 千字 |
| 版　　次 | 2023 年 7 月第 1 版 |
| 印　　次 | 2023 年 7 月第 1 次印刷 |
| 定　　价 | 99.00 元 |

# 前 言

　　根据适用的场景，口译可分为会议口译、联络口译、讲座口译、商务口译、健康口译以及法律口译六大类。其中法律口译（legal interpreting）泛指发生在法律场景下的口译，如法庭、律师事务所以及与法律相关的学术交流、国际会议、新闻发布会等。在法庭上发生的传译被称为司法口译（judiciary interpreting）或者法庭口译（court interpreting），在法庭外的其他法律场所发生的传译被称为准司法口译（quasi-judiciary interpreting）。

　　法庭话语作为机构性话语一种特殊的功能语域，具有很强的即席性、互动性和规约性，在本质上是言语行为的类聚系统。法庭口译的要求是忠实于原语，这种忠实要求译文达到原语的效果，真实表达原语者的意图，严格保留原语的形式、风格、语气以及言外之力。但要从法律和语言两方面来实现译文与原文的"法律上的对等"，对法律口译员来说是极大的挑战。从言语交际的角度来看，法庭口译是实现操不同语言、有不同文化背景的诉讼各方以及庭审法官、合议庭或陪审团成员之间互相理解沟通的桥梁与中介。从法律沟通的角度讲，法庭译员经常肩负着沟通不同法系之间差异性的重任。与此同时，法庭口译也是维护和保障法律赋予诉讼各方的公民权和法律平等的必要条件。

　　西方的许多国家都是移民大国，如美国、加拿大、澳大利亚等。移民潮导致了大量说各种语言的人员的涌入，移民潮导致这些国家各色人俱全，造就了"一法多语"（One Law, Many Languages）现象。在这样的背景之下，法律口译就显得非常重要，并成为必然。我国是一个多民族、多语言、多法系的国家。许多少数民族依然保留自己的语言，在这些少数民族聚居地区的法院，通常使用当地通用的语言进行审讯。对于不懂当地通用语的诉讼参与人，应当提供诉讼参与人所用语言和该地区方言之间的法庭翻译服务。随着经济全球化步伐的加快，特别是中国加入世界贸易组织以来，中国的对外交往大大增加，经贸来往也更加频繁。与此同时，在经济、贸易、文化方面不可避免地会产生一些纠纷以及由此产生的诉讼。中国法庭将会越来越多地处理涉外纠纷案件，由此产生的对于法律口译人员的需求也会大量增加。

美国国会早在 1978 年即通过了《法庭口译人员法》，并于 1988 年进行了第二次修订，该法为民事和刑事诉讼中使用庭审口译服务提供了依据，从而保障了使用不同语言者在法律上平等的权利。该法同时也制定了联邦法庭口译人员考试（The Federal Court Interpreter Certification Examination，简称 FCICE）。该考试为法庭口译实践引入了"以表现为基础的口译员测试"（performance-based interpreter testing）这一概念，要求参加考试者做大量针对该测试的操练，反映了从事法庭口译实践所需的知识、能力、技巧以及其中的难点。只有通过考试的口译人员才能获得庭审口译员证书，成为法庭口译人员，这项规定从制度上确保了法庭口译的质量。自此，其他移民国家纷纷出台相关的法律，规范了法庭口译的过程，保证了公民获得公平、公正审判的权利。我国自 1954 年的宪法开始，直至现行宪法的 2004 年修正案以及其他法律，多次立法为少数民族使用其语言文字的权利和当事人享有法庭翻译的权利提供保障。我国《刑事诉讼法》和《民事诉讼法》中也有涉及法庭翻译人员条款，主要涉及翻译作为诉讼参与人的义务的规定，但对如何选择和聘请翻译人员，翻译人员应当具有的资格、翻译性质、翻译操作过程等均未提及。可见，中国法律口译的立法工作仍然任重道远。

本书是针对翻译硕士专业学位（MTI）教指委所颁布的指导性教学大纲规定的选修课法律口译而开发的，凸显口译训练的高层次、专业性和应用型的导向。本书的主编系广东外语外贸大学翻译学研究中心主任、高级翻译学院教授，法律语言学博士，翻译学博士生导师，主持和参加了多项法律语言学和法律翻译的国家社科及省级以上科研项目；参与本书编写和审阅的团队成员均有多年的法律口译实践经验，其中主审张新红博士是广东外语外贸大学国际商务英语学院法律英语系主任、法庭口译专家，执行主编张鲁平博士是中国政法大学法律话语研究中心研究员、资深法律翻译。

全书分为 14 个单元，围绕五个宏观法律专题板块展开。这五个板块分别是法律交流、法律体制、中国庭审口译、英美庭审口译以及替代性争议解决方式（ADR），基本上涵盖了法律口译的主要领域，并为口译学员提供了系统全面的学习及实训内容。每个单元均由专题知识、热身练习、实战训练、参考译文和句子精炼等组成。专题知识（legal knowledge）主要是给读者提供一些与各单元口译训练相关的法律知识，可以和各单元第二部分的词汇热身结合使用。本书附录将各单元的词汇整理为英汉对照表，便于读者查阅。参考译文则便于读者自我检查或进行双向口译训练，而句子精炼使读者就一些关键的句型和知识点开展针对性强化训练。

鉴于与 MTI 系列的其他口译类图书有一定的衔接性和区分性，本书有较强的专业针对性，以法律知识专题为线索进行编排，不再对一般性的口译技巧做细致的讲解和归纳，但在编写时充分考虑了语言的循序渐进，由简而繁。在选材上，凸显口译的实践性、真实性和时效性，选取真实的语料和场景，既有时下的法律访谈、新闻发布会、全真的大会演讲，也有庭审准备、法庭辩论和宣读判决等。在不同的法律专题下，各单元依据口译实践的技巧规律选取和编排练习，兼顾英汉、汉英互译训练，由对话口译、段落口译向连续传译乃至同声传译过渡，穿插一些核心的口译技巧点评。口译能力的提高离不开口译技能和专题知识，因此本书的特点是知识性为主，读者通过学习要逐步建立属于自己的"词汇库"（glossary），译者的成功不外乎"功到自然成"，只有"do your homework"（苦练内功），才能做到"no surprises"（有备无患）。

本书的读者定位主要是已经选修过基础口译和交替传译的翻译专业本科及硕士学员，该阶段的重点是进行法律主题内容的训练。此外，本书也可以供法律英语高年级学生、英汉双语程度较高的法律专业毕业生及对法律口译感兴趣的法律从业人员使用。

本书得到了中国政法大学专业学位研究生培养专项及教育部人文社会科学规划基金项目（18YJAZH131）资助，谨致谢忱！

本书引用的材料尽量在参考文献中有体现，若有遗漏之处敬请指正并与我们联系，不胜感谢。

由于时间仓促，本书在编写的过程中难免存在遗漏和不足，欢迎读者诸君在使用时提出宝贵意见建议。

编者谨识

2023 年孟夏

# 目 录

CONTENTS

前　言 ··························································· 001

第一单元　法律访谈 ········································· 001

第二单元　立法听证会 ······································ 023

第三单元　记者招待会 ······································ 047

第四单元　中国法律体制 ···································· 078

第五单元　大陆法系及普通法系 ···························· 097

第六单元　庭审前奏 ········································· 116

第七单元　法庭交锋 ········································· 131

第八单元　法庭审判 ········································· 159

第九单元　法庭调查（英美法系） ·························· 184

第十单元　法庭交锋（英美法系） ·························· 209

第十一单元　最后陈述及评议判决（英美法系） ············ 227

第十二单元　诉讼外争端解决 ······························ 245

第十三单元　调解与仲裁 ···································· 267

第十四单元　司法体制改革 ·································· 280

附　录　法庭口译词汇对照表（按单元分） ··············· 283

参考文献 ······················································ 310

后　记 ························································· 312

# Ⅰ. 专题知识 Legal Knowledge

公职律师是在国家行政部门设立的政府律师，由政府支付薪水，属于国家公务员序列，主要办理本机关法律事务，以提高政府机构依法行政水平，在法律上维护国家利益，公职律师不得为社会提供有偿法律服务。

## 一、公职律师的性质

（1）身份的双重性。既是律师，又是公务员。这一特征将公职律师与一般公务员区别开来。公职律师的身份在现实中多数是公务员，有的是政府雇员，有的是依照公务员管理的事业单位人员（如城市管理行政执法局中的公职律师）。

（2）服务的特定性。提供的是公共产品服务，与国家公权力有关，禁止对外执业。在这一点上，要将公职律师同社会律师和法律援助律师区别开来。公职律师不得从事有偿法律服务，不得在律师事务所和法律服务所兼职，不得以律师身份办理本级政府或部门以外的诉讼与非诉讼案件。

（3）管理的双重性。公职律师本身要受所属政府部门的管理，既要接受每年的公务员年度考核，又要接受司法行政机关的资质管理和业务指导，在党纪、政纪方面比社会律师要接受更为严格的约束管理。

（4）工作的特殊性。按照现有公职律师的职责，可以把公职律师概括为行政机关及其首长的"参谋助手"。在为本单位和部门决策提供法律意见时，起着"参谋"的作用，在办理具体法律事务时，又是领导的"助手"。当公务员执行公务时，认为上级的决定或者命令有错误的，可以向上级提出改正或者撤销该决定或者命令的意见；上级不改变该决定或者命令，或者要求立即执行的，公务员应当执行该决定或者命令，执行的后果由上级负责，公务员不承担责任。

（5）服务的无偿性。公职律师在提供法律服务时不向服务对象也即行政机关收取费用。公职律师的工资、福利待遇等由财政部门比照一般公职人员解决。

## 二、公职律师存在的重要性

1. 公职律师的存在有利于提高政府依法行政水平

建设法治国家首先要求有一个法治政府，法治政府的核心是依法行政。依法行政首要在于对行政权力的运作进行有效规范，从而为公民权利的行使提供充分保障，实现公平、正义、自由、秩序等价值目标。在我国，依法行政尚处在初级阶段，无论是观念上还是制度上都面临着挑战。随着法治观念的深入人心，依法行政已逐渐为我国广大人民所熟知，"民告官"的事例不断增多，这对行政机关公职人员法律素质的专业化和普遍化提出了更高的要求。公职律师制度的推行，正是为了适应行政体制改革，适应"管理型"政府向"服务型"政府转变，适应"依法治国"深入开展，适应全民法治意识普遍提高这一系列新的时代特点。公职律师制度推行后，公职律师履行职责、参与行政活动，将有利于提高政府依法行政水平，提升政府形象，降低决策成本。

2. 公职律师的存在有利于维护社会稳定

法律援助制度是国家司法制度的重要组成部分，是国家保障公民合法权益和司法公正不可缺少的重要手段，是社会民主与法治健全程度的反映，是社会文明进步的重要标志。在改革开放和发展社会主义市场经济条件下，法律援助制度对推动民主与法治建设，维护社会稳定，保护公民合法权益，起着极其重要而独特的作用。但是，目前我国开展法律援助的现状还不能满足弱势群体对法律援助需求的日益扩大，存在着力量整合缺乏、经费人员严重不足、机构不够健全等诸多问题。为受援人提供法律援助属公职律师的职责范围。建立公职律师制度，充分发挥公职律师在法律援助工作中的作用，能缓解当前法律援助人员严重不足的压力，促进社会公平与公正，维护弱势群体的合法权益，维护社会稳定。

3. 公职律师的存在有利于服务经济建设

政府是市场经济的宏观管理者，政府对经济的管理水平在很大程度影响着国民经济的发展速度。我国在加入世界贸易组织（WTO）后，对政府管理经济的水平提出了更高的要求。在 WTO 的 29 个协议中，除个别条款涉及企业，其余均与政府有关，尤其是政府的立法与决策。政府决策水平的重要性可想而知。政府行为的法治化是"入世"后社会主体对政府行为的必然要求，也是政府面临的一次深刻挑战。市场经济是法治经济，各种主体都有明确的法律规范，我国加入 WTO 后，经济一体化的趋势更迫切需要政府将自己的行政活动纳入法治化轨道。而公职律师的主要职责正是在于当好各级政府职能部门法律方面的参谋和助手；在于规范行政行为，提高政府的决策水平以促进经济建设的稳步进展。

## II. 词汇热身 Vocabulary Warm-up

*Directions*：*Give the English equivalents of the following Chinese expressions*：

| | | |
|---|---|---|
| 依法治国 | 普法规划 | 润滑剂 |
| 法律援助 | 互谅互让 | 依法执政 |
| 弱势群体 | 改造罪犯 | 公职律师 |
| 人民调解 | 法律顾问 | 应运而生 |
| 便民措施 | 公证员 | |
| 拖欠工资 | 和谐社会 | |

*Directions*：*Give the Chinese equivalents of the following English expressions*：

| | | |
|---|---|---|
| chief judge | adjudicative | delinquent |
| chamber | multiple | squander |
| judiciary | murder | out of hand |
| appeal court | levelheaded | consuming |
| appellate | anguishing | |
| vandalism | juvenile | |

## III. 课文口译 Text for Interpreting

### ◆ *Passage 1*

**Directions**：*Listen to the passage and interpret from Chinese into English at the* *end of each segment.*

（下面是记者于 2006 年就公职律师、公司律师制度试点对司法部前部长张福森进行的专访。）

**问：**司法部提出开展公职律师和公司律师制度试点的背景是什么？//

**答：**我们提出开展公职律师、公司律师制度试点，主要是基于两点考虑：一方面，是发展社会主义市场经济和依法治国的客观要求。依法治国方略的实施、社会主义市场经济体制的建立和社会主义法律体系的健全，以及加入世界贸易组织和经济全球化的趋势，对政府依法行政和企业依法经营管理提出了更高的要求，政府机关和企业面临越来越多更为复杂的法律事务，迫切需要建立公职律师、公司律师这种专门的律师队伍来提供法律服务，以维护国家利益和企业的合法权益。// 另一方面，是进一步完善律师组织结构的需要。建立中国特色律师制度既要从国情出发，也需要借鉴国外的有益做法。从一些律师制度比较发达的国家的情况来看，这些国家大多设有公职律师和公司律师制度。而我国除了军队律师外，只有社会律师一种形式，律师结构需要进一步发展和完善，逐步形成社会律师、公职律师、公司律师等队伍并存、相互配合、优势互补的格局。以此为基础，进一步完善我国律师制度。//

**问：**公职律师、公司律师同社会律师有什么不同？//

**答：**公职律师、公司律师与社会律师最明显的区别有两点：一是身份的双重性。公职律师供职于政府职能部门或行使政府职能的部门，公司律师属企业的内部人员。因此，公职律师既是国家公务员又是律师，公司律师既是企业的职工或雇员又是律师。// 二是服务对象的固定性。公职律师、公司律师只能为本单位提供法律服务，不得面向社会从事有偿法律服务，不得在律师事务所和法律服务所兼职，不得以律师身份办理本单位以外的诉讼与非诉讼案件。//

公职律师、公司律师有着自己独特的优势：一是专门的法律职业资格。公职律师、公司律师必须具有律师资格或法律职业资格，接受更为严格的继续教育和执业纪律、职业道德培训。// 二是职责和权利广泛。公职律师、公司律师可以深入、广泛地参与到本部门、本单位工作的决策、执行、监督等环节之中，而且在调查取证、查阅案件材料，以及加入律师协会、参加律师职称评定等方面与社会律师享有同等的权利。// 三是地位明确。当今的律师业已是发展较为成熟的法律服务行业，建立公职律师、公司律师制度更容易得到社会的认同，也有助于构筑以律师为主体的法律服务业平台。// 四是符合国际惯例。当今世界上一些法制比较健全的国家，其政府部门和大的企业都有自己专门的律师。我国建立公职律师、公司律师制度，可以便于对外交往。//

**问**：作为主管部门，请谈谈司法部将以何种形式对公职律师、公司律师的责权利进行明确界定？//

**答**：现行律师法对此尚未作出明确规定，目前公职律师、公司律师制度作为一项改革措施，正处于试点阶段。为保证试点工作规范、有序进行，司法部于去年制定了开展公职律师和公司律师试点工作的意见，明确了公职律师、公司律师的职责范围、权利和义务。// 下一步，我们将及时总结试点工作的经验，抓紧研究起草相关的工作规范。一旦条件成熟，我们将及时提出修改律师法的建议，尽快把公职律师、公司律师制度纳入我国律师制度的整体框架。//

**问**：公职律师、公司律师的发展前景如何？//

**答**：一个制度是否有生命力，我认为最重要的就是看这个制度是否有产生、存在和发展的客观基础，也就是说社会需不需要这个制度。法律制度也不例外。实践证明，一个法制比较健全的国家，必然要求：政府必须依法行政，企业必须依法经营。律师作为法律的实践家，深谙各种法律、制度和规则，必然在其中扮演重要角色。// 我国的公职律师、公司律师制度正是在深入推进依法治国伟大进程中和全面建设小康社会这一大背景下出现的，可以说是应运而生。现在，无论是政府职能部门还是大的公司企业都非常关注、重视这项制度的试点工作，有些单位已经颁证挂牌，有些单位正在抓紧做试点的准备工作。// 从目前情况来看，发展势头很好。我认为，这项制度是一个具有旺盛生命力的制度，实践必将证明，它会对我国的政治生活、经济发展和社会进步产生积极而深远的影响，同时也必将进一步推动我国律师制度的发展和完善。//

## ◆ *Passage 2*

**Directions**：*Listen to the passage and interpret from English into Chinese at the end of each segment.*

(*The following is an interview with New York's Chief Judge Judith S. Kaye, who was appointed by Governor Mario Cuomo in* 1983 *to the New York Court of Appeals, she became the first woman to serve on the state's highest court. When sworn in as chief judge on March* 23, 1993, *she became the first woman to hold New York's highest judicial office. She retired in December* 2008 *under New York's mandatory retirement rules.*)

**Justice Timmons-Goodson**: Some have described you as having risen from a "modest beginnings". Would you share a bit about your early life and how it shaped your career choice? //

**Chief Judge Kaye**: My little granddaughter one day startled me by saying, "Tell me about your life." I began, "I was born on a farm. My parents came from Poland and settled in upstate New York." She interrupted and said, "No, no, I don't mean that. Tell me about your life since yesterday." So I ask, do you really want me to go all the way back to the farm, and then the ladies' clothing store, the village of Monticello, New York? It could take days! I'll start in high school, in Monticello, where my burning ambition was to be a journalist. // That took me to New York City and Barnard College, in the shadow of the Columbia Journalism School. I nurtured that ambition, but the world of journalism was not welcoming to women back in the late 1950s. I took a job as a social reporter and decided to burnish my résumé with just a touch of law school, never intending to be a lawyer. But after a year in law school, I was bitten. My poor parents back in Monticello! They were bereft about my journalism ambition, but even more so about my becoming a lawyer. A woman lawyer? Who would marry me? //

**Justice Timmons-Goodson**: In appointing you Chief Judge of the State of New York in 1993, Governor Mario Cuomo entrusted you with the leadership of the New York state court system. You had been on the bench less than ten years at the time. Were you prepared for the responsibility? If not, how did you prepare yourself? //

**Chief Judge Kaye**: No one can fully prepare to be chief judge—the demands are huge and different as every day society deposits its cutting-edge problems at the courthouse doors. The unexpected is the norm. It was nice to have had those years on the bench with my colleagues, who were always tremendously supportive, and to be known within the court system. Looking back, I think the two greatest helps were terrific assistants (especially my chambers staff and a very knowledgeable chief administrative judge I get to appoint) and deep breaths. So much can be upsetting if you allow it to be. I also became active in the Conference of Chief Justices and the National Center for State Courts. There's a lot of support and a lot of information available from colleagues like that. //

**Justice Timmons – Goodson:** Roberta Kaplan, your former clerk and the author of a recent tribute to you, has said you have your own jurisprudence, one mindful of the "human dimension" and of how your decisions will affect people's everyday lives. Would you tell us more about your judicial philosophy and how you have approached the decision-making process? //

**Chief Judge Kaye:** I resist the label "philosophy" —maybe that's something other people impose on a judge, like the "activist judge" label if you want to be really critical of a judge's performance. For me, a decision begins with intensive study of the briefs, the record, and the law, and ends with the "common sense" check. The judiciary is, after all, a stare-decisis, precedent-bound, stable institution, but we function in today's world, and we attempt, as well, to anticipate tomorrow in our decisions. A difficult, delicate balance—but, oh my, what a privilege! //

**Justice Timmons–Goodson:** I must ask the question that every female judge is invariably asked: Has your gender made a difference in your judging? //

**Chief Judge Kaye:** I don't think so. We are now four women and three men on the Court of Appeals and we have split on just a couple of issues—like "fees on fees" in shareholder derivative actions. No, I sense no gender boundary on our court. I have observed, however, that during my years as Chief Judge of the State— the executive/administrative, rather than adjudicative, role— there has been a long-overdue awakening to the importance of family law issues and "problem – solving courts" across the nation. And I do note the coincidence of that phenomenon and the arrival of women on the bench—and women chiefs—in large numbers. It's hard to deny a relationship. //

**Justice Timmons – Goodson:** In a 2004 law review article entitled Women

Chiefs: Shaping the Third Branch, after pointing out that one-third of state court chiefs are women, you commented that numbers matter a lot. Why? //

**Chief Judge Kaye:** Absolutely numbers matter. There's comfort in numbers—the company of people who have faced similar challenges and struggles is confidence building. While we can—we do, and we must—persevere alone, there's a natural alliance among us, different as each of us is, that is very strengthening. Not that we are by any means isolationists. //

**Justice Timmons-Goodson:** You were one of the few women to graduate from law school in the 1960s and enter what was then a male-dominated profession. In what ways has your personal struggle been reflected in the New York court system under your leadership? //

**Chief Judge Kaye:** I take no personal credit, but I have to believe that any woman who came through the struggles of the 1960s (and 1970s) would be mindful of the need to hold out a hand to those who come after us. By the way, I do not see the struggle as over, by any means. We make a mistake to assume that it is. I have written about this in my recent Fordham Law Review article. //

**Justice Timmons-Goodson:** You once described your judicial role as a judge of the Court of Appeals as "lawyer heaven". Why? //

**Chief Judge Kaye:** Serving as a judge of the Court of Appeals—one of seven equals—is absolutely the pinnacle of our profession. Every day we are faced with an array of legal issues—from a slip and fall on an icy sidewalk, to multiple murders, and everything in between—that profoundly affect the lives of the particular litigants and the law that governs our society. The colleagues over these past twenty-five years have been superb judges and wonderful friends, and our task is, in collegial fashion, to reach the wisest, best result. The court staff and facilities are excellent. All in all, Lawyer Heaven, don't you agree? //

**Justice Timmons-Goodson:** As chief judge, your role has been twofold: one as a judge and the other as an executive dealing with the administrative aspects of the New York judiciary. Focusing on your executive role, please tell us about your experience running one of the world's largest and most complex court systems. //

**Chief Judge Kaye:** I do have two roles. As Chief Judge of the New York Court of Appeals, I perform an adjudicative role as a member of a great common law court. The other role — that of chief judge of the State of New York — is the executive/administrative role. I head our huge, sprawling judicial branch, with close to 15, 000 employees, 365 courthouses, and roughly four million filings annually. I spend about 80 percent of my time as chief judge of the Court of Appeals, and the other 20 percent as chief judge of the State of New York. Although my adjudicative responsibilities surely present anguishing dilemmas, it is the demands of that second box of stationery—those of the chief executive officer role — that are consistently the most bedeviling. It presents the most headaches — simultaneously providing tremendous opportunities to improve the delivery of justice and to find ways to better serve emerging social realities within our stable, tradition-bound system. And I know you will forgive me if I sidestep the most bedeviling issue of my entire tenure — critically inadequate judicial compensation. // Of course, in the chief executive role, I have help that is not available in my other role; in the executive role I have a chief administrative judge, administrative teams, technological advances to improve the effectiveness of what we do, and innumerable opportunities for collaboration with the bar, with our partners in government, and with the broader community. But two consuming initiatives, the first being jury reform and the second being problem-solving courts, can give you a sense of the kind of endeavors I have been involved with in my executive capacity. //

**Justice Timmons-Goodson**: Let's talk about a few of your initiatives as chief judge. I know that issues involving children have been a central focus of your professional life. Would you tell us more about how you viewed your role as chief judge with respect to issues involving children? //

**Chief Judge Kaye**: I came to the court in 1983 from a commercial litigation practice, and when my predecessor chief judge some years later asked me to chair his newly formed Commission on Children, I rejected the invitation out of hand. After all, I knew nothing of the field. But he persisted, and I accepted. (It's hard to turn down a chief judge, I'm pleased to say!) To this day I chair the commission — it's been positively life altering for me. I see how much we can, and must, do for children in our Family Courts. And, as I discovered, we can do so much to give them a chance at life, whether it's early intervention with health services, or early permanency, or keeping them in school, or even giving them a new book when they come to court. So many of the children — foster care children — in fact are technically in "our" care. //

**Justice Timmons – Goodson**: Your enthusiasm for jury innovation is well-known. Why are you so passionate about juries and jury innovation? How can advances in modern technology improve our jury system? //

**Chief Judge Kaye**: Our prized American jury system is a core element of our great democracy. It is astounding to think that the United States in the twenty-first century has more than 95 percent of all jury trials in the entire world, that more than a third of all Americans are likely to be empanelled as jurors during their lifetime, that tens of millions of jury summonses are sent annually. We have close to 150, 000 jury trials each year in state courts across the nation, more than 10, 000 annually in New York State alone. // Given the enormous importance of jury trials to the parties and to the law, we naturally want the jury system to function as effectively as humanly possible. But there is an additional lure for chief judges. We call a huge number of citizens into the courts, many having their own first personal encounter with us. Never mind the terrible things they see on TV and read in popular fiction. Jury service offers us a unique opportunity to promote public trust and confidence in our courts, to show a cynical, distrustful public a government institution that really does work well and that values them. It is truly a rare opportunity in today's world — an opportunity we simply cannot afford to squander. // Unquestionably, technological change has helped drive us forward, and it will continue to do so. Today the public can use the Internet to complete qualification questionnaires. Summoned jurors can use the Web to request a postponement and to check whether their service is needed the following day. Computer software can help us better predict how many jurors we'll need and, in our busiest courthouses, where to assign them. We're making service much more convenient. But as important as technology has been in improving the system, it has also brought us new problems. I think of the ways in which it can jeopardize the functioning of a trial or violate a juror's privacy. Technology is also part of the reason that so many of us learn differently in this new age and here again, there are new challenges. //

**Justice Timmons-Goodson**: You have been a leader in the development of problem-solving courts. What is the current state of problem-solving courts, and what further developments, if any, would you like to see? Are there other ways in which our legal system can, as you've put it, more effectively deliver justice? //

**Chief Judge Kaye**: One of our biggest challenges centers on today's dockets and most especially on the repeat low-level offenders, often drug-addicted, in our state courts who corrode their own lives and the vitality of our neighborhoods. And the domestic violence cases, too often beginning with an assault and a court-issued order of protection and ending with murder/suicide. And the child neglect and abuse cases, foster care cases, juvenile delinquents, children with children of their own—generation after generation of poverty, homelessness, mental illness, unemployment and crime, graduating from Family Court to Criminal Court. What a waste of lives. What a waste of resources. So as we study our court dockets, we can simply watch the numbers rise. Or we can ask: Are we using our resources as effectively as possible? Can repeated court interventions perhaps help to stop the downward spiral of these lives? Are we simply counting cases, or can we make each case count? // New York's first problem-solving court, the Midtown Community Court, opened about fifteen years ago smack in the middle of the Manhattan theater district. It focused on quality-of-life crimes—shoplifting, illegal vending, vandalism, prostitution—the sort of repeat conduct that angers and erodes neighborhoods, overfills court dockets, and sends offenders on a steady descent into an abyss of worsening criminal conduct. //

Today we have eight community courts in New York State, each necessarily its own local product but with the same core elements, beginning with a dedicated judge in the leadership role of judicial decision maker and convener of all the collaborators necessary to assure maximum information and maximum opportunity for a meaningful resolution. // Offenders, after pleading guilty, typically receive sentences of community service designed to help restore the neighborhood harmed by the offense—like removing graffiti—and those sentences are closely monitored and actually served. There is cognition that these offenders most often need additional help—which is made available through the court and may include drug treatment, mental health referrals, job interview training, and employment services. //

And here I think the issue is especially relevant for all of us. Collaboration is essential to every problem-solving initiative, collaboration among the justice system leaders, the lawyers, the social service providers, and community groups — even law school clinical programs. Vital as independence is in judicial decision making, it is our strong collaborations with the bar and the community that enable us to build edifices that honor the past, settle the present, and anticipate the future. //

**Justice Timmons-Goodson**: As women, early on we did all we could to conform and blend in with our male colleagues in the legal profession, whether at a law firm or in a government office. This desire to conform was reflected in our dress, our hair, and our professional conduct. We did not want to call attention to ourselves. Yet today, you can often be found wearing red dress shoes. What, if anything, can or should we take from this? //

**Chief Judge Kaye**: I do love red shoes! My reference to the need for more "red shoes" on the bench was a way of urging more women to step forward and aspire to the judiciary. I do agree, however, that "Be yourself" is the guiding principle. That is reflected in how we dress, how we behave, how we think. It's hard enough to be yourself — impossible to be someone else too! //

**Justice Timmons-Goodson**: You have called for judicial pay raises and you currently have a lawsuit pending against the New York legislature for failing to raise judicial salaries in the last ten years. Why does the issue of judicial salaries warrant taking such measures? //

**Chief Judge Kaye**: Now you've touched on something that really hurts. As I look back on a really great fifteen years as chief judge, I am reminded of the question: "Other than that, Mrs. Lincoln, did you enjoy the show?" The compensation issue has been nothing short of devastating. Governors George Pataki, Elliot Spitzer, and David Paterson have all heartily agreed— indeed, everyone agreed — that the judges deserve a raise, but year after year after year, it fails for reasons having nothing to do with us. We negotiated strenuously, and ultimately I was left with no alternative but to file suit. //

**Justice Timmons – Goodson**: What will you miss the most about being the chief judge? //

**Chief Judge Kaye**: Everything! Fortunately I live in New York City, where I frequently hear, "Out of my way, lady!" That keeps me levelheaded, though I will miss immediate return calls and the ability to convene people. When the chief judge calls a meeting, people come! On a more serious note, it's the people in the courts that I will miss most. They will continue, as friends, of course, but I will miss our collaborations—whether on cases or on initiatives. It just won't be the same. //

**Justice Timmons–Goodson**: What are your plans upon leaving the bench? //

**Chief Judge Kaye**: That's a subject I am deferring for the moment. I know what I do not plan to do: nothing. And I know that initiatives for children always will be part of my life. Beyond that, I'm busy simply filling every minute of these last chief-judge-ly days with the tasks, and opportunities, of the office. //

# Ⅳ. 参考译文 Reference Versions

## ◆ *Passage 1*

(*Government lawyer and corporate counsel system reform is currently a hot issue which has attracted the great concern of the society. On such issues, the reporter held an interview with the former Minister of Justice Zhang Fusen.*)

**Q**: What's the background when the Ministry of Justice launched a trial government lawyer and corporate counsel system? //

**A**: Mainly based on two points, we propose to carry out the trial government lawyer and corporate counsel system. On one hand, it is the objective requirements of the development of socialist market economy and the rule of law. The implementation of the strategy of rule of law, the establishment of socialist market economic system, improvement of the socialistlegal system and the accession to the WTO and economic globalization, all of these pose a higher demand for the law-based government administration and enterprise management. Government organs and enterprises are facing more and increasingly complex law affairs; there is an urgent need to build government lawyer and corporate counsel team to provide legal services and legal rights and interests. // On the other hand, that is the need to further improve the organizational structure of the lawyer system. To build lawyer system with Chinese characteristics, we need to learn good practices both from the national conditions and from abroad. In some countries where the lawyer system is mature, most of them have government lawyer and corporate counsel. In addition to the military lawyers, we only have social lawyer, and lawyer structure calls for further development and perfection to the formation of mutual benefits between social lawyers, government lawyers and corporate lawyers. On this basis, we further improve China's lawyer system. //

**Q:** What is the difference between social lawyers, government lawyers and corporate lawyers? //

**A:** The most obvious difference between social lawyers, government lawyers and corporate lawyers is twofold: First, the duality of identity. Government lawyers serve in government organs or the department exercising governmental functions. Corporate lawyers are a company's internal staff. Therefore, government lawyers are civil servants but also lawyers, company lawyers are employees and lawyers. // Second, the fixity of the clients. Government lawyers and corporate lawyes only provide legal services to their own units. They are not allowed to engage in onerous legal services for the community and do part-time job in law firms and legal services agencies. Also, in a lawyer's capacity they shall not engage in the litigation and non-litigation cases outside their own organization. //

Government lawyers and corporate lawyers have their own unique advantages: First, professional legal qualification. Government lawyers and corporate lawyers must be qualified lawyers or have legal professional qualifications, facing more stringent continuing education, practice discipline and professional ethics training. //The second is broad responsibilities and rights. Government lawyers and corporate lawyers can be thoroughly and extensively involved in decision-making, implementation, monitoring and other links of the organization, and have equal rights compared with the social lawyers in the investigation, evidence collection, and access to case materials, joining the Bar Association and participating in job evaluation. // Third, clear position. Today's lawyer industry has been a more developed legal services industry, the establishment of government lawyer and corporate lawyer system can be more readily accepted by the community, but also help to build a legal services platform with the lawyer as the mainstay. // Fourth, in line with international practice. In countries where legal system is developed, its government departments and large enterprises have their own lawyers. Establishing government lawyer and corporate lawyer system can facilitate communications with foreign countries. //

**Q:** As a department in charge of the job, what form the Ministry of Justice will take to define the responsibilities, rights and interests of the government lawyers and corporate lawyers? //

**A:** The current Law of Lawyers has not yet made it clear. As a reform measure, it is in the pilot phase. To operate the job in a standard and orderly manner, the Ministry of Justice established guidance last year for the lawyers and corporate counsel to carry out the pilot work which clarify the responsibilities, rights and obligations the of the government lawyers and corporate lawyers. // Next, we will promptly sum up the experience of pilot work and payclose attention to the work of the drafting of relevant norms. Once the conditions are ripe, we will promptly proposal to amend the Law of Lawyers so as to bring the government lawyer and corporate lawyer system into the overall lawyer framework. //

**Q:** What are the prospects for the government lawyers and corporate lawyers? //

**A:** Whether a system is viable or not, I think the most important is to see whether this system has an objective basis for its existence and development, that is to say, the society needs this system. Legal system is no exception. Practice shows that a sound legal system of a country has one necessary requirement: government must function in accordance with law; companies must operate in accordance with law. Lawyers as legal practitioners, familiar with various laws and rules, will have to play a key role. // China's government lawyer and corporate counsel system emerge against the background of promoting the rule of law and building a moderately prosperous society which can be said to come with the tide of fashion. Now, whether it is government organs or large companies, they attach great importance to this pilot system. Some organizations have been given the certificate; others are doing the preparation work without hesitation. // From the current situation, the prospects are bright. I believe this system is of great vitality. Practice will prove that it is to exert positive and profound influence on China's political activities, economic development and social progress, and to further promote the development and improvement of China's lawyer system. //

◆ *Passage 2*

（以下是与纽约首席法官朱迪·凯伊的访谈录，她在 1983 年被州长任命为纽约上诉法院法官，她成为第一位担任州最高法庭首席法官的女性。）

**蒂蒙斯-古德森**：有人形容您从一个"一般的开始"起步，可以分享一下您早期的生活以及它是如何塑造你的职业选择的吗？//

**朱迪·凯伊**：我的小孙女有一天让我吓了一跳，说："告诉我你的生活。"于是我就开始，"我出生在一个农场。我的父母来自波兰，在纽约州北部定居。"她打断我的话说："不，不，我不是那个意思。从昨天告诉我你的生活。"所以我就说，你真的想让我一下子从农场开始讲，然后到女装服装店，蒙蒂塞洛村庄，最后到纽约？这可能需要数天时间！我将从蒂塞洛的高中讲起，在那里我雄心勃勃地希望以后成为一名记者。// 这一梦想把我带到了纽约市和巴纳德学院，然而却被笼罩在哥伦比亚新闻学院的光辉之下。我一直怀抱着那个梦想，但新闻界在 20 世纪 50 年代末是不欢迎女性的。我做了一名社会新闻记者，并决定学一点法律从而充实一下我的简历，那时却没有打算成为一名律师。但学习一年法律后，我感受到了内心的痛苦。我在蒙蒂塞洛可怜父母！他们对于我新闻事业的雄心不屑一顾，就更别提我要成为一名律师了。一个女律师？会有人娶我吗？//

**蒂蒙斯-古德森**：州长马里奥·科莫于 1993 年委任您为纽约州的首席法官，让您领导纽约州法院系统。您当时做法官还不到 10 年。您做好接受这一职务的准备了吗？如果没有，您是怎么准备的？//

**朱迪·凯伊**：成为首席法官，没有人能做到充分准备，因为成为首席法官的要求是巨大的而且各不相同，每天这个社会都将前沿问题放到法院里去寻求解决。出乎意料的事情是家常便饭。作为法官的这些年很高兴能够得到同事的巨大帮助，这一点在法院系统是众所周知的。回想起来，对我帮助最大的一个是我拥有非常棒的助手（尤其是我办公室工作人员和我任命的知识渊博的行政法官），另一个就是深呼吸。如果你听之任之，很多事情都会让你心烦忧虑。我同样在首席大法官会议和州法院国家中心中表现积极。因为你会从这里的同事中得到很多帮助和大量的信息。//

**蒂蒙斯-古德森：**罗伯塔·卡普兰，您的前任秘书，她最近撰文赞扬您，说您有您自己的法学思维，而且这是一个关注人性的法律思维，并且提到您的决定是如何影响人们的日常生活。您能告诉我们关于您的司法哲学以及您的决策过程是怎样的吗？//

**朱迪·凯伊：**如果你真的对一名法官的表现表示怀疑，我反对加贴"哲学"的标签，也许这是一些人强加给法官的，像"法官活动家"的标签。对我来说，一个决定开始于对案情、记录、法律细节的仔细研究，并用常识来进行检验，司法部门毕竟要遵循先例的约束，是稳定的机构，但在当今世界的运行过程中，我们同样尝试预测我们的决定。一个困难、微妙的平衡，但是，噢，上帝，多么荣幸！//

**蒂蒙斯-古德森：**我要问的是每一位女性法官总是被问到的问题：请问您的性别是否会影响到您的判断？//

**朱迪·凯伊：**我认为不会。在上诉法院我们现在是 4 名女性和 3 名男性，我们只是在个别问题上观点有分歧。我们法院没有性别的界限。在我作为州首席法官（担任行政职务而非审判职务）的这些年里，在全国范围内人们很久才终于意识到家庭法律的重要性。我确实注意到了这种现象和女法官甚至女首席法官大量出现的这种巧合。这是不容否认的关系。//

**蒂蒙斯-古德森：**2004 年，在一篇题为"女首席法官：塑造第三分支"的法律评论文章中，您指出 1/3 的州法院首席法官是女性，您说数字很重要。为什么？//

**朱迪·凯伊：**数量绝对重要。在数字里面人们会找到舒服感，会与同你一样面临着类似的挑战和斗争的人建立信任。我们能够做到并且必须做到——一个人坚持下来，我们之间有一种天然的联盟，虽然我们不相同，但这个联盟却十分巩固。但我们绝不是孤立主义者。//

**蒂蒙斯-古德森：**您是为数不多的在 20 世纪 60 年代从法律学校毕业并进入了当时以男性为主的行业的女性。您的个人奋斗的哪些方面反映在了您领导的纽约法院系统呢？//

**朱迪·凯伊：**我没有自我吹捧的意思，但我相信，任何经历过 20 世纪 60

年代（和70年代）的女人会意识到为我们后来者伸出援手是多么的必要。顺便说一下，这场斗争并没有结束。我们犯了一个错误，以为这已经结束了。对于这个，我最近已经写在福德姆法律评论文章上面了。//

**蒂蒙斯-古德森：**您曾经形容您在上诉法院的工作为"律师的天堂"。为什么？//

**朱迪·凯伊：**作为7个上诉法院其中之一的法官，绝对是我们专业的顶峰。每一天我们都面临着一系列法律问题，从冰冷的人行道上的一次跌倒到多重谋杀，以及介于两者之间各种各样的事情，这些都深刻地影响到当事人和贯穿我们社会生活的法律。过去这25年的同事都是出色的法官和很好的朋友。我们的任务是，以合议的方式，达到最明智、最佳的结果。法院工作人员和设施都非常优秀。总之，律师天堂，你不同意吗？//

**蒂蒙斯-古德森：**作为首席法官，您的角色有两个：一名法官和一个处理纽约司法部门行政事务的执行官。现在让我们来关注一下您的行政角色，请告诉我们您运行世界上最大和最复杂的诉讼法院系统之一的一些经验体会。//

**朱迪·凯伊：**我确实有两个角色。作为纽约上诉法院的首席法官，我履行作为一个伟大的普通法法院法官的职务。除了纽约州的首席法官，另一个是我的行政的角色。我领导着近15 000名员工，365座法院大楼，大约每年有400万份档案。我用80%的时间当上诉法院的首席法官，另外20%的时间当纽约州的首席法官。虽然我的审判职责带来了极度痛苦的困境，但它是我第二个角色，即行政事物执行官所需要的，这始终是最为困扰我的。它带来了最头痛的事情——同时提供巨大的可能来确保司法的公正，并且在传统的约束系统中更好地解决不断出现的社会问题。而且我知道你会原谅我，如果我回避了我的整个任期内最困扰的问题——严重不足的司法赔偿。// 当然，在行政长官的这个角色里，我得到了在其他角色里所有没有的帮助；在行政机关的角色，我有一个首席行政法官，行政团队，还有提高我们工作成效的先进技术，以及无数与大律师合作的机会，我们在政府有合作伙伴，并可以更广泛地参与到社区里。但有两个迫切的倡议，首先是陪审团的改革，其次是高效率的法院，这是在行政长官的身份里，我一直努力参与的。//

**蒂蒙斯-古德森：**让我们谈谈您作为首席法官而倡导的一些措施。我知道，涉及儿童的问题一直是您的职业生涯中的焦点。您能告诉我们更多关于您作为首席法官如何看待涉及儿童的有关问题吗？//

朱迪·凯伊：我 1983 年从商业诉讼领域来到现在的法庭，几年后当我的前任首席法官要我主持他新成立的儿童事务委员会时，我立即拒绝了邀请。毕竟，对于该领域我一无所知。但在他的坚持下，我还是接受了。（我很高兴地说，拒绝一个首席法官是很难的！）直到今天我仍然担任着该委员会主席——它给我的生活带来了积极改变。我能看到在家庭法院我们能够以及必须为我们的孩子做多少。而且，我发现，我们可以给他们很多生活中的机会，无论是附带医疗服务的及早介入，还是留他们在学校，甚至当他们来法院时给他们一本新书。因此，很多儿童——寄养儿童——其实严格来说处于"我们的"关怀中。//

蒂蒙斯–古德森：您对陪审团创新的积极性是众所周知的。您为什么对陪审团和陪审团的创新抱有这么大的热情？怎样才能利用现代技术的进步提高陪审团制度？//

朱迪·凯伊：我们珍视的陪审团制度就是我们伟大民主的核心要素。人们吃惊地发现，进入 21 世纪以后，在世界上所有陪审团的审判美国拥有全世界 95% 以上的陪审团审判，有超过 1/3 的美国人在其一生中可能被选任为陪审员，每年发送数百万陪审团传票。每年我们在全国各地拥有近 15 万次陪审团审判，仅在纽约州就超过 10 000 次。// 由于陪审团审判对于各方和法律极为重要，我们当然希望陪审团制度有效地、人性地发挥功能。但是，对首席法官来说，还有一个额外的诱惑。我们呼吁众多市民到法院旁听，其中很多人与我们第一次见面。更别说他们通过电视和小说得知的可怕事情了。陪审团的服务为我们提供了一个独特的机会，促进公众的信任和信心，从而让愤世嫉俗、缺乏信任感的市民看到我们的政府勤于工作，重视他们的意见。这确实是当今世界难得的机遇——一个我们根本不能浪费的大好机会。// 毫无疑问，技术的变化，有助于推动我们前进，而且会一如既往地发展下去。今天，市民可利用互联网来完成资格问卷。陪审员可以使用网络请求延期，并检查第二天是否需要他们的服务。计算机软件可以帮助我们更好地预测需要有多少陪审员和在我们最繁忙的法院大楼中如何分配他们。我们正使服务更加方便。但系统的完善，也给我们带来了新的问题。它可能危及审判职能或侵犯陪审员的隐私。科技也是我们许多人在这个新时代和这里以不同方式学习的部分原因。在这里，有新的挑战。//

蒂蒙斯–古德森：您一直是高效率法院的领导者。对于高效率法院的现状以及进一步发展，您有什么想法？是否还有其他方法，使我们的法律制度可以像您所说的那样，更加有效地提供司法服务？

**朱迪·凯伊**：我们最大的挑战之一，反映在今天的案卷上特别是在低级别惯犯中，就是经常吸毒，他们腐蚀了自己的生命和我们的社区活力。而家庭暴力案件，往往一开始伴随着殴打和法庭发出保护命令，但最终以谋杀罪或者是自杀结束。忽视和虐待儿童案件、收养案件、少年犯、一代一代的贫困、无家可归、精神疾病、失业和犯罪的产生，从家庭法院发展到刑事法院。这真是生命的浪费，同样也是浪费资源。所以，当我们研究法院日程时，我们可以简单地看到数字上升。或者我们可以问：我们尽可能有效地利用我们的资源了吗？法院的反复干预也许可以有助于制止这些生命的恶性循环？我们仅仅是计算案件，还是能够使每个案件都有意义？// 纽约的第一个高效率法庭——中城社区法院——15 年前在曼哈顿剧院区的中间成立。它集中于审理生活质量犯罪，店铺盗窃、非法贩卖、破坏、卖淫，这些行为反复激怒和侵蚀附近的地区，填满了法院日程，并使这些冒犯者的犯罪行为滑向日益恶化的深渊。//

今天，在纽约州，我们有 8 个社区法院，虽然都是独立的法院，但它们有着共同的核心价值，从司法决定中尽职尽责的法官到法院合作者之间的召集人，确保每一次有意义的判决都得到最多信息和给予最大的机会。// 罪犯认罪后，通常会收到旨在帮助恢复受损的邻里社区刑罚的罪行，如消除涂鸦。这些刑罚的执行会受到密切的监视，并切实得到履行。有人认为，这些罪犯往往需要额外的帮助，这可以通过法院得到实现如药物治疗、精神健康、工作培训以及就业服务。//

在这里，我想这个问题与我们息息相关。协作是每一个问题都必不可少的解决措施，这些合作存在于司法系统领导者、律师、社会服务机构、社区团体，甚至是法学院的案例之间。司法独立非常重要，它与律师公会和社区有着紧密的联系，这样可以使我们建立至高无上的准则，从而缅怀过去、解决现在和预测未来。//

**蒂蒙斯-古德森**：作为女性，从很早开始，不论是在律师事务所还是在政府办公室，我们都努力使自己符合并且融入男性同事的圈子。这个愿望反映在我们的着装、我们的头发，以及我们的职业操守之中。我们并不想让别人注意自己。然而，今天，你经常可以看到有人身穿红色礼服鞋。我们可以或

应该从中看到什么呢？//

朱迪·凯伊：我喜欢红色的鞋子！我所指的需要"红鞋子"是想督促更多的女性向前一步，参与司法工作。不管怎样，我同意，"做自己"是指导原则。这反映在我们如何着装、我们如何表现、我们如何想。成为自己就已经很难了——不可能成为别人了！//

蒂蒙斯-古德森：您要求提高工资，并且目前您就过去 10 年司法机关没有提高工资而状告立法机构。为什么对于司法人员的工资问题要采取这个措施？//

朱迪·凯伊：现在你已经触及一些实在令人伤心的东西。正如我回顾作为首席法官精彩的 15 年一样，我想起一个问题："除了这个，林肯夫人，你享受这个节目吗？"薪酬问题是让我非常心痛的一点。乔治·柏德基州长，埃利奥特·斯皮策，大卫·帕特森都由衷同意，事实上，每个人都同意——法官应该得到更高的报酬，但是年复一年，都因与我们无关的原因而流产。我们艰苦谈判，最终只好向法院提起诉讼了。//

蒂蒙斯-古德森：作为首席法官，什么是您最怀念的？//

朱迪·凯伊：一切！幸运的是我住在纽约市，在这里我经常听到，"让开，女士！"这让我头脑冷静，虽然我会怀念立即回电话，并能够召集人。当首席法官召开紧急会议，人们都能来！更值得怀念的是法院的同事。当然，我们将继续做朋友，但我会怀念我们的合作，无论是个案还是倡议。感觉不一样。//

蒂蒙斯-古德森：离开法官这个职业后您会做什么？//

朱迪·凯伊：这个问题我暂时还没想好。我没有不打算做的事。而且，我知道，为了孩子们的倡议将永远是我生活的一部分。除此之外，我只是正忙着填补作为首席法官的每一分钟的工作任务和机会。//

# V. 句子精炼 Sentences in Focus

**Directions**：*Interpret the following sentences alternatively into English or Chinese*：

1. 我国除了军队律师外，只有社会律师一种形式，律师结构需要进一步发展和完善，逐步形成社会律师、公职律师、公司律师等队伍并存，相互配合、优势互补的格局。

2. 公职律师、公司律师只能为本单位提供法律服务，不得面向社会从事有偿法律服务，不得在律师事务所和法律服务所兼职，不得以律师身份办理本单位以外的诉讼与非诉讼案件。

3. 一旦条件成熟，我们将及时提出修改律师法的建议，尽快把公职律师、公司律师制度纳入我国律师制度的整体框架。

4. No one can fully prepare to be chief judge—the demands are huge and different as every day society deposits its cutting-edge problems at the courthouse doors. The unexpected is thenorm.

5. The judiciary is, after all, astare-decisis, precedent-bound, stable institution, but we function in today's world, and we attempt, as well, to anticipate tomorrow in our decisions. A difficult, delicate balance—but, oh my, what a privilege!

6. I have observed, however, that during my years as Chief Judge of the State—the executive/administrative, rather than adjudicative, role — there has been a long-overdue awakening to the importance of family law issues and "problem-solving courts" across the nation.

7. Although my adjudicative responsibilities surely present anguishing dilemmas, it is the demands of that second box of stationery — those of the chief executive officer role — that are consistently the most bedeviling. It presents the most headaches — simultaneously providing tremendous opportunities to improve the delivery of justice and to find ways to better serve emerging social realities within our stable, tradition-bound system.

8. Jury service offers us a unique opportunity to promote public trust and confidence in our courts, to show a cynical, distrustful public a government institution that really does work well and that values them. It is truly a rare opportunity in today's world — an opportunity we simply cannot afford to squander.

9. Collaboration is essential to every problem-solving initiative, collaboration among the justice system leaders, the lawyers, the social service providers, and community groups — even law school clinical programs. Vital as independence is in judicial decision making, it is our strong collaborations with the bar and the community that enable us to build edifices that honor the past, settle the present, and anticipate the future.

# 立法听证会

## Unit 2 Public Hearings

# Ⅰ. 专题知识 Legal Knowledge

作为一种程序性民主形式，立法听证制度是指立法机构在制定涉及公民、法人权益的法律法规时，借助某种程序性的形式，听取有关人员的意见，赋予利益相关人表达自身利益的机会，并将这种利益表达作为立法依据或参考的制度形式和实践。在现代民主政治中，立法听证制度是实践人民主权原则、维护公民政治参与权利的重要途径。

## 一、我国建立立法听证制度的法律基础

（1）宪法依据。在现代理念中，宪法体现了国家的政治宣言和法律理性，是公民权利的保障书，其根本目的在于规范国家公权力的行使。在我国的体制下，国家的一切权力属于人民。《宪法》[1]虽然没有明确规定立法听证制度，也没有类似美国"正当法律程序"的规定，但其第 2 条第 3 款规定："人民依照法律规定，通过各种途径和形式，管理国家事务，管理经济和文化事业，管理社会事务。"这就要求国家机关在作出任何涉及公民权利和义务的规定或决定时都应当通过民主的形式听取人民的意见，也表明人民有权通过各种途径参与国家事务管理和向国家机关提出意见和建议。该规定为立法听证制度的建立提供了宪法依据。

（2）行政法基础。在现代行政法治中，公众参与已占据十分重要的地位，这对保障行政机关依法公正行使职权及维护行政相对人的合法权益都有着特

---

[1]《宪法》，即《中华人民共和国宪法》。为表述方便，本书中涉及我国法律文件直接使用简称，省去"中华人民共和国"字样，全书统一，后不赘述。

殊、重要的意义。作为行政法特别是行政程序法的基本原则，公众参与是民主立法的根本体现，是公民对立法的启动、过程和结果感到满意并使之"合法化"的一种力量，保障了公民意愿的自由表达，体现了依法行政与科学行政的基本要求。立法听证制度正是公众参与在立法层面上的集中体现，保障了行政法基本原则的实现。

## 二、立法听证制度的功能

（1）使立法主体广泛收集信息，为提高立法质量提供了制度保障。从信息学角度讲，立法就是决策者在获取广泛信息的基础上进行决策的行为。信息是决策的依据，信息的质和量影响着立法决策的质和量。开明的立法者应该广泛地收集不同的信息。在立法听证过程中，经过各方参与者的意见陈述和辩论，可使立法主体全面了解事实、正确决策，也有助于将立法决策过程纳入公众的监督之下。

（2）使立法直接体现民主，有利于人们对法律的遵守和执行。尽管近代以来代议制民主一直是民主的主要实现形式，但其毕竟是一种间接实现民主的方式。随着现代社会民主的发展，许多国家都越来越多地注意发展直接民主。立法听证制度就是直接体现民主的一种方式。立法听证不仅能够提升立法的科学化与民主化水平，而且符合"人民是国家的主人"的宪法原则，同时也可极大地拓展法律的可信度与权威性。

（3）有助于在立法中平衡各相关主体的利益，促进社会资源的有效配置。立法决策过程的实质是一个协调利益、配置社会资源的过程。立法听证制度的建立给予不同力量以制度性的表白途径，实现了以理性的沟通途径来化解冲突的目的。

## 三、完善我国立法听证制度的建议

（1）明确立法听证的对象范围。在选择立法听证的对象时应当坚持两个原则：一是公共利益优先原则。任何一项立法都会涉及利益的分配，且须作出恰当的选择，这就要求立法主体必须均衡各种利益关系。设立立法听证程序虽然有时可以有效地保护个人利益，但很可能损害公共利益，这也是各国在国家安全、军事、外交领域及紧急情况下均不适用听证程序的原因。二是收益大于成本原则。在确定听证范围时，必须充分考虑听证程序所必须承担的人力、物力、财力，保障所取得的社会经济综合效益高于支出成本。

（2）设置可操作的听证程序规则。在法治社会里，正义不仅应得到实现，而且应以人们看得见的方式得到实现。立法听证制度在运行过程中必须始终贯彻公开的原则，使之处于社会的监督之下，以最大限度地排除恣意和偏执。立法听证制度实施的结果在很大程度上取决于对听证参与人的选择。如果没有公开的听证参与人选择机制，不能保证与立法事项有重大利害关系的各方代表都能参与听证会，那么立法听证的结果就容易被听证主持机构的主观性所主导，立法听证制度的公正性和代表性就必然难以实现。因此，在制定全国性的法律时应当充分考虑不同地域、不同收入阶层的代表比例，明确听证会参与人的选拔标准，公开选拔的过程并对选拔结果进行公示，增强透明度，以最大限度地体现民意。

（3）保障实效性，防止立法听证制度流于形式。应当建立听证回应制度。听证主持机构要认真归纳各方听证参与人的意见，对合理的意见应当采纳，对不合理的尤其是反对的意见不予采纳时应给予书面答复并阐明理由。

# Ⅱ. 词汇热身 Vocabulary Warm-up

**Directions**：*Give the English equivalents of the following Chinese expressions*：

| | | |
|---|---|---|
| 立法听证会 | 拆迁 | 专门委员会 |
| 个人所得税 | 知情权 | 座谈会 |
| 起征点 | 见义勇为 | 公用设施 |
| 舶来品 | 立法机关 | |

**Directions**：*Give the Chinese equivalents of the following English expressions*：

| | | |
|---|---|---|
| contentious | legislative | rebuttal |
| hearing procedure | record | deliberation |
| spelled out | publication | warrant |
| statute | ordinance | apolitical |
| overturn | transcript | proceedings |
| testimony | testify | disturbance |

# III. 课文口译 Texts for Interpreting

## ◆ *Passage 1*

**Directions**: *Listen to the passage and interpret from English into Chinese at the end of each segment.*

Public bodies, such as city councils, boards of county commissioners, and planning commissions, are sometimes required by state law to hold public hearings. Since the issues addressed in these public hearings are frequently contentious, may involve due process rights of private parties, and generate litigation, it is important to know and follow proper hearing procedures. Because these procedures are not generally spelled out in the statutes that require hearings, there is no ready guide for public bodies to follow when conducting hearings. // This focus issue discusses what is legally required for public hearings, with an emphasis on quasi-judicial hearings, and summarizes the basic procedures that should be followed. While following proper hearing procedures may not eliminate litigation over the issues addressed in hearings, it will help prevent having the decisions made following public hearings overturned by the courts on procedural grounds. Following proper procedures also helps insure that public hearings are conducted fairly. //

A public meeting generally occurs whenever a quorum of a public body, and sometimes less than a quorum, meets together and deals in any way with the business of that body. Public meetings, whether regular or special meetings, are governed by the procedures of the Open Public Meetings Act in chapter 42. 30 RCW. Although the public often is allowed to participate in regular or special meetings, public participation is not required by state law. Two basic legal requirements of a public meeting are that the public be notified and be allowed to attend. //

Although a public hearing is also a public meeting, the main purpose of most public hearings is to obtain public testimony or comment. A public hearing may occur as part of a regular or special meeting, or it may be the sole purpose of a special meeting, with no other matters addressed. An "open record hearing" under 1995 regulatory reform legislation (chapter 36. 70B RCW) is a public hearing, while a "closed record appeal" is a public meeting. //

There are two types of public hearings, legislative and quasi-judicial, and it is important to understand the distinction between them. The purpose of a legislative public hearing is to obtain public input on legislative decisions on matters of policy. Legislative public hearings are required by state law when a city or county addresses such matters as comprehensive land use plans or the annual or biennial budget. Legislative public hearings are generally less formal than quasi-judicial public hearings. They do not involve the legal rights of specific, private parties in a contested setting, but rather affect a wider range of citizens or perhaps the entire jurisdiction. // The wisdom of legislative decisions reached as a result of such hearings is not second-guessed by the courts; if challenged, they are reviewed only to determine if they are constitutional or violate state law. For example, a court will not review whether the basic budgetary decisions made by a city council or county commission were correctly made. On the other hand, comprehensive plans in Growth Management Act (GMA) counties may be reviewed by a growth management hearings board, and maybe later by a court, for consistency with the GMA. //

On certain controversial legislative issues, it can be important to conduct a thoughtful public process in advance of any public hearing. Hearings often occur late in the process and may leave citizens with the impression that local officials do not want to hear their ideas. Council or board chambers are formal and can be intimidating to citizens who are not accustomed to public speaking. The format of hearings often leaves little, if any, room for reasonable discussion, give or take, or response to prior testimony. //

While beyond the scope of this focus issue, here are some brief thoughts on public process. Involve citizens in the early stages of the policy development process. Small group processes work well for truly involving interested citizens. Make sure that there is plenty of opportunity for people to get answers to questions; this usually does not happen at a formal public hearing. Consider using a trained facilitator to facilitate discussion on really controversial issues. Good public process can be time consuming and expensive. However, these processes increase the potential to arrive at solutions that have strong support in the community. //

Quasi-judicial public hearings, unlike legislative ones, involve the legal rights of specific parties, and the decisions made as a result of such hearings must be based upon and supported by the "record" developed at the hearing. Quasi - judicial hearings are subject to stricter procedural requirements than legislative hearings. Most quasi-judicial hearings held by local government bodies involve land use matters, including site specific rezones, preliminary plats, variances, and conditional uses. //

A public hearing is required only when a specific statute requires one. Of course, a local government may hold a public hearing in other instances, such as when it desires public input on asensitive or controversial policy issue. If you have any question as to whether a public hearing is required for a particular matter, we recommend that you consult with your city attorney or county prosecutor. //

## ◆ *Passage 2*

**Directions:** *Listen to the passage and interpret from English into Chinese at the end of each segment.*

Welcome to the Iraq Inquiry's first day of public hearings. For those of you who do not know me, I am Sir John Chilcot, chairman of the Iraq Inquiry. I am joined by my colleagues Professor Sir Lawrence Freedman, Professor Sir Martin Gilbert, Sir Roderic Lyne and Baroness Usha Prashar. Together we form the Iraq Inquiry Committee. Next to me is Margaret Aldred who is the Secretary to the Inquiry. //

The Iraq Inquiry was set up to identify the lessons that should be learned from the UK's involvement in Iraq to help future governments who may face similar situations. //

To do this, we need to establish what happened. We are piecing this together from the evidence we are collecting from documents or from those who have first hand experience. We will then need to evaluate what went well and what didn't, and crucially, why. //

My colleagues and I come to this task with open minds. We are apolitical and independent of any political party. We want to examine the evidence. We will approach our task in a way that is thorough, rigorous, fair and frank. //

The Committee and I are also committed to openness and are determined to conduct as much of our proceedings in public as possible. I welcome those members of the public who join us here today — thank you for taking the time and effort to travel here this morning. I also welcome the media present here at the QEII. For those not physically present, I am pleased that the Inquiry proceedings are available for broadcast and are being streamed on the Internet. //

These public hearings are the activity which will attract the most publicity but they form only one part of our work. //

Over the past months we have requested and received mountains of written material from Government departments involved in Iraq during 2001-09. We have spent many hours combing through these official records—and will continue to do this in the months ahead. We are confident that we will have access to all the material that we need. //

But we don't want to, and are not, just hearing from the "official" representatives. We value hearing a broad spectrum of views from a wide range of people and organizations. We want to know what people across Britain think. We want to get a range of challenging perspectives on the issues we are considering. We've already made a start on this by holding: //

Five meetings with the families of those who were killed or are missing in Iraq. We are very grateful to all those who came to talk to us. //

Preliminary meetings with Iraqveterans two seminars with a range of experts. We hope to have a further seminar early next year. //

We have also asked anyone who has information, or who wants to make points, relevant to our terms of reference to contact us. We thank all those who have already been in touch. //

The next phase begins today. We have called as witnesses those with first-hand experience of the development and implementation of UK government policy in Iraq. Our first round of public hearings begins today and runs until early February 2010. We will then take a break from public hearings, returning to our analysis of written material. We will hold some private hearings: to take evidence on matters which if disclosed in public would cause harm to the public interest, or where there are other genuine reasons why a witness would have difficulty being frank in public. The circumstances in which we will hold private hearings are set out in the Protocols published on the Inquiry website. //

There will be a further round of public hearings in the middle of 2010. We expect to invite back some previous witnesses and, where relevant, call some new ones. What I would like to stress now is that people should not jump to conclusions if they do not hear everything they expect to in the first round of hearings: there will be more to follow. //

Once we have collected all the evidence we need, we will be in a position to draw conclusions and make recommendations. We plan to report by the end of 2010. It is not in our, or the country's, interest to delay the process. Our objective, however, is to produce a thorough analysis that makes a genuine contribution to improving public governance and decision making. If that takes a bit longer, I hope people will bear with us. //

That is for next year. For now it might be useful to set out today what we aim to cover in the initial phase of public hearings, and how we plan to conduct our business. //

We want to establish a clear understanding of the various core elements of the UK's involvement in Iraq, and how these developed over time. We will start by hearing from the senior officials and military officers who had a key role in developing advice for Ministers and/or implementing government policy. We want them to take us through the main decisions and tasks. That will give us a clear understanding of the various strands of British policy development and implementation since 2001. We will learn the reasons why particular policies or courses of action were adopted, and what consideration was given to alternative approaches. //

Once we have heard that initial evidence, we will begin to take evidence from Ministers and other officials about issues which run throughout the period we have been asked to consider. In some cases, we will be able—on the basis of the evidence we have heard from officials earlier in the session—to get into considerable detail. In other cases, we may need to return to a number of the issues at a later stage. It will be during those hearings in the New Year—and not before—that we will be hearing about the legal basis for military action. //

In all our questioning we will be drawing on the vast number of documents that we have already read. This has given us a good sense of the main events of the period, the issues and pre-occupations. Oral evidence will build on our previous knowledge. It will help develop our lines of inquiry—these, I must stress, are still developing. We remain, as we have been from the outset, open minded. What we are committed to, and what the British general public can expect from us, is a guarantee to be thorough, impartial, objective and fair. //

Perhaps this is an appropriate moment to set out our expectations of how these proceedings will run. //

Iraq Inquiry Committee members will ask the questions. Witnesses will respond for themselves. We expect them always to give evidence that is truthful, fair and accurate. We do not intend to ask questions today that will involve evidence that might harm national security or other important public interests as described in the Protocols we have published. In the extremely unlikely event that evidence moved towards such matters sensitive to national security, I would intervene to halt the proceedings. //

As I have said before, we are not a court or an inquest or a statutory inquiry; and our processes will reflect that difference. No one is on trial. We cannot determine guilt or innocence. Only a court can do that. But I make a commitment here that once we get to our final report, we will not shy away from making criticisms where they are warranted. //

Finally, as I said earlier, we are pleased that these are public sessions. We welcome those who join us today and will do so over the coming weeks. These are, however, serious matters that we examine; we want to get to the heart of what happened and do not wish to be distracted in our task by disturbances. We have set out on our website and to all here today the behaviours we expect from those present in the hearing room. They are not different from those expected of the public when they attend Parliament. Just as there, those who fail to meet them will have to leave. //

And so to the proceedings of today: as I set out above the first five weeks of these hearings aim to establish the main features of UK involvement in Iraq 2001 - 2009. We have invited to give evidence those senior officials and military personnel who (by the posts they occupied) had a unique perspective on UK government decision making and the implementation of those policies. Today we start in 2001. Before me sit Sir Peter Ricketts, who in 2001, was Director General Political in the Foreign and Commonwealth Office; Sir William Patey who was the Head of the Foreign Office's Middle East Department and Simon Webb who was Policy Director in the Ministryof Defense. //

◆ *Passage 3*

**Directions**: *Listen to the passage and interpret from Chinese into English at the end of each segment.*

全国人大法律委员会近日发布公告，决定将于 9 月 27 日举行立法听证会，就个人所得税修正案草案中的个人所得税"起征点"问题向社会广泛征求意见。这将是全国人大及其常委会举行的首次立法听证会，也是全国人大常委会工作历史上的第一次听证会。它意味着我国最高立法机关对实现立法科学化与民主化的一次重大探索，标志着我国民主立法进入了一个全新的发展阶段。//

随着我国立法事业的发展和立法观念的更新，立法听证对于地方立法而言已不再是一个新鲜的"舶来品"。自 2000 年《立法法》颁布至 2004 年底，全国已有 24 个省级人大常委会共对 39 件地方性法规草案举行过 38 次立法听证会。立法听证的内容涵盖了市场管理、消费者权益保护、环境资源保护、城市公用设施建设、拆迁管理和见义勇为等诸多方面。由此可见，立法听证在我国地方立法过程中已经普遍开展起来。然而，一直以来，全国人大及其常委会还没有就全国性立法举行过立法听证会。从这个意义上说，这次就个税法举行听证会，是本届全国人大常委会以实际行动积极拓展公众参与立法的途径和形式，彰显立法民主价值的重大举措。它对于真正落实人民依法管理国家事务的宪法权力，推进民主立法进程具有十分重要的意义。//

全国人大及其常委会在进行国家立法过程中，以往听取意见的常用方式主要有三种：一是向各省、自治区、直辖市、较大的市、中央有关部门、有关教学科研机构等征求相关草案的书面意见；二是召开座谈会征求有关人士的意见；三是对一些重大法律草案在报刊上发布，向全社会征求意见。立法听证会不同于以往的这些方式，它源于英美普通法的"自然公正"原则，是指立法机关在开展受到社会普遍关注的立法活动的过程中，为了直接、公开听取社会意见，邀请草案起草人代表、专家学者、当事人、与议案有关的利害关系人作为听证人或陈述人到会，就相关立法焦点问题充分表达意见和展开辩论，并以此作为审议法律草案的重要依据和参考的一项立法制度。立法听证作为立法机关经常运用的一种颇具实效的程序性民主形式，目前已成为许多国家提升立法民主化程度和广泛获取相关立法信息的重要途径。//

在我国，建设社会主义市场经济和民主政治的国情为立法机关实行立法听证制度创造了条件。《立法法》专门就全国人大常委会立法过程中引进立法听证作出如下明确规定："列入常务委员会会议议程的法律案，宪法和法律委员会、有关的专门委员会和常务委员会工作机构应当听取各方面的意见。听取意见可以采取座谈会、论证会、听证会等多种形式。"这可以被看作是在全国人大常委会全面实行立法听证制度的明确规定。实行立法听证会制度，其本身所具有的制度价值和社会意义在于：//

第一，立法听证制度有利于实现立法过程的公开、公正和透明，是保障公民对国家和社会重大立法事务知情权的重要方式。立法听证会完全向社会公开，进行听证的事项和焦点问题一般事先以公告的形式向全社会公布，符合报名条件的公民可以按规定方式自愿报名为陈述人或旁听人。立法听证会对新闻媒体开放，也可以使更多未亲自到会的公众了解草案的情况和各方面意见。//

第二，立法听证制度为民众提供了一个公开陈述、辩论和举证的论坛，为立法者、执法者与守法者之间搭起一个信息交流的平台，是在立法过程中充分反映民意和集中民智，实现立法民主化的有效环节。通过听证会，不同观点的代表能够直接陈述自己的希冀与要求，立法机关也能够全面了解各方利益和矛盾所在，从而使立法更好地反映社会主体的合理心声，使法律这一"公共产品"更好地为民众服务，从根本上维护社会的稳定与和谐。//

第三，对于广大人民群众而言，立法听证制度提供了一个行之有效的进行民主训练、民主宣传和民主教育的活生生的"课堂"。听证会不同于座谈会、论证会的一个重要特征在于其严格的程序性和规范性。为了保证陈述人的广泛代表性和平等的发言机会，每次听证会都制定有严格的听证规则，对陈述人的遴选，参加人数，听证会的发言顺序，发言内容、发言时间和主持人、记录人等都有明确规定。普通群众通过这样的方式实质参与立法过程，可以直接获得在一个规范化的场所，以程序化的手段表达各自诉求的机会，真正享受民主的国家生活和社会生活，进一步增强民主法治意识和主人翁责任感，从而间接推动中国民主政治的进程。//

第四，立法听证制度有利于提高立法质量，可以在尽可能的范围内保证所立之法的科学性和可行性。立法机关可以通过听证会广泛收集立法资料，发现事实真相，了解有关的背景知识及社会各界的反应，以及法律如获通过后应有的社会效益，从而有助于立法符合实际并获得广泛的社会认同。这既兼顾了立法的民主与效率，又可防止立法的偏颇与缺失，形成对立法机关的某种制约，从根本上保证所立之法的科学性和可行性。//

个人所得税的"起征点"问题不仅涉及国家对社会财富的合理调节，而且关系广大工薪收入者的切身利益，关系个人利益与社会福利的平衡。它在任何国家都是政策选择和立法调整的难题，相关立法的制定和审议也必然意味着一个极其复杂和困难的博弈、权衡过程。这次，全国人大常委会以个税法修改为突破口，通过听证会形式让更多的社会成员直接参与税收立法的过程，向立法机关直接表达意见以维护自身权益，必将大大增强最高立法机关在论证、拟订和审议法律草案过程中与社会、公众的沟通，保证相关立法决策、立法审议存在科学、真实的客观依据，从而使最后出台的法律能够充分获得普遍的社会理解和民众支持。这也充分表明，全国人大就个税法举行听证会，尽管针对的只是一个"起征点"问题，但其象征意义已远远超出了个税法本身。它是对立法民主价值的一次彰显，是我国民主法治进程中的一个重要里程碑。//

全国人大法律委员会、财政经济委员会和全国人大常委会法制工作委员会，就修改个税法定于 2005 年 9 月 27 日在北京举行关于得税工薪所得减除费用标准立法听证会。//

本次听证会主持人：全国人大法律委员会主任委员杨景宇、全国人大财政经济委员会副主任委员刘积斌、全国人大常委会法制工作委员会主任胡康生。//

听证会纪律：参加听证会的人员应当遵守下列纪律：①按指定区域就座。②关闭手机、寻呼机。③听证陈述发言应当事先得到听证主持人许可。④不得随意走动和喧哗。⑤新闻记者不得在听证过程中对参加听证会的人员进行采访。⑥不得有妨碍听证会正常进行的其他活动。违反听证会纪律的，听证主持人应予以制止；拒不改正的，可以责令其离开会场。（省略）//

刘积斌：在今天的听证会上，28 名听证陈述人围绕确定的听证事项发表了意见，阐述了理由和论据。大家的发言代表和反映了不同的观点和要求，体现出了强烈的社会责任感和主人翁意识，今天的听证会是社会主义民主的生动体现。在此，我代表全国人大法律委员会、全国人大财经委员会和全国人大常委会法制工作委员会向各位陈述人表示由衷的感谢。同时，也借此机会通过新闻媒体向报名参加本次听证会，但因名额所限未能参加的人士表示感谢。希望大家继续关心和支持国家的立法工作，为国家立法积极建言献策。对今天听证会上的意见和建议，我们将在会后及时进行认真的整理和研究，提出听证报告，提交给全国人大常委会，作为立法时的重要参考和依据。现在我宣布，本次听证会结束。谢谢大家！//

# Ⅳ. 参考译文 Reference Versions

## ◆ *Passage 1*

公共机构，例如市议会、县议会委员会、规划委员会，根据国家法律规定在某些情况下需要举行公开听证会。因为这些听证会所要解决的问题往往具有争议性，可能涉及私人当事方的正当程序权利，并导致诉讼，所以了解和遵循正确的听证程序是很重要的。因为要求听证的这些法规通常是不会详细说明具体操作步骤的，没有现成的指导公共机构举行听证会时应该遵循的准则。本文正是关注于此，讨论了什么是法律所要求的召开准司法性听证会所要遵循的规则，并总结了应遵循的基本程序。虽然经过正当的听证程序可能无法消除听证会所要讨论解决的问题的诉讼，但将有助于防止因为程序上的原因而推翻在听证会上作出的决定。经过正当的程序也有助于确保公众听证会公正进行。//

一个公众集会只要符合一个公共机构的法定人数一般就可以进行，有时比法定人数少，一起开会，并处理任何与该机构有关的经营方式。公众会议，无论是定期还是特别会议，均受公开会议法程序的约束。虽然市民经常被允许参加定期或特别会议，但国家法律并未规定这点。公开会议的两项基本法律要求是通知公众并允许公众参加。//

虽然公开听证会也是一次公开会议，但大多数公众听证会的主要目的是获取公共证言或意见。公众听证会可能会作为一项经常性或特别会议的一部分来召开，也可能是一个特别会议的唯一目的，且不处理任何其他事项。根据 1995 年的监管改革立法（第 36 章 70B），"开放的记录听证会"属于公开的听证会，而"而封闭记录上诉"属于公开的会议。//

公众听证会有两种类型，即立法的和准司法性的，而且重要的是要了解它们之间的区别。采用立法听证的目的是获得关于作出立法政策事项决定的公众意见。立法听证会是由国家法律规定，例如一个城市或县城处理诸如综合土地利用计划，或年度，或两年期预算等事项。立法听证会一般不如准司法听证会正式，且不涉及竞争的背景下当事人具体的私人的合法权益，但会影响到更广泛的公民区域或者整个管辖权。对以这种听证会的形式而达成的立法决策，法院事后不会给予评论；如果受到质疑，审查只会确定它们是否符合宪法或违反国家的法律。例如，法院不会检查由县级市议会或委员会提出的基本预算的决定是否正确无误。此外，参与成长管理法案（GMA）全面计划的县可以由成长管理听证委员会审查，其后会由法院检查其与 GMA 的一致性。//

对于某些有争议的立法问题，在任何公开听证会之前经历周到的公共过程是非常重要的。听证会在这个过程中经常较晚出现，并可能给市民留下当地官员不愿了解他们想法的印象。理事会或商会虽然正式，但是对于不习惯公开演讲的市民来说可是让人生畏。听证的过程往往没有留下合理讨论的空间或是对之前的证词给予的回应。//

虽然超出了这个重点问题的范围，但这里有一些关于公开程序的简单的想法。让公民参与到政策制定过程的早期阶段是有必要的。对于真正感兴趣的公民而言，以小组的形式参与程序是非常有效的。通过这个方式，可确保有机会参与的公民得到答案，而这通常不会发生在一个正式的公开听证会上。另外，可考虑雇用一个训练有素的主持人，以便在遇到真正有争议的问题时能够推进讨论的进行。正式的公开程序可能非常耗时和昂贵。然而，这些程

序有助于推动达成能得到社会大众支持的解决方案。//

　　准司法听证会与立法措施不同，涉及具体当事人的具体合法权益，这种听证会得出的结果必须依据听证会的"记录"。准司法听证会受到较严格的立法听证会的程序要求。大多数由当地政府举行的准司法机构听证会涉及土地使用，包括特定选址、初步绘图、变量和条件使用事项。//

　　只有当特定的法规有要求时，才有必要举行听证会。当然，当地政府可能在其他情况下举行听证会，如一些关于敏感或是需要寻求公众意见的争议性政策问题。如果您对一件事情是否需要举行公开听证会不清楚，我们建议您咨询您所在城市或县的检察官和律师。//

◆ *Passage 2*

　　欢迎您来到伊拉克问题调查第一天的公众听证会。你们里面也许有人不认识我，我是约翰·齐尔考特，伊拉克问题调查委员会主席。和我一起的还有我的同事，劳伦斯·弗里德曼教授、马丁·吉尔伯特教授、罗蒂·克莱恩和乌莎·普拉莎尔男爵夫人。我们一起组成了伊拉克问题调查委员会。我旁边的是委员会助理玛格丽特·阿尔德雷德。//

　　成立伊拉克问题调查委员会的目的，是查找从英国参与伊拉克战争的经验教训，从而为政府可能会面临的类似情况提供帮助。//

　　要做到这一点，我们需要确定发生了什么。我们根据从文件和直接经历此事的人员那里收集的证据将整个时间联系起来。然后，我们需要知道在整个事件中，我们什么做得好，什么不好，并且关键的是为什么。//

　　我和我的同事本着开放的思想开展这个工作。我们没有政治立场并且不隶属于任何党派。我们用证据说话。我们将彻底、严格、公正、坦率地着手我们的工作。//

　　我本人以及调查委员会致力于以开放的态度行事，并决心尽可能使我们的过程公开化。我欢迎加入我们的市民，感谢你们今天上午花时间和精力来到这里。我也欢迎来到伊丽莎白二世中心的媒体。我很开心地看到对于那些没有亲自到场的朋友，调查程序可通过广播和互联网传播。//

　　这些公众听证会的活动将得到最密切的关注，但他们只是组成我们工作的一部分。//

　　在过去的几个月里我们已经要求并获得了大量 2001 年 9 月期间政府部门

涉及伊拉克的书面材料。我们花了大量时间梳理这些官方记录，并会继续在未来数月继续这项工作。我们相信，我们能够获得所需的所有材料。//

但是，我们不希望也不会仅仅听取官方代表的看法。我们重视听取具有广泛代表性的民众和组织的意见。我们想知道英国各地人的看法。对于我们正在考虑的问题，我们希望得到具有挑战性的观点。通过若干次会议，我们已经开始了这项工作：//

我们与那些在伊拉克被打死或失踪人员的家庭举行了 5 次会面。我们非常感激所有那些与我们交谈的人们。//

我们与伊拉克老兵举行了预备会议，与各方面专家举行了两次研讨会。我们希望明年年初能有进一步的讨论。//

我们还希望任何拥有信息的人，或者与我们的工作相关的愿意发表个人见解的人与我们联系。我们感谢所有已经联系我们的人。//

今天开始下一阶段。我们呼吁对于英国在伊政策的发展和实施有第一手经验的人作为证人。我们的第一轮听证会今天开始，一直到 2010 年 2 月初。然后，我们的公众听证会将暂停一下，回到对书面材料进行的分析。我们将举办一些不公开听证会，来对那些一旦公开就会损害公共利益的事项进行取证，或者对那些有难言之隐的证人进行取证。对于在什么情况下将举行不公开听证会，大家可以查询委员会网站上公布的议定书。//

2010 年，我们将举行新一轮听证会。我们打算邀请一些先前的证人，并邀请一些与所谈话题相关的新证人。我现在想强调的是，在第一轮听证会上，如果人们没有了解到他们所期望了解的任何事情，那么他们就不应该妄下结论：因为将有更多新的情况出现。//

一旦我们收集了所需要的所有证据，我们便可以得出结论并提出建议。我们计划于 2010 年年底前形成报告。拖延这一进程无论对于个人还是对于国家都是不利的。然而，我们的目标是提供一个全面的分析，从而为改善公共治理和决策作出贡献。如果这需要多一点的时间，我希望大家谅解。//

以上是明年的计划。现在需要制定出在公共听证会的初步阶段我们计划讨论的内容，以及我们计划如何开展这项工作。//

我们要建立一个对英国在伊拉克的各种核心要素明确的认识，以及这些核心要素如何随着时间的推移而发展。我们首先从对部长们形成和实施政府政策起到关键作用的高级官员和军官的意见开始。我们希望通过他们了解作出决定和执行任务的过程。这将使我们对自 2001 年以来英国制定政策和实施的各个方面有清晰的认识。我们将了解为什么个别的政策或行动方针被采纳，以及采用其他途径都被给予了哪些考虑。//

我们一旦了解到初步证据，将就有关问题向部长和其他官员收集证据，这将贯穿整个过程。在某些情况下，我们会根据早些时候收集到的证据，而进行详细的讨论。在其他情况下，我们可能需要在稍后阶段重新回到这些问题。在新的一年，将是那些在听证会期间，而不是之前，我们将对军事行动的合法性举行听证会。//

我们的质证过程会用到大量我们已经审查过的文件。这给了我们对这一时期主要事件的良好认识，问题和预先处理的事务。口头证据将建立在我们以前的知识上。这将有助于发展调查的路线，但我必须强调，这些路线处在发展之中。我们依然采取一开始的开放态度。我们承诺，以及英国的普通市民可以期待从我们这里得到的是彻底、公正、客观和公正的保证。//

也许这是一个适当的时机去规划我们对程序如何进行的预期。

伊拉克问题调查委员会的成员会问一些问题。证人会为自己回答。我们希望他们始终提供真实、公正和准确的证据。我们今天不打算提涉及可能危害国家安全或其他重要公共利益证据的问题，我们在已经发布的协定中对此作过描述。在极不可能的情形下，如证据指向诸如国家安全等敏感事项的时候，我会停止诉讼。//

正如我以前说过，我们不是法庭、审讯或法定调查，我们的流程将反映这种差别。没有人是在受到审判。只有法院能确定有罪或无罪，而我们不行。但我在这里作出承诺，一旦我们作出最终报告，如果事出有因，我们不会回避对他们的批评。//

最后，正如之前所说，我们高兴地看到这些都是公开会议。我们欢迎今天以及今后几个星期参加听证会的朋友。这些都是我们要研究的重要问题，我们希望深入事件中心，不希望我们的工作因为一些骚乱而被干扰。对于我们希望今天在座的各位所应作出的具体行为我们都已经写在了我们的网站上面。这与大众参与议会时对其的希望没什么不同。和那里一样，没有达到要求的人必须离开。//

对于今天的听证会也一样：正如我上面所说的，前 5 个星期的听证会的目的是明确 2001 年至 2009 年英国参与伊拉克的主要特点。我们已邀请对英国政府的决策和政策执行有独特视角的高级官员和军事人员（根据他们的任职）提供证词。今天，我们从 2001 年开始。坐在我面前的是彼得·里基茨先生，他在 2001 年任外交和联邦事务部政治总干事；威廉·帕蒂先生，他曾是外交部中东局局长；西蒙·韦伯，他曾是国防部政策室主任。//

## ◆ *Passage 3*

NPC Law Committee recently issued a notice that a legislative hearing will be held on September 27, widely seeking advice on the matter of personal income tax "threshold" in the draft amendment to Law of Personal Income Tax. This will be the first time that NPC and its Standing Committee hold hearings on legislation and also the first in the work of the NPC standing committee. It signifies a major exploration by China's top legislature on the implementation of scientific and democratic legislation and indicates that China has entered into a new development stage of democratic legislation. //

With the development of legislation and legislative mentality, in terms of local legislation, legislative hearing is no longer a fresh "import". Since the promulgation of Legislation Law in 2000 to the end of 2004, the country has a total of 24 provincial-level standing committee of People's Congress holding 38 legislative hearings for the draft of 39 local laws and regulations. Legislative hearings cover a wide range of market management, consumer protection, environment protection, urban public facilities construction, demolition, gallantly rising to the occasion and other many aspects. Thus, legislative hearings have been generally set up in the local legislative process. However, the NPC and its Standing Committee has not yet held hearings on a nation-wide legislation. In this sense, the hearing on tax law, embody concrete steps by National People's Congress to expand means and forms of public participation in legislation, demonstrating major legislative initiatives of democratic values. It is of great significance for implementation of constitutional authority by the people to manage state affairs in accordance with the law and to promote democratic legislative process. //

In the past, there used to be three ways of seeking advice for NPC and its Standing Committee in the process of national legislation. First is to seek the relevant written comments on the draft to the provinces, autonomous regions, municipalities directly under the Central Government, larger cities, the central authorities and the teaching and research institutions; Second is to hold a forum to solicit views of the people concerned; Third, some of the major draft laws will be released in the press, seeking advice from the whole society. Unlike the past, legislative hearing comes from Anglo-American common law of "natural justice" principle which refers to the fact that during the legislative process of law of common concern, in order to directly and openly solicit the views of the society, the legislature will invite representatives of the drafters, experts and scholars, stakeholders concerned with the motion as a hearing person or the realtors to the meeting to air their views and debate, which forms an important reference for the legislation. Legislative hearings often used by legislature as a rather effective procedural form of democracy has become an important way in many countries to enhance the effect of democratization and to get broad access to information relevant with the legislation. //

In China, building a socialist market economy and democratic political conditions create the conditions for the legislature to implement the hearing system legislation. Legislation Law has specified the practice of the legislative hearing by NPC and its Standing Committee that: "The Constitution and Legislative Affairs Committee, the special committee and the Standing Committee shall listen to the views on the legislative bill included into the agenda of the Standing Committee meeting. Seeking views can be through holding forums, seminars, hearings and other forms. " This can be seen as the clear stipulation on the full implementation of Legislative Hearing System by the NPC Standing Committee. Implementation of legislative hearings system has its own system of values and social significance: //

First, the legislative hearing system is conducive to achieving an open, fair and transparent legislative process and is an important way to protect the citizens' right to learn the truth about the major legislation affairs by the state and society. Legislative hearings will be completely open to the community. The focus and the matter of the hearing will be announced to the whole society in advance through notice. Qualified citizens can sign up for the realtors or audience. Legislative hearings open to the news media will also allow more people to know about the draft and opinions from various sides. //

Second, the legislative hearing system provide a public presentation forum for debate and evidence for people and put up an information exchange platform between the legislators, law-executor, and law-abiding people which is an effective link in democratic legislation to reflect public opinion and pool their wisdom. Through the hearings, representatives of different points of view can directly state their hopes and requirements and the legislature can fully understand where the interests and conflicts lie so that the legislation can better reflect the reasonable aspirations of the public and make the "public goods" better serve the public. The fundamental objective of safeguarding social stability and harmony can be finally achieved. //

Third, for the majority of the people, the legislative hearing system provides an effective democratic training, education, promotion and living democratic "classroom". An important feature of difference between hearing and seminars lies in its strict and normative procedures. To ensure broad representation and equal opportunity to speak, each time a hearing is governed by strict rules on realtor's selection, the number of participants, the order of speech, the content of the speech, timing of speeches, the host and the recorder, all of which are clearly defined. Ordinary people participate in the real legislative process in such a way that can directly obtain an opportunity to express their aspirations in a standardized place through procedural means. Then the people can really enjoy social life in the country of democracy and further enhance the democratic and legal awareness and sense of master, thereby indirectly promoting the process of democratic politics in China. //

Fourth, the legislative hearing system will help improve the quality of legislation and can ensure scientificity and feasibility of the legislation within the scope of the law as much as possible. Through legislative hearing the legislature can extensively collect legislation material, find the truth, understand the relevant background knowl-edge, the community's response, and the social benefits after the passage of laws so as to make the legislation consistent with the social reality and receive wide recogni-tion. This not only takes into account the legislative democracy and efficiency, but will also prevent the bias and deficiency of legislation, which forms a curb on the legislature, fundamentally ensuring scientificity and feasibility of the legislation.

"Threshold" issue of personal income tax is related not only to a reasonable regulation of social wealth by the country, but also to the vital interests of the majority of income-earner, and to the balance between personal interests and social welfare. It is a hard nut both in policy-choice and in legislation-adjustment in any country, and the formulation and consideration of relevant legislation is also an extremely complex and difficult weighing process. This time, the NPC Standing Committee chooses tax law amendment as a breakthrough. The hearings allow more members of society direct involvement of the process of tax legislation and to express their views directly to the legislature to protect their own interests. This will greatly enhance the communication between the legislature and the society in the process of demonstration, drafting, and review of the law so that it will ensure the law being made have solid bases and will gain universal social understanding and public support after its passage. This has sufficiently shown that although the hearing carried out by NPC is only for a "threshold" issue, its symbolic significance is far beyond the personal income tax law itself. It is a demonstration of democratic value of legislation and an important milestone in the process of rule of law in China. //

NPC Law Committee, Financial and Economic Committee and the Legislative Commission of the NPC Standing Committee are scheduled to hold hearing on the standard of personal income tax deduction in personal income tax law, on September 27, 2005, Beijing. //

The anchorpersons of the hearing: Yang Jingyu, chairman of the NPC Law Committee, Liu Jibin, Vice Chairman of the NPC Financial and Economic Committee, Hu Kangsheng, Director of Legislative Affairs Commission of NPC Standing Committee. //

Hearing disciplines: participants in the hearing shall observe the following disciplines: First, sit at designated areas. Second, turn off cell phones, pagers. Third, Hearing statement should be permitted by the anchorperson. Fourth, do not move around and make noises. Fifth, journalists can not interview participants during the hearing. Sixth, no other activities affect the normal hearing. The chairperson should stop those violating the disciplines; those who refuse to correct can be ordered to leave the venue. (Omitted) //

Liu Jibin: In today's hearing, 28 realtors of the hearing aired their views and elaborated on the reasons and arguments. Participants' speeches reflect different perspectives and requirements, displaying a strong sense of social responsibility and sense of master. Today's hearing was a vivid manifestation of socialist democracy. Here, on behalf of the NPC Law Committee, the NPC Financial and Economic Committee and the Legislative Affairs Commission of NPC Standing Committee, I would like to express my heartfelt thanks to all the speakers. At the same time, through the media I also would like to take the opportunity to extend my thanks to those who registered but did not attend the hearing because of limited number of speakers. I hope that people will continue to support national legislation by offering positive words and ideas. We will carefully and timely sort out and study today's opinions and suggestions in the hearing. We will produce the hearing report submitted to the NPC Standing Committee, as an important reference for legislation. Now I declare that the hearing is closed. Thank you! //

# V. 句子精炼 Sentences in Focus

**Directions**: *Interpret the following sentences alternatively into English or Chinese*:

1. While following proper hearing procedures may not eliminate litigation over the issues addressed in hearings, it will help prevent having the decisions made following public hearings overturned by the courts on procedural grounds.

2. An "open record hearing" under 1995 regulatory reform legislation (chapter 36. 70B RCW) is a public hearing, while a "closed record appeal" is a public meeting.

3. For example, a court will not review whether the basic budgetary decisions made by a city council or county commission were correctly made. On the other hand, comprehensive plans in Growth Management Act (GMA) counties may be reviewed by a growth management hearings board, and maybe later by a court, for consistency with the GMA.

4. Quasi‐judicial public hearings, unlike legislative ones, involve the legal rights of specific parties, and the decisions made as a result of such hearings must be based upon and supported by the "record" developed at the hearing.

5. Of course, a local government may hold a public hearing in other instances, such as when it desires public input on a sensitive or controversial policy issue. If you have any question as to whether a public hearing is required for a particular matter, we recommend that you consult with your city attorney or county prosecutor.

6. I welcome those members of the public who join us here today—thank you for taking the time and effort to travel here this morning. I also welcome the media present here at the QEII. For those not physically present, I am pleased that the Inquiry proceedings are available for broadcast and are being streamed on the Internet.

7. Over the past months we have requested and received mountains of written material from Government departments involved in Iraq during 2001 – 09. We have spent many hours combing through these official records—and will continue to do this in the months ahead. We are confident that we will have access to all the material that we need.

8. We will hold some private hearings: to take evidence on matters which if disclosed in public would cause harm to the public interest, or where there are other genuine reasons why a witness would have difficulty being frank in public.

9. What I would like to stress now is that people should not jump to conclusions if they do not hear everything they expect to in the first round of hearings: there will be more to follow.

10. We have invited to give evidence those senior officials and military personnel who (by the posts they occupied) had a unique perspective on UK government decision making and the implementation of those policies.

11. 自 2000 年《立法法》颁布至 2004 年底，全国已有 24 个省级人大常委会共对 39 件地方性法规草案举行过 38 次立法听证会。立法听证的内容涵盖了市场管理、消费者权益保护、环境资源保护、城市公用设施建设、拆迁管理和见义勇为等诸多方面。

12. 立法听证会不同于以往的这些方式，它源于英美普通法的"自然公正"原则，是指立法机关在开展受到社会普遍关注的立法活动的过程中，为了直接、公开听取社会意见，邀请草案起草人代表、专家学者、当事人、与议案有关的利害关系人作为听证人或陈述人到会，就相关立法焦点问题充分表达意见和展开辩论，并以此作为审议法律草案的重要依据和参考的一项立法制度。

13. 通过听证会，不同观点的代表能够直接陈述自己的希冀与要求，立法机关也能够全面了解各方利益和矛盾所在，从而使立法更好地反映社会主体的合理心声，使法律这一"公共产品"更好地为民众服务，从根本上维护社会的稳定与和谐。

14. 立法机关可以通过听证会广泛收集立法资料，发现事实真相，了解有关的背景知识及社会各界的反应，以及法律如获通过后应有的社会效益等，从而有助于立法符合实际并获得广泛的社会认同。

15. 在此，我代表全国人大法律委员会、全国人大财经委员会和全国人大常委会法制工作委员会向各位陈述人表示由衷感谢。同时，也借此机会通过新闻媒体向报名参加本次听证会，但因名额所限未能参加的人士表示感谢。希望大家继续关心和支持国家的立法工作，为国家立法积极地建言献策。对今天听证会上的意见和建议，我们将在会后及时进行认真的整理和研究，提出听证报告，提交给全国人大常委会，作为立法时的重要参考和依据。

# 记者招待会

## Unit 3　Press Conference

# I．主题知识 Legal Knowledge

记者招待会，又称新闻发布会。是社会组织或个人，根据自身的某种需要，邀请有关新闻单位的记者、编辑、主持人以及社会听众，宣布某一消息，并接受参加者提问的一种特殊会议。它是公关人员与新闻界联络的重要形式，是一种极具影响力的公共关系活动。记者招待会的功能和作用概述如下。

## 一、具有提供信息和沟通协调的功能

记者招待会是主办者就某方面重大问题予以公布或作出解释或接受记者集体采访而专为记者举行的会议，具有极强的目的性。因而记者招待会也是信息的集散地。记者招待会提供信息的功能主要表现在：一是不同类型、种类的记者招待会如政治类、经济类、军事类、外交类、教育类、体育类、文化娱乐类等的记者招待会可以提供内容不同、形式多样的信息；二是在某一个单一的记者招待会（专题性记者招待会除外）上，由于会议的议题一般是分散的、模糊的，记者们通过提出不同的问题，也可以得到回答各异的信息。所谓记者招待会的沟通协调功能，主要是指记者招待会为主办方和公众构筑了一个交流联系的平台，通过记者招待会，公众可以了解到主办方发布或澄清的信息，而主办方亦可迅速接收到公众的反馈，更好地做好工作。

## 二、具有解疑释惑和稳定社会的功能

记者招待会还具有解疑释惑和稳定社会的功能。这一点在政府运用记者招待会处理突发事件时表现得尤为明显。当突发事件发生后，各种舆论、声音通过不同的渠道在"观点的自由市场"上展开交锋。这个时候，如果权威部门"集体失音"，那么各种流言、谣言就会乘机兴风作浪，占领"观点市场"阵地，误导大众舆论。由于此类谣言完全是在传谣者不了解事实真相情况下的一种负向猜测的结果，因此辟谣的关键即是以最广泛、最权威、最及时的方式向公众公布事实真相。记者招待会作为一种直接与受众见面的权威发言，它通过权威机构举行，由权威人士就当前瞩目的重要问题、重大事件向记者发表公开谈话，回答记者提问，阐明政府的立场、观点、态度，介绍情况，提供新闻信息，回答群众关心的问题，利用广播、电视、报纸等大众传播工具向社会广为宣传、扩大影响，在排除受众疑虑、消除谣言传播、稳定社会方面具有其他传播形态无法替代的作用。

### 三、具有保障公民知情权的功能

知情权指的是民众享有通过大众传媒了解政府工作信息和社会公共信息的法定权利。在现代社会中，随着政治多元化和社会信息化，公民知情权的有无和多少成了衡量一个民主自由程度和信息化程度的重要标志之一。了解政府决策、施政及各种工作情况的信息，了解立法和司法机关立法和执法情况的信息，了解与其利益相关的各种社会公共信息，是公民知情权的内涵和本质所在。保障、维护公民的知情权重要举措之一就是建立和完善新闻发言人制度，确保政府信息公开、透明。

### 四、具有社会监督与环境监测的功能

记者招待会的传播具有开放性，新闻发布会大都是公开举行，且有多种媒体参与报道，有关方面所论及的政策、立场、观点、态度，以及重要问题和重大事件的经过、细节等通过电视、广播报等大众传播工具为千百万人所了解，具有很强的开放性和透明度。并且，记者提出的问题大多是社会瞩目的"热点""焦点""尖端"问题。对此，答问者必须立即作出回答，这对增强民众与政府机构、社会团体等的相互信任，加强公众对政府部门、机构官员、社会集团、知名人士的监督都有重大的作用。

### 五、具有塑造和调整形象的公关功能

新闻传播能够扩大和提升个人、团体和社会活动的知名度和影响力，增

强其显著性，授予其显赫的社会地位，令受众关注，有利于报道主体意志的最终实现。记者招待会的功能和作用更是如此。记者招待会自诞生以来便与公共关系结下了不解之缘，它对于塑造和调整政府、集团、企业、个人的形象都具有重要的作用。

# Ⅱ. 词汇热身 Vocabulary Warm-up

**Directions**: *Give the English equivalents of the following Chinese expressions*:

| | | |
|---|---|---|
| 庭审直播 | 当庭释放 | 共同犯罪 |
| 裁判文书 | 疑罪从无 | 明星代言 |
| 人民陪审员 | 模拟审判 | 医疗器械 |
| 错判错杀 | 首席大法官 | 突发事件 |
| 抗诉 | 国家赔偿 | 非法行医 |
| 《人权白皮书》 | 精神赔偿 | 定罪量刑 |

# Ⅲ. 课文口译 Text for Interpreting

◆ *Passage 1*

**Directions**: Listen to the passage and interpret from Chinese into English at the end of each segment.

（下面内容节选自 2005 年第 22 届世界法律大会中国组委会秘书长万鄂湘介绍大会筹备工作时答记者问）

**CCTV 社会与法频道记者**：15 年以前，世界法律大会在我国成功召开了一次，15 年以后，第 22 届世界法律大会再次在我国召开。请问万院长，在这 15 年当中，我国在立法、司法和法学研究、法学教育各个方面所取得的重大成就是什么？//

**万鄂湘**：谢谢这位记者的提问。的的确确，时隔 15 年，1990 年大会时，我是第 14 届世界法律大会的联络员，现在我成了这次会议的秘书长。我从自己人生走过的 15 年中体会到，中国的立法、司法和行政、法律教育和法学教育都取得了非常重要的成果。从立法方面来看，在 15 年当中一个非常重要的制度体现刚好也是在 15 年前，从那年开始，我们的行政诉讼制度确立了。也就是说有了行政诉讼法，我们国家公民权的保护得到了一个实质性的飞跃。还有最近几年，我们以人为本的概念出现，特别是去年，我们宪法修正案把国家尊重和保护人权写进去，还有一系列法律方面的修改，都已经达到了一个新的高度，这是立法方面的进展。//

从司法角度来看，我们司法的制度性改革也进入了非常重要的程序。我个人体会最深的就是我们司法的透明度大大地提高了，特别是借助于 WTO 的加入程序。WTO 程序当中有一个非常重要的要求，就是提高透明度。大家对我们司法审判改革体会最多的就是透明度的增加，特别是很多审判在很多国家都不一定能够做到庭审直播，还有很多案件的裁判文书在宣判的当天或者第二天就可以在网上查到。我跟其他国家的法官们共同谈论这个话题的时候，他们感觉到，的的确确，中国司法的透明度和民主化达到了一定的高度。特别值得一提的是，从今年 5 月 1 日开始，我们要实行一个非常重要的人民陪审员制度，这也是司法民主和公开的一个非常重要的进展。//

从法学教育看，我也是有亲身体会的。5 年前，我还是一个法学教授。从一个法学教授到一个法官，我也亲历了这十多年来我们法学教育的飞速发展。我们的法学教育从无到有，从有又到无，再从无到有，现在是蓬勃发展的时期。并且，法学教育的国际化或者相互之间的交流、交往越来越多。我们中国法学界在世界上发表重要的研究论文或者是发表重要研究成果的机会也越来越多。同时，我们还看到，更多的法学教授也正在加入司法队伍，我本人是之一，还有最高人民法院的常务副院长曹建明教授，现在也成了司法界非常有名的人物。在高级人民法院、中级人民法院有越来越多的学者加入司法改革的过程中或者加入司法队伍当中。//

最后，我想提一点，就是我国司法界与国际司法界同仁们的交往日益增多。我们每年都要邀请 20 位左右的各个国家的首席大法官和最高法院的院长到中国来访问。每年我们也会派出 300 多名各级法院的法官到各个国家去学习和参加国际会议。每年我们要接待的其他国家司法机关到中国来访问的人员将近 800 人。这样频繁的交流和访问使我们国家的司法体制改革和我们国家有关的法学研究、教育和交流合作达到了一个新的高度。//

**新京报记者：**万院长介绍时提到这次世界法律大会有一个议题就是人权，

我想提一个现在大家比较关心的问题。现在大家都比较关注"湖北杀妻案"，有专家评论"湖北杀妻案"折射出了在司法实践中的错判错杀。案件有一个共性，就是审判机关的价值取向是疑案从轻，而不是疑案从无，从互相配合到互相制约。请问万院长，在司法实践中是否存在这些问题？最高人民法院在司法保障人权方面有哪些举措？如何完善和改进？谢谢。//

**万鄂湘：**谢谢这位记者的提问。的确，现在很多媒体的头条新闻都涉及"湖北佘某林杀妻案"再审的结果。非常巧合的是，昨天国务院新闻办也发表了人权白皮书，当中有一项很重要的内容就是司法的保障问题。在谈有关情况的时候，我想简单向大家讲讲我们国家司法体制上级别管辖的问题，由于佘某林案件最早是以谋杀罪或者命案的概念提出来的，它的第一审是荆州市中级人民法院。这样的案件最早由中级人民法院审理，二审就到了省高级人民法院。在审查荆州市中级人民法院有关案件的时候，办案人员感觉到存在疑点，就发回重审。//发回重审以后，有疑点存在的情况下，他们就把这个案件又发回到原审最基层法院，即京山县人民法院审理。也就是说，在起诉的时候，这个案件就已经不是作为一个谋杀罪确定的、能够判死刑或者是死缓或者是无期的案件起诉，已经是作为一般的案件或者是案情不是非常肯定的案件。因此，就出现了这个案件又回到京山县人民法院审理的情况。这是我们在案件管辖方面要向大家介绍的程序方面的情况。//

从昨天上午的审判结果来看，佘某林最后被宣告无罪，当庭释放。如果当事人不提出上诉，宣告无罪再上诉的可能性几乎没有。反过来还要看检察院是否提出抗诉，如果检察院不抗诉，当事人不上诉的话，这就是生效的判决。生效判决从审判机关的角度来看，有一些值得总结和归纳的经验和教训，我想至少有下面三点值得我们考虑。//

这三个方面就是有关司法理念方面调整和变更的。//

第一，对刑法的功能和刑事诉讼制度的作用的全面认识问题。除了惩罚和打击犯罪、维护公共秩序和安全，是否还有一个更重要的功能，或者是同等重要的功能，那就是保护无辜和维护人权？这也是司法特别是刑事司法的双重功能当中一个非常重要的功能。//

第二，我们要用司法的手段来保护人权、保护无辜，那么就要有一个选择，出现疑罪的时候我们如何作出取舍？是疑罪从无还是疑罪从轻？//

第三，在疑罪或者疑罪比较多，对案件事实有很多疑问的情况下，我们

到底是从民意还是从事实？这也是我今天上午听有关新闻评论的时候听到的一个非常有价值的问题。//

也就是说，这三个问题都是非常有逻辑关联性的。不管我们将来观念有什么改变或者发展到什么程度，我们都有一个原则，那就是审判机关必须严守底线，无论是死刑案件还是其他任何案件，审判机关作为公平和正义的最后一道防线，必须严把事实关，确保程序公正和实体公正。//

**中国日报记者：** 请问万院长，第 14 届世界法律大会在北京召开的时候，中国国家领导人出席并致辞，请问是什么样的领导人？本届大会是否按同样的级别举行？//

**万鄂湘：** 有关哪一级国家领导人出席开幕式的问题，历次世界法律大会都是由东道国的国家主要领导人出席开幕式，第 14 届世界法律大会的开幕式是由当时的国家主席杨尚昆主席出席开幕式的。我们正在做有关方面的工作，也希望这次出席会议的国家领导人的层次能够跟以往一样，也希望来的代表是各个国家的首席大法官。至少从目前看来，已经有了确定回复的有美国、英国、法国、德国、俄罗斯、西班牙的代表，还有亚洲和非洲很多重要国家的首席大法官和大法官都已经确定要参加这次大会。有些国家的首席大法官将率领非常大的代表团，有的国家则是由总检察长或司法部部长率团出席这次重要的会议。//

**新华社记者：** 第一个问题，请问万院长，刚才您在介绍中说，这次大会将在北京和上海两地进行，请问这两地是如何进行分工的？怎么样安排议程？第二个问题，我们看到昨天佘某林的案子已经得到了重审，佘某林无罪释放。据当地的媒体报道，佘某林和他的家人会就这个案件申请一些赔偿。依您的看法，按照国家的赔偿法，他本人有没有可能获得赔偿？这个赔偿有没有可能包含精神赔偿？谢谢。//

**万鄂湘：** 首先回答你第一个问题，关于在北京和上海两地会议议程的分配问题。我刚才已经简单地提到了，在北京的时间是 2 天半，在上海是 2 天，北京主要是开幕式、专题研讨、法律纪念日，还有模拟审判。在北京有 15 个专题，在人民大会堂各分厅三个议题同时举行，所有的代表都可以在这三个议题中选择一个感兴趣的议题去听。在上海有一个简短的开幕式，有 7 个议题，7 个中有 1 个是重要议题，就是"法律、法治与法院"，专门占了一个下午的时间，由各个国家的首席大法官或其代表发表演讲，包括肖扬首席大法官。另外 6 个是同时在不同的两个厅进行分题讨论，代表也可以在这两者中选择感兴趣的议题参与讨论，这样代表按照兴趣的分流和不同的专题可以共同进行，也可以节省一些时间，大家发言的机会也会更多一些。上海除了这些有关的讨论活动，由于一些首席大法官第一次来中国，我们的外事接待部门还会安排他们到我们的基层人民法院、高级人民法院看看我们人民法院的建设情况，这些是前后穿插活动的安排。//

第二个问题，有关佘某林的案件，对他是否有权或者是否有可能提出国家赔偿的问题，昨天宣告他无罪的同时，京山县人民法院的法官、审判长已经告知佘某林，你有这个权利，可以提出国家赔偿的请求。数额的多少将由中国一直以来的司法实践决定。至于精神的赔偿问题，我们也有司法解释。我相信，各级人民法院会根据最高人民法院制定的司法解释，对他就精神损害或者是其他有关方面提出的赔偿要求给予合理、公正的判决。//

**人民日报记者：**万院长，您介绍说，这次世界法律大会的专题设置一共是 6 个大类，共 22 个专题。请问这 6 个大类 22 个专题是怎么选择出来的？对中国的法治建设有什么积极意义？//

**万鄂湘：**非常好的问题。这 6 个大类 22 个专题是围绕着一个主题提出来的，就是构建和谐社会。和谐社会不只是我们中国国内的和谐社会，而是把它延伸到在国际上有一个共同的、大家所期望的主题，那就是法治与和谐社会。//

"和谐"这两个字是 WJA 也就是世界法学家协会异口同声说出来的，这次的主题就是追求国际和谐。这个主题刚好和我们国家所追求的国内的和谐社会是相关联的。和谐的概念包括民主法治、公平正义、诚信友爱、充满活力、安定有序、人与自然的和谐相处，我想这不是偶然的巧合，而是国际社会共同的兴趣所在。//

如果把这 22 个专题分开，大家手上的资料中都有介绍，跟我们 6 个大主题相比较的话，恰好都是有共同目标的。中国作为一个负责任的大国，在国际社会当中，正在发挥日益重要的作用，在建设国内和谐社会的同时，也愿意为国际和谐社会或者是和谐的国际社会作出自己的贡献和努力。//

**主持人：**
新闻发布会到此结束。//

## ◆ *Passage 2*

（以下内容节选自 2009 年国新办就假药、劣药刑事案件应用法律情况举行的发布会。5 月 26 日，最高人民法院副院长熊选国先生、最高人民检察院副检察长朱孝清先生和国家食品药品监督管理局副局长边振甲先生，向大家介绍这一司法解释的有关情况，并回答记者们的提问。）

**中国日报记者：**此次新颁布的司法解释规定，为生产、销售假药、劣药犯罪分子提供广告等宣传的行为将被以共犯论处，这是否意味着以后假药、劣药广告将会接受更严格的审查和更严格的惩处？//

**熊选国：**司法实践中对于生产、销售假药、劣药的共同犯罪行为，要依法严厉打击，这也是群众反映比较突出的问题。所以，在司法实践中，对于生产、销售假药、劣药的一些共同犯罪行为，向生产、销售假药、劣药的犯罪分子提供方便条件，比如提供资金、账号等，也包括刚才提到的为其提供广告宣传活动，针对这些共同犯罪行为，这次解释对生产、销售假药、劣药的共犯行为进行了具体的规定。//

我相信，司法解释对于共犯行为进行具体、明确的规定，将为司法机关惩治生产、销售假药、劣药的共犯行为提供具体的法律依据，同时这也是一种规范，对于为生产、销售假药、劣药的犯罪提供方便和便利条件的人也是一种警示。假药、劣药的广告行为确实一直是老百姓反应十分强烈的问题，那些明知他人生产、销售假药、劣药而在各种媒体上为其提供广告的宣传活动，在群众中造成了十分恶劣的影响。为了使老百姓免受假药、劣药广告的误导和侵害，这一次我们在司法解释中将广告行为专门列举出来，作为共犯来打击。对于假药、劣药的广告等宣传行为，今后要加大审查力度和打击力度，要进行更为严格的审查、更为严厉的惩处。同时欢迎广大群众对这种行为进行举报，协助有关部门依法开展调查和处理。//

**凤凰卫视记者：**第一个问题，请问食药局的边先生，因为我们知道，现在甲型流感感染人数增加，我们也看到这个司法解释也特别强调在这个特别时期会依法从重处罚这些制售假劣药的行为。请问针对这次甲型流感，有哪些药品或者是医药用品属于我们加强审查的范围的？对于中间可能出现的制售假药的行为，现在有没有相关的统计结果？我们会有什么针对的加强措施？

第二个问题，针对上一个广告从重处罚的问题，请问明星代言行为是否包含在其中？//

　　**边振甲：**国家食品药品监督管理局在防控甲型 H1N1 流感的工作中，主要履行了四项职责：

　　第一，加强监管，确保防治药品和医疗器械的质量安全。对合法的药品生产企业、医疗器械生产企业生产的防控甲型 H1N1 流感的药品、医疗器械要加强质量监管。我们已经发出了一些通知，包括派人到相关的工厂进行监督检查，主要是确保防控药品和医疗器械的质量安全。//

　　第二，做好甲型 H1N1 流感疫苗研发和生产的准备工作。在准备工作中，我们配合生产企业做好准备，提前介入，提前和他们一起沟通如何符合国家的规范要求，如何符合国家规定的申报注册的程序，在安全有效的前提下进行审查。//

　　第三，做好特别审批工作。在防控工作中，涉及防控甲型 H1N1 流感的药品、医疗器械，我们建立了特别审批渠道，不受节假日的限制，只要符合程序，是安全的、有效的，在这样的前提下我们都会启动特别审批程序，以满足国内防控甲型 H1N1 流感的需要。//

　　第四，加大打击假劣药品力度。凡是发现和甲型 H1N1 流感防控工作有关的假药、医疗器械，我们坚决予以打击。尤其是在当前全国都在防控甲型 H1N1 流感过程中，我们将更加严密地做好打击假劣药品和医疗器械的相关工作，一旦发现违法犯罪行为，我们都会严厉打击，确保防控药品、医疗器械的安全。//

　　**熊选国：**关于第一个问题，我补充两句。这次解释明确规定在自然灾害、事故灾难、公共卫生事件等突发事件发生时期，生产、销售用于应对突发事件药品的假药、劣药要依法从重处罚。司法解释这样规定主要也是考虑到老百姓对假药、劣药深恶痛绝，在自然灾害、公共突发事件这个特定时期，生产假药、劣药更是直接危害人民群众的生命健康安全。不仅危害个体人员的生命健康安全，而且会对整个救灾、抢险工作产生直接的危害。所以，司法解释这次规定要依法从重处罚。我相信这个规定也会增强我们防控甲型 H1N1 流感病毒、保障药品安全的信心。//

　　对于你提到的明星代言行为，从司法解释角度来看，首先还是提供广告宣传这样一个行为的定位问题。根据《刑法》的规定，生产、销售假药、劣药犯罪，是故意犯罪，构成共犯是以知道或者应当知道他人生产、销售假药、劣药为前提的。所以，对于明星的代言行为，如果是明知他人生产、销售假药、劣药，符合《刑法》规定，作为共犯处理是可以的，但是这个前提很重要。//

　　**新京报记者：**第一个问题，司法解释第1条规定了生产、销售假药"足以严重危害人体健康"的认定标准，2001年的时候，"两高"也发布过一个司法解释，第3条也作了一些规定，这次解释里的规定和那个相比有哪些调整和补充？主要基于什么考虑？//

　　第二个问题，想请问熊院长，关于广告宣传的问题，如果媒体被新闻出版部门界定为非法出版物，是否包含在这个范围内？刚才讲到明星，我们经常在电视里看到或者在广播里听到的一些节目，如果最后被认定为做了非法假药劣药的广告宣传，这个节目的参与人，包括主持人、嘉宾和专家是否也要被界定为共犯？您刚才讲到一个很重要的前提就是"故意""知道或者应当知道"，那么怎么界定其是"知道或者应当知道"？//

　　**朱孝清：**我来回答第一个问题。生产、销售假药，只有达到"足以严重危害人体健康"的程度才构成生产、销售假药罪。这次"两高"的解释对"足以严重危害人体健康"的规定与2001年的司法解释相比有比较大的调整。主要有三个方面的情形：//

　　第一种情形，对原来的规定加以补充，使其更加全面。比如2001年的解释将"含有超标准的有毒有害物质"作为"足以严重危害人体健康"的一种情形，但是实践中还存在"不应含有有毒有害物质而含有"的情况。这次司法解释对这两种情况都作了规定。//

　　第二种情形，原来的解释没有作规定，这次作了增加。属于这种情形的有4项标准，现在解释第1条第2项到第5项，这几项都属于社会危害性比较严重、群众反映强烈、司法实践需要解决的情形。//

　　第三种情形，原来的解释作了规定，这次作了删除。属于这种情形的有3项，比如原来解释第3条第2项规定的"不含所标明的有效成分，可能贻误诊治的"，从司法实践来看，"不含所标明的有效成分"是界定这个药是不是假药的一个条件，因为生产、销售假药罪的条件有两个，一是假药，二是足以严重危害人体健康。某一个药品不含有所标明的有效成分，是认定该药品是否为假药的条件。"可能贻误诊治"，从司法实践来看，界定、认定是比较

困难的，可操作性比较差，所以这次把这一项删除了。//

　　总的来说，这次的修改调整，主要是为了适应打击生产、销售假药、劣药犯罪的需要，使司法解释更加完善。//

　　**熊选国：** 我来回答第二个问题，看来记者朋友们对广告很感兴趣。第二个问题实际上是两个问题，第一个问题是非法广告的问题，算不算广告，我想也要包括进来，尽管打广告的行为没有得到有关部门的批准，但实际上也在进行一种广告行为，像路边上或者墙上经常看到贴的"小广告"，肯定没有得到有关部门的批准，但是其实施了宣传行为，应该是司法解释规定的提供广告宣传的方式。//

　　第二个问题，怎么认定行为人知道或者应当知道。因为生产、销售假药罪首先要知道是假药，朱孝清先生刚才介绍了，首先是假药，然后是足以造成或者已经造成严重后果，才追究刑事责任。司法解释作为规定来讲，"知道或应当知道"是主观的东西，司法实践中"知道"一般是指行为人的供述或者有关的证人证言，都证明他是知道的，这当然就是"知道"。有些行为人不供述，就要靠客观证据，证明他是知道的。所以，"应当知道"实际上是通过客观证据来判断的，他知道是生产、销售假药，只不过被告人自己不承认、不供述。举一个例子，司法解释中有一条"没有或者伪造药品生产许可证或者批准文号，且属于处方药的"，作为广告来讲，你知道它没有批准文号，而且是处方药，那我就可以认定你是知道的。//

　　**美联社记者：** 这次司法解释的出台是否会使有关机关审判生产假药的工作变得更加容易呢？您是否认为今后法院审理相关案件的数量会上升？//

　　**熊选国：** 应该说您这个说法是正确的。这次解释总结了实践审判经验，把涉及生产、销售假药罪和生产、销售劣药罪的定罪标准进一步明确，而且把这两种犯罪的量刑标准也进一步明确了，所以为我们检察机关依法提起公诉，为法院依法审判（包括定罪量刑），提供了更为明确的依据。我相信随着该解释的发布实施，行政机关将进一步加大查处力度，司法机关将依法审判，对于这类案件我们都会依法给予惩处。//

　　**北京电视台记者：** 第一个问题，请问最高人民法院的熊院长，对于持有GMP证书的大企业生产的假劣药品，这次解释中有没有更新、更具操作性的细则，对于责任人的惩处是否有细化标准？第二个问题，最近很多药品在销售方式上出现了新方式，比如通过互联网进行销售，司法解释对于互联网销

售假劣药品的行为有没有更细化的管理细则和标准？//

**熊选国：**第一个问题，对于正规厂家，如果发生了生产、销售假药、劣药的情况，这里的情况也是比较复杂的，如果是故意生产、销售假药、劣药，按照司法解释就要以生产、销售、假药、劣药犯罪来定罪处罚，单位和个人犯罪的标准都是一样的。有些可能是过失行为，是一种渎职行为，按重大责任事故或者渎职犯罪依法定罪处罚，这些就要适用另外的定罪处罚标准。生产、销售假药、劣药犯罪是故意犯罪，不管是正规厂家还是个人，只要是故意生产、销售假药、劣药，法律都将给予严厉的惩处。//

第二个问题，互联网销售假药、劣药的问题，这是一种行为的方式，只要你销售，不管你通过什么方式，只要你销售的是假药，只要这个假药足以危害人体健康，不管是通过互联网还是其他的渠道销售，达到司法解释中规定的定罪量刑标准的，都要给予处罚。//

**中央电视台记者：**请问院长，该解释专门对医疗机构销售假药、劣药规定要追究刑事责任，这一点我们是怎么考虑的，如何执行？//

**熊选国：**医疗机构是救死扶伤、百姓最为信赖的地方，这些年也出现了个别医疗机构明知是假药、劣药而使用的情况。这种坑害百姓、蒙骗患者的情形是百姓最不愿意看到、最深恶痛绝、最难以理解的。这次司法解释针对医疗机构违法行为规定了专门条款，要严厉打击，这也是基于维护人民群众根本利益的需要。在执行过程中，应主要注意以下三点：//

第一点，该解释规定医疗机构知道或者应当知道是假药而使用或者销售，首先要达到定罪标准，如果是假药，要足以危害人体健康，这是司法解释第1条的规定，有6种情况，要符合这个标准。如果是劣药，要造成严重的后果。司法解释第3条对此有规定，要达到规定的定罪量刑标准。//

第二点，这里的医疗机构包括医院这些医疗单位，也包括个体行医者，不光是正规医院，还包括个体诊所、个体行医者。//

第三点，它是一种故意犯罪，主观上是知道或者应当知道是假药、劣药而使用或者销售的，按生产、销售假药、劣药犯罪来定罪处罚。//

**郭卫民：**最后一个问题。//

**香港文汇报记者：**按照该解释的规定，生产、销售假药罪，要求足以对人体健康造成严重危害，请问这些是否需要药监部门出具鉴定结论？如果不足以对人体健康造成严重危害，是否就不用承担刑事责任？//

**朱孝清**：是否要请药品检验机构出具鉴定结论涉及两方面的内容：一是生产的是不是假药、劣药，对这个问题一般要请药品检验机构出具鉴定结论。二是生产销售的假药有没有达到"足以严重危害人体健康"的程度，对这个问题，这次司法解释列举了 6 种情形。这 6 种情形，根据实际需要来确定是否要请药品检验机构来鉴定。如果说专业性比较强，通过专业机构才能判明的，要请药品检验机构来鉴定；如果专业性不是很强，司法人员直接能够判明它足以严重危害人体健康的，则不需要请药品检验机构鉴定。//

总的来说，是否要请药品检验机构鉴定，要看实际需要。如果司法机关认为需要请药品检验机构鉴定，就请他们鉴定；如果司法人员认为不需要请他们鉴定，司法机关能够直接判明就不用请他们鉴定。当然，我们在办案过程中不请检验机构鉴定，还可以请他们做专业咨询，这也是办案中经常有的情况。//

生产、销售假药如果达不到"足以严重危害人体健康"的程度将不构成生产、销售假药罪，但是如果构成了其他犯罪，还是要追究刑事责任的。比如根据《刑法》第 149 条和有关司法解释的规定，如果销售金额达到 5 万元以上，或者药品的货值金额达到 15 万元以上，就要按照《刑法》第 140 条，以生产、销售伪劣产品罪来追究刑事责任。再比如，这次司法解释第 6 条规定"实施生产、销售假药、劣药犯罪，同时构成生产、销售伪劣产品、侵犯知识产权、非法经营、非法行医、非法采供血等犯罪的，依照处罚较重的规定定罪处罚"。根据这个规定，如果生产、销售假药达不到足以严重危害人体健康的程度，但构成非法经营罪、假冒商标罪、非法行医罪、非法采供血罪，就按照行为人所触犯的罪名来追究刑事责任。//

另外，还要说明的是，行为人生产、销售假药，如果不构成犯罪，不追究刑事责任并不等于其可以不受处罚，因为药品监督管理部门还要依法追究其违法责任。//

**郭卫民**：明天下午 3 点在这里举行新闻发布会，请监察部、发改委、财政部、审计署的领导介绍中央扩大内需、促进经济增长政策落实的检查情况，欢迎大家出席。今天的发布会到此结束，谢谢各位。//

# IV. 参考译文 Reference Versions：

## ◆ *Passage 1*

**CCTV 12**：Fifteen years have passed since the 14th World Law Congress, so could you comment on the major achievements China has made during the past fifteen years in terms of the legislation, judiciary, law studies and the law education? //

**Wan**：Thank you for raising this question. Indeed fifteen years have passed. In 1990, at the 14th World Law Congress, I served as a coordinator for this congress, fifteen years later, now I serve as the secretary-general of the 20th World Law Congress. According to my personal experience, I feel that great achievements have been made in China in such areas as legal, judicial, administrative and law educational matters. For example, since 1990 to the current year, with fifteen years passed, we have established such a system as administrative lawsuits, procedures, which mean a great leap forward for the protection of the civil rights for our citizens, and we also put in place such a concept of putting people first. Last year in our constitution, we have included such a clause as respecting and protecting human rights. I think this is a clear demonstration of the great progress China has made in the legislative area and we have also remanded quite a lot of laws which are also clear indication of the improvement of our legislative work. //

In judicial area, we have pushed forward the institutional reform in a great matter. We have greater transparency of our judicial trials. That is partly thanks to China's WTO membership, because according to the WTO rules, one of the most important principles is the improvement of transparency, and you can see that nowadays we have live broadcast of some important trials, and you can look up those results of trials from the Internet. When I discuss these matters with my colleagues from other countries, they also express such an impression that the transparency and democracy of the judicial trials and matters of China have been increased greatly. Another important development is that since May 1 this year, we will have such an important system as the citizen jury system, which means great improvement in our judicial matters. //

Concerning the law education matter, indeed according to my personal experience, five years ago, I personally was a law professor, and during my transformation from a law professor to Vice President of Supreme People's Court, I deeply felt the rapid development of China in this regard, it is to say that the law development in China is a process from new to a dynamic progress. Nowadays we have seen frequent exchanges and cooperation in the law education. And law professionals in China have published their important research achievements or study results in the international community. Many law professors now have joined the contingent of legal professionals. Another example is the Executive Vice President of Supreme People's Court, Mr. Cao Jianming, who also was a law professor, and also in the high people's court and intermediate people's court, we have now many legal professionals who are to law professors or educators. //

Last, what I also want to mention is that the exchanges between China's judicial community and international judicial community have been more and more frequent. Every year we invite about 20 chief justices or presidents of supreme courts to visit China and every year we send more than 300 judges of courts at different levels to other countries to studies or participation in international conferences. We also receive nearly 800 foreign judges to China for such information sharing and exchanges. Such frequent interactions and cooperations are conducive to pushing the judicial reform and law education in China. //

**New Beijing Daily**: Mr. Wan, just now in your briefings you have said that one of the specific topics of the upcoming 22th World Law Congress will be humanized, so I would like to raise a question on human rights. Which is related to the acres in which an offender who is convicted of committing homicide of killing his wife in Hubei Province, and this case is connected with such phenomena that in the trial practices or judicial practices in China, there are some problems, such as in the process of making trials, there are some issues related to the moral selection, and in the process of the criminal procedures, the judges show such attendance as they pay more attention to the dimension with each other and pay less attention to mutual restriction or mutual restrained. So if there indeed are such phenomena, and how will the Supreme People's Court improve the protection of human rights from the judicial perspective and how will you improve your work? Thank you. //

**Wan**: Thank you for asking me this question. Indeed the case you mentioned nowadays have become the headlines of many major newspapers, and it is also a co-incidence that yesterday the Information Office of the State Council issued the White Paper on the Human Rights Situation in China in the year 2004, which also mentioned in judicial protection of human rights. Before answering your question, I would like to brief you aspects on the procedures of the jurisdiction over such cases in China. Because this case at the very beginning, involves the crime of murder, it was tried in the intermediate people's court of Jingzhou. And for the second trial of this case, it was raised to the provincial high court of Hubei Province. At this high court the judges there found that there were some suspicious aspects in this case, and so they returned this case to the original court which has the jurisdiction over this case. // This case happened in to be Jinshan County course level, that is to say, for the filing of this case, the case was not with hard evidence, and rather it was taken as a case where there is still suspicious evidence that still need to be cleared out. Therefore the case was returned to the grassroots level people's court. That is the common procedure for handling such cases in China.

According to the court trial yesterday's morning, this man has been announced his crimes and was released from the court. If the man involved does not raise appeals, and the people's procuratorate does not challenge such ruling, then the case will be ended and the man will be free of crime and innocent, and such court trial verdict will take effect. Therefore, according to this case, I think we can summarize three points and experience, which need to be further studied. //

All these three points are adjustment of our judicial concepts. //

First is that we should have full review on the function of our criminal law and the criminal procedure law. In addition to such roles and functions as cracking down on crimes and maintaining public security and social stability. I think the other functions of such law should be to protect innocent and preserve human rights. This is also one of the roles of our criminal law in particular. //

The second related issue is that if you want to adopt judicial measures to protect humanrights and the innocent citizens, there is such a case the suspicious, what principles should we choose? Should we choose the principle of if there are suspicious or they are assumed or involved as innocent or the crime should be lighter or miner? //

The third point is that in the case where there are suspicious, then what aspects should we follow? Should we strictly adhere to the facts? Or should we clearly adhere to those suspicious aspects? So I heard many news coverage on this case and I think what the media has covered was worthy our great attention. //

Despite the adjustments of those judicial aspects or concepts I have mentioned just now, I think when the principle should be strictly adhered to for the people's court for the trial organs, that is, for all the cases, no matter death penalties is involved or not, as the trials organ we should clearly and strictly abide by the hard evidence and the facts, and we should ensure the 100% justice of the law itself and the procedures. //

**China Daily**: Mr. Wan, in 1990, at the 14th World Law Congress, a state leader delivered an opening remark at the opening ceremony. What was the level of that leader? And will the participation of the leader be the same of the upcoming congress? //

**Wan**: As to the question about the level of the state leader to the ceremony for all the previous congresses, the common practice is that one of the major leaders of the host country will attend the opening ceremony. In the year 1990 at the 14th congress, the then president of China Mr. Yang Shangkun attended the opening ceremony. Now we are coordinating with the relevant departments and we hope that the level of the state leader attending this ceremony will be the same. On the level of the representatives to the congress, now we have received information from many chief justices of such countries as the United States, the UK, Germany, Russia, Spain and many other important countries in Asia and Africa, and some of them will lead a very big delegation and for other countries the attorney – general, ministers of justice, the chief prosecutors will attend this congress. //

**Xinhua News Agency**: Mr. Wan, I have two questions. Just now you have said that the upcoming congress will be held in Beijing and Shanghai, so how will these two cities share the workload of this congress and what will be the arrangement of the agenda of the upcoming congress? And I also want to go back the case my colleagues raised just now. The case has already retried and the offender was acquitted. And according to some news report, Mr. She and his family wish to get some compensation according to the law on the national compensation, so do you think he will get the compensation? Do you think he will get the compensation for mental harm? Thank you. //

**Wan:** On your question about the arrangement of the agenda in Beijing and Shanghai, as I said the Congress will last two and a half days in Beijing and two days in Shanghai. In Beijing there will be a world day of law celebration, and then we will have the opening ceremony, the panel discussions and the mock trial. In Beijing we will have panel discussions on 15 specific topics which will be held in the Great Hall of the People. The panel discussions on three specific topics will be held at the same time and participation in which one to choose in accordance with their specific interest. As to the agenda of the congress in Shanghai, there will be an opening ceremony and the panel discussions on seven specific topics will be held. One of the seven is an important one, which is the panel discussion on the rule of law in the court. And chief justices from other countries of the world and the chief justices of China, Mr. Xiao Yang will give the keynote speech. As to the other six topics, they will be held in two different meeting rooms and the participation will also be able to choose which to attend with their interest. In addition to these agenda items of the congress in Shanghai, some chief justices paid their first visit to China, therefore, the departments also arrange such itineraries for them to pay inspections to the grassroots, people's courts and high courts in Shanghai, so they will have first-hand information of the legal system of China. //

As to the case, whether Mr. She will get compensation, I think it has been very clear that when the court trial result was announced, the chief justice has already told that Mr. She has the right to apply for compensation. As to the concrete amount of the concrete compensation he can have, that will be carried out in accordance with the provisions of the law as to the mental compensation. I think the Supreme People's Court has already released the judicial interpretation for that. The relevant judges and the courts concerned will have their work done in accordance with such judicial interpretation in a just and accurate way. //

**China Daily**: Mr. Wan, just now you have said at this congress there will be 22 specific topics which can be summarized to six categories, so my question is how did you choose this six categories of 22 specific topics? What is the significance of the specific topics for the legislative or the judicial system improvement in China? //

**Wan**: Very good question! Indeed the selection of these six categories of 22 specific topics is chosen centering on the major scene of the congress that is building harmony in the international society. By harmony we mean not only a harmonious domestic society, instead, we extend this concept to the harmony in the international society and the rule of law. //

In fact, this concept "harmony" is unanimously raised by the WJA and indicated the wishes that they want to identify the theme of the congress as the building of harmony in the international society and I find that this tells us to build a socialist harmonious society which are democratic, an rule by law which features justice and equality, credibility, friendship as well as dynamism and in such a harmonious society man and nature coexist in great peace and coordination. I think the selection of this theme is not coincidence; instead it is a common goal for both China and international community. //

If you consult the brochure that you have on these 22 specific topics, you will find that what I said just now is the common goal for these six categories. China as a major responsible country is now playing an increasingly important role in the international community and China's ready to make contribution to build the international community or society of harmony while making great efforts to set up an internal or domestic society which also features great harmony. //

**Host**: That is the end of the press conference. Thanks for coming. //

## ◆ *Passage 2*

**China Daily**: In the current judicial interpretation, those who provided assistance like advertising or other means of publicity for the production and selling counterfeit and substandard drugs will be handled as an accomplice. I would like to know whether such activities like advertising or publicity shall be subject to more stringent screening or review and receive heavier punishment in the future. //

**Xiong**: To provide facilitation and assistance for the production and selling counterfeit and substandard drugs will be handled seriously in accordance with law. It is also an issue that has immediate concern of our general public. Therefore, in judicial practice, the act of complicity to provide facilitation for the production and selling counterfeit and substandard drugs will be handled in accordance with law. These activities including offering financial support, accounting numbers, advertising, and other means of publicity for the production and selling counterfeit and substandard drugs. In the judicial interpretation this time, there has been specific stipulation in this regard. //

I believe the clearly identified stipulation in the document this time has offered a legal ground for us to handle those accomplices who offered facilitation and assistance to those accomplices who offered facilitation and assistance to those criminals who engage in the production and selling counterfeit and substandard drugs. It has also regulated behaviors in this regard as acted as the determined for those would-be criminals. To provide advertising and other kinds of publicity for the production and selling counterfeit and substandard drugs has always been an acute concern among the general public. Those who are acutely aware that the drugs used, produced or sold counterfeit drugs, but still make advertising, or provide publicity for such drugs has always been the target for the art pry and protest. It has caused very negative consequences. In order to ensure that the general public will not be misled or suffered from such behaviors, we have signaled out advertising in this judicial document as a target for campaign and punishment. We believe that in the future such activities as advertising for the production and selling counterfeit and substandard drugs will surely be handled with harsher terms. It will receive more stringent screening and will receive heavier punishment. We would like to see the general public will be involved in this process to help us discover and dispose more cases like such or coordinate with relevant departments in their legal investigation and handling such cases. //

**Phoenix TV**: I would like to get this question to Mr. Bian Zhenjia, Deputy Commissioner from State Food and Drug Administration, we see that people affected by the AH1N1 flu virus have been increased and we also noticed that in this judicial document. It is clearly mentioned that during the outbreak of natural disasters, public health hazards, more heavier punishment will be mediated out on making or selling counterfeit and substandard drugs, so what kind of drugs or drug products will be subject to more stringent screening or examination this time specially with the consideration of AH1N1 flu virus? What specific measures will be taken by the administration to combat such fake drugs? And also the second question for the previous one making advertising for such drugs, will the stars or celebrities advertisement be included in such behavior? //

**Bian**: As for the work of the State Food and Drug Administration, there are mainly four responsibilities in terms of our efforts in preventing the spread of AH1N1 flu virus. //

First, we have strengthened our efforts in supervision especially with regard to the quality and safety of the products and medical devices being produced. We have had even more strict quality supervision and inspection on qualified enterprises that produces relevant products and medical devices that are intended in our current fight against AH1N1 flu virus. We have issued notice to relevant plants and pharmaceuticals and we have carried out checks on the qualities of their products in order to ensure that all drugs and medical devices to be used in this prevention and treatment of academic standard are in standard and safe. //

Second, we have also closely with relevant enterprises and pharmaceuticals in making preparation for the IND and production and relevant excellence. We have started very earlier and discussed with them about the procedures how to meet the relevant requirements for making such vaccines and how to apply for the registration and application of the use of such vaccines, so all the review work shall be done with regard to safety and efficiency. //

Third, we have also set up an extraverted approval mechanism for relevant products and medical devices to be poured out of the factories. We have set up a special approval mechanism in this regard. We will carry out our work on normal work days and holidays or weekends in order to facilitate and expertise relevant approval procedures as long as those products are safe and effective. //

Fourth, we have also strengthened our campaign against substandard or counterfeit drugs. As long as we found the drugs are fake or not up to standard, we will trace it down and follow through and also seriously handle those drugs. We are sure that during this special period, the spread of AH1N1 flu virus, more stringent measures will be taken to prevent and the currency of counterfeit drugs in order to ensure the safety of our people. //

**Xiong:** I also want to add some points on the previous question in this current judicial interpretation, it is clearly stipulated that during the outbreak of public e-mergencies, such as natural disasters, accidents, and public health hazards. The production and selling counterfeit and substandard drugs will receive heavier punishment according to the law. The major considerations are that to make fake products itself is a very responsive act. However, it is even awful during the outbreak of public emergency, because it directly poses threat to the life and well-being of the general public. It will normally endanger the life and health of the people, and will also undermine our rescue relief and operations during this period. Therefore, to meet out heavier punishment according to the law on these activities is of great significance and we also believe that by pouring these regulations and measures that will boost our confidence in ensuring drug safety, especially in the current preventing the spread of AH1N1 flu virus. //

As for the second part of the question, the advertising for the fake and substandard drugs by celebrities, I will say it has to be approved by the perspective of judicial aspect and take it as an act of making advertising or other means of publicity in this regard, because according to the Criminal Law, to have such crime convicted should have the prediction of its intentionality, that is to say, any accomplices who provide facilitations must be aware or should have the knowledge that the products sold or produced are counterfeit and substandard drugs, so if the celebrity who made advertising for the drugs did fully aware about the nature of such drugs, then he or she shall be handled as an accomplice. This is very clearly defined. //

**Beijing News:** The first question is about the interpretation of this document. We have noticed that Article 1 in this document provides very clearly the circumstances of the standards or criteria for the conviction of such crimes as produce or sell counterfeit or substandard drugs. We also noticed that in 2001, Supreme People's Court and Supreme People's Procuratorate has also issued a similar document. In this document No. 3 article also dealt with the counterfeit and shoddy drugs. Is there any difference between them? Is there any adjustment or edition being added to the current document? What is the consideration behind it? //

The second question is for Mr. Xiong, also about advertising that if a media affiliation is categorized as an illegal publication by the press and publication authorities, will it fall into this category? And another question is about, in these recent days, we see on televisions and radio programs, there are a number of programs or shows that involve in the promotion of several drugs, will these guests, hosts, media anchors, and experts be considered a part of accomplice if these programs involve the promoting or marketing such drugs? And what measures will be taken to evaluate or verify that their acts are complicity because you just mentioned that intentional actions are very important in this regard. //

**Zhu:** Let me take the first question. With regard to the criteria against which the conviction can be made and the crimes of producing and selling counterfeit drugs, there is a criteria, that is this crime should cause serious harm to human health, this is very basic standard, so that the crime can be established. Well, in the legal interpretation issued by the Supreme People's Court and Supreme People's Procuratorate is also relevant regulations that in the current one, we have made adjustments, there are mainly three parts. //

First, we have supplemented the original stipulations and make it more complete, for example, in the 2001 document, it has made defined the toxic and poisonous substances that exceed the requirements. It makes it as a standard for saying this is a counterfeit or toxic or poisonous drug. However, in viewing practice, there are also substance and drugs that should not contain toxic or poisonous substance but have them instead. //

And the second adjustment is that we have made editions to the original interpretation. There are major mainly four standards. The original Article 1, Item 2 to Item 5 are newly added, because they are activities that will cause very negative social consequences. And issues of strong concern of the general public should be immediately dealt with by judicial agencies. //

The third adjustment we have done to the current document to delete original stipulations in the 2001 document. There have been major mainly three stipulations in this regard. First is the Article 3 Item 2 of the 2001 document. There have been stipulations with regard to drugs that do not contain indicated effective ingredients so as to delay the process of diagnosis and treatment. However, we have found that for these standards, it includes obviously two parts: the first one the drugs that do not contain indicated effective ingredients. This is the counterfeit actually for identifying the counterfeit drugs, if the drugs do not contain very clearly identifications or labels they will cause serious harm to human health, and then they will be identified as counterfeit drugs. However, as for the second part, it will delay the process of the diagnosis and treatment, we found it very difficult to verify in the real judicial practice, and it's very hard to be applied into reality. Therefore, we have deleted it. //

In the general sense, the edition and adjustment to the current document is to meet the requirement for strengthening efforts against the production and selling counterfeit and substandard drugs. And it will also try to make the relevant legislations more complete. //

**Xiong**: Let me take the second question, also about the advertising. It seems that the media has tremendous interest in this regard; well I think there are two approaches and perspectives in looking at this question. The first is that illegal advertising in advertisement promoting or marketing without approval will not fall into the category of advertising or not. Well, I think for a lot of circumstances there are posters and advertisements posted on the walls and street poles, obviously they haven't obtain the approval from relevant authorities. That they are an act of advertising, so they shall be subjective to relevant legal punishments and the criminal responsibilities, if they abide by the law. //

And second how to verify that the persons involved are fully aware or should have the knowledge about the drugs they used or sold. Yes, this is a difficult question and I have just mentioned that it involves first of all the drug used is counterfeit drugs, and it is serious or not to cause harm to human health, but to have to knowledge or should have the knowledge about the nature of the drugs is a very subjective in nature, but in viewing judicial practice, how can we say this person is fully aware or should have the knowledge about it in real practice. Obviously sometimes we can get this fact from the state holders, and the offender himself, and sometimes they don't admit that they know about the drugs, but all the objective evidences or point to the fact that they should have the knowledge about it. Let me take an example, for instance, in this current document, there is specific provision with regard to the production of prescribed drugs without the license number or faking license number or approval number, and a drug serious is not to cause harm to human's health, and if an advertiser who do not have the license number or number for the drug he is going to promote, and provide such activities for them, then we think we can judge that these activities involve intentionality and this is an act constituting the crime. //

**AP**: Just wonder the recent interpretation will be easier to sentence all those production of fake drugs to expect the number of criminal cases to rise as a result of this interpretation. //

**Xiong**: As you say this is a very correct observation, the Interpretation of this time has summarized the trial experiences of courts of the parts previous out work, and it has further clearly identified the criteria for the conviction and sentencing of the crime of the production and selling counterfeit and substandard drugs. Therefore, it will provide very clear benchmark for the procuratorial departments in filing relevant cases and easier for people's courts to handle and investigate relevant cases, and provide sentencing, so I believe with the release and promulgation and relevant document, the administrative authorities were strengthened their investigation efforts, the judicial organizations will also handle the relevant cases according to law. //

**BJ TV**: This question is for Mr. Xiong from the Supreme People's Court, I would like to know is there any new applicable measures being adopted with the coming of this judicial document, with regard to this enterprises with GMP to produce fake and substandard drugs. And what kind of specific standards will be applied to hold those criminal offenders into accountable, and also with regard to the marketing those products, we see that there are new methods in marketing very kind of products. For example, through Internet, are there any specific methods or criteria being adopted to regulate such activities? //

**Xiong**: I think the first question involves the enterprises obviously are legitimate enterprise. If they are engaged in the productive and selling counterfeit and substandard drugs, obviously with intention, that they will be held criminal responsibility, for the crimes and production and selling counterfeit and substandard drugs. the criteria employed by these enterprises are same employed to the individuals who offended these crimes and second, obviously if these enterprises that do not have the intention, for example, in major accidents or dereliction of duty in producing or using that substandard drugs, they should also be handled in accordance with law, but with other criteria and other laws. I have just stressed the importance of this crime that it should have the subject intentionality of the subjects as well as they have the knowledge or they have the knowledge that they have the drugs used are counterfeit and substandard drugs, and then they have constituted the crime. If the products used or sold has caused enormous serious harm to human health. //

And second question involve the Internet promotion of drugs. I think Internet is a way of marketing products and no matter what measures employed, as long as the drugs promoted are counterfeit and substandard drugs, and they cause serious harm to human health, be it in the Internet, newspapers or other ways of media as well as the compliance with relevant standards set up by the judicial interpretations, it will be handled according to the law. //

**CCTV**: In this Interpretation, there is specific stipulations with regard to medical institutions that engaged in the production and use of counterfeit and substandard drugs, and they shall be held criminal responsible in this regard. What is the consideration behind, and how it will put into practice? //

**Xiong**: Medical institutions, in our opinion, should be a place to treat the wounded and rescue the dying. It's one of the places that win the utmost trust about people and trust. However, in recent years, some individual medical institutions knowingly use counterfeit and substandard drugs to the detriment of the interests of the patients. This has been very responsive. This is a very last scene that people wish to see, and we found it very difficult to understand accept the very thing they hate most. Therefore, there has been special stipulation in the current document to regulate behaviors of medical institutions and efforts to seriously combat the crimes made by the medical institutions and to safeguard fundamental interests for the general public. Three points should be paid attention to during the implementation. //

Firstly in the current document, it is made very clear that there are some preconditions for convicting medical institutions of making such a crime if it is that the counterfeit drugs cause serious harm to human health. Substandard drugs issue also lead to very negative and serious social consequences as provided for Article 3 in the current interpretation. //

And second by medical institutions, not only include hospitals and other medical institutions, it also include health practitioners. //

And third, we have just mentioned the intentional actions of this crime. It's to say that the act should know or must have the knowledge that the drug used or sold is counterfeit and substandard and in accordance with this requirement, can make conviction and sentencing crimes. //

**Guo**: One last question please. //

**HK Wenhui Daily**: With regard to this interpretation, it mentioned very clearly that the production and selling of counterfeit and substandard drugs that causes serious harm to human health will be held criminal responsible, but we would like to know does this require expert evaluation from the Food Drug State Administration? If they do not meet relevant standards, will they be shied away from receiving relevant punishment? //

**Zhu**: As for the expert evaluation offered by the State Food and Drug Administration, I think there are mainly two aspects, the first one is as regard to the production substandard and counterfeit drugs, we normally will use an expert evaluation when it conforms to a relevant technical issues, because when this is very technical in nature, and it requires expert evaluation from the food and drugs authorities, then such an expert evaluation is an necessity. The second issue is whether the counterfeit drugs produced and sold have reached the level of "serious harm to human health". This judicial interpretation lists six situations regarding this issue. These six situations are determined based on actual needs, and whether to invite a drug inspection institution for identification. If it is not technical in nature and judicial personnel can make judgment about whether it is serious or not to cause harm to human health, then there is no need to make Food and Drug Administration involvement to make such a judgment. //

So I have to say all in all whether there is a need to ask FDA to involve making their expert evaluation. It all depends on the need and situation on the ground. If the judicial agencies found it there is a need to ask a food regulatory staff to make an expert evaluation, they will ask them to be involved, and otherwise if there is not such a need, they shall not be involved to make such an evaluation. And it is also very common in our judicial practice that sometimes there is no need for official expert evaluation from food regulatory authorities, but we will also seek expert advice from relevant professionals. //

whether the drugs being produced or sold is enough to cause harm to human health, well I have to say in this case, they will not constitute the crimes of production and selling counterfeit drugs. But if they also violated some other standards in other kinds, they shall also be held responsible according to other laws and regulations. For example, No. 149 of the Criminal Law as well as the relevant interpretation have all made it clear that if the products sold exceeded 50, 000 RMB in its proceedings and the overall capital of drugs involved exceeded 150, 000 RMB, then this activity will be handled in accordance with Article 140, that is the crime of production and distribution shoddy and counterfeit products. Another example is according to Article 6 of the current interpretation for the production and selling counterfeit and substandard drugs if the drugs sold or produced are substandard or counterfeit, obviously they will be held criminal responsible according to this regulation, but also when they do not offense this regulation, but they violate the lawful operation, distribution, collection, offering blood samples, they shall also be seriously handled according to relevant regulations. In this case, even if the drugs used do not cause serious harm to human health, but if they fell to other offense in this relevant regards, they shall also be handled responsible. //

Even if these criminal activities are not serious enough to cause harm to human health and do not constitute criminal offenses, that doesn't mean the offenders are safe in sound. They shall also be subject to relevant regulations and punishments meet out by food and drug departments. //

**Guo**：There will be another press conference at 3：00 tomorrow afternoon. Leaders from the Ministry of Supervision，NDRC（National Development and Reform Commission），Ministry of Finance，Administration of Audit will introduce the implementation situation of central government's policy on expanding domestic demand and economic promotion. This is the end of the press conference. Thank you！//

# Ⅴ. 句子精炼 Sentences in Focus

**Directions**：*Interpret the following sentences from Chinese into English*：

1. 最近几年，我们以人为本的概念出现，特别是去年，我们宪法修正案把国家尊重和保护人权写进去，还有一系列法律方面的修改，都已经达到了一个新的高度，这是立法方面的进展。

2. 在起诉的时候，这个案件已经不是作为一个谋杀罪确定的、能够判死刑或者是死缓或者是无期的案件起诉，已经是作为一般的案件或者是案情不是非常肯定的案件。

3. 不管我们将来观念有什么改变或者发展到什么程度，我们都有一个原则，那就是审判机关必须严守，无论是死刑案件还是其他任何案件，审判机关作为公平和正义的最后一道防线都必须严把事实关，确保程序公正和实体公正。

4. 我们要用司法的手段来保护人权、保护无辜，那么就要有一个选择，出现疑罪的时候我们有什么取舍？是疑罪从无还是疑罪从轻？

5. 在上海有一个简短的开幕式，有 7 个议题，7 个中有 1 个是重要议题，那就是"法律、法治与法院"，专门占了一个下午的时间，由各个国家首席大法官或其代表发表演讲，包括肖扬首席大法官。

6. 至于精神的赔偿问题，我们也有司法解释。我相信，各级人民法院会根据最高人民法院制定的司法解释，对其就精神损害或者其他有关方面提出的赔偿要求给予合理或者是公正的判决。

7. "和谐"这两个字是从 WJA 也就是世界法学家协会异口同声说出来的，这次的主题就是追求国际和谐。这个主题刚好和我们国家所追求的国内的和谐社会是相关联的。和谐的概念包括民主法治、公平正义、诚信友爱、充满活力、安定有序、人与自然的和谐相处，我想这不是偶然的巧合，而是国际社会共同的兴趣所在。

8. 我相信，司法解释对于共犯行为进行具体明确的规定，将为司法机关惩治生产、销售假药、劣药的共犯行为提供具体的法律依据，同时这也是一种规范，对于为生产、销售假药、劣药的犯罪提供方便和便利条件的人也是一种警示。

9. 在防控工作中，涉及防控甲型 H1N1 流感的药品、医疗器械，我们建立了特别审批渠道，不受节假日的限制，只要符合程序是安全的、有效的，在这样的前提下我们都会启动特别审批程序，以满足国内防控甲型 H1N1 流感的需要。

10. 这次解释明确规定在自然灾害、事故灾难、公共卫生事件等突发事件发生时期，生产、销售用于应对突发事件药品的假药、劣药要依法从重处罚。

11. 司法解释第 1 条规定了生产、销售假药"足以严重危害人体健康"的认定标准，2001 年的时候，"两高"也发布过一个司法解释，第 3 条也作了一些规定，这次解释里的规定和那个相比有哪些调整和补充？

12. 司法解释作为规定来讲，"知道或应当知道"是主观的东西，司法实践中的"知道"一般是指行为人的供述或者有关的证人证言，都证明他是知道的，这当然就是"知道"。有些行为人不供述，就要靠客观证据，证明他是知道的。

13. 这次解释总结了实践审判经验，把涉及生产、销售假药罪和生产、销售劣药罪的定罪标准进一步明确，而且把这两种犯罪的量刑标准也进一步明确了，所以为我们检察机关依法提起公诉，为法院依法审判，包括定罪量刑，提供了更为明确的依据。

14. 互联网销售假药、劣药的问题，这是一种行为的方式，只要你销售，不管你通过什么方式，只要你销售的是假药，只要这个假药足以危害人体健康，不管是通过互联网还是其他的渠道销售，达到司法解释中规定的定罪量刑标准的，都要给予处罚。

15. 这次司法解释第 6 条规定"实施生产、销售假药、劣药犯罪，同时构成生产、销售伪劣产品、侵犯知识产权、非法经营、非法行医、非法采供血等犯罪的，依照处罚较重的规定定罪处罚"。根据这个规定，如果生产、销售假药达不到足以严重危害人体健康的程度，但构成非法经营罪、假冒商标罪、非法行医罪、非法采供血罪，就按照行为人所触犯的罪名来追究刑事责任。

# 第四单元 中国法律体制
## Unit 4 The Legal System of PRC

# I . 专题知识 Legal Knowledge

当代中国法律制度的发展是一个艰难曲折的过程，在中国人民反对帝国主义、封建主义和官僚资本主义反动统治的革命斗争中孕育，在社会主义国家建立以后正式确立，并在社会主义建设过程中发展。党的十一届三中全会以后，法律制度进入了迅速发展的新时期，立法、执法、司法和法律监督制度不断完善，一个以宪法为基础的、具有中国特色的社会主义法律体系正在形成。

## 一、中国法制建设的曲折历程

（1）新中国成立初期的法制建设。新中国成立后，加强法制建设被提上了议事日程，制定了一些保护人民的法律法规，如在 1950 年至 1952 年期间，陆续制定了婚姻法、土地改革法、惩治反革命条例、惩治贪污条例等。

与此同时，新中国也逐步建立起了比较完备的法制。1954 年，由全国1.5 亿人参与讨论和修改的《宪法》经第一届全国人民代表大会通过，新中国第一部国家根本大法诞生，为中国法律体系的完善奠定了基础。之后制定了 5 部国家机构的组织法，它包括全国人大、国务院、地方人大和人民委员会、法院和检察院的组织法。就立法工作来说，全国人大常委会成立后，在起草法律方面，组织各方面力量，进行刑法、民法、诉讼法等法律的调查研究和起草工作。

（2）法制遭到破坏的"文革"时期。由于当时对法制建设重要意义的认识不够深刻，党的八大提出的正确方针没能一贯坚持，对法制建设时而重视，时而放松，从 1957 年反右派，到后来 1966 年"文化大革命"，几个重要法律的起草工作一度停顿下来，人大常委会机关人员精简，新中国成立后逐步建立起来的社会主义法制遭到破坏。"文化大革命"的教训很多，其中之一，就是没有重视社会主义民主和法制建设。为了防止类似"文化大革命"的混乱局面重演，邓小平同志在十一届三中全会前召开的中央工作会议上，针对过去存在的问题，明确指出："必须使民主制度化、法律化，使这种制度和法律不因领导人的改变而改变，不因领导人看法和注意力的改变而改变。"

（3）法制建设的繁荣期。健全社会主义法制，首先要抓立法工作。1979年以来，全国人大及其常委会把立法工作摆到重要议事日程上来。1982年制定了新宪法，并先后制定了138部法律，对10部法进行了修改，包括一系列有关国家机构的法律、民法通则和一系列单行民事法律、刑法、三大诉讼法（刑事诉讼、民事诉讼、行政诉讼）以及一批经济方面的、保障公民权利的、涉外方面的、行政管理方面的重要法律。特别是1992年以来，全国人大及其常委会根据十四大、十五大精神，加强立法工作，围绕建立和完善社会主义市场经济体制的目标，先后制定了104部法律，对57部法进行了修改，通过了8件法律解释。目前，中国现行法律已达200多件、行政法规600多件、地方性法规8000多件。以宪法为核心的中国特色社会主义法律体系初步形成。同时，确立了依法治国的基本方略。1999年全国人大以宪法修正案的形式，将"依法治国，建设社会主义法治国家"正式写进了国家根本大法。这是中国法制建设史上的重要里程碑。法治是社会文明进步的重要标志，法律在保障社会的安宁与稳定、促进经济的发展与繁荣等方面都具有其他任何社会调节手段不可替代的重要作用。

## 二、以宪法为核心的中国特色社会主义法律体系初步形成

宪法是基本法，规定了国家最基本的政治制度。宪法以下有六大基本部门：

（1）民商法。民商法从法律角度来说，解决的是平等主体间的法律关系，包括市场经济关系、家庭关系、婚姻关系和其他劳动关系。

（2）经济法。经济法的概念是国家通过政府的控制手段来干预经济。这种干预分两个方面：一个是宏观调控，对外汇、金融、外贸、税务、资源等方面的宏观管理；第二个是微观的、市场的管理。在市场机制下，这一方面也非常重要。

（3）行政法。这是国家对于行政权行使中一些权力的制约和监督，以使行政权能顺利行使又不过分膨胀。

（4）社会法。这是当代法律中相当重要的一部分，是 20 世纪世界上提出的一个新兴的法律部门。从市场经济来看，如果我们强调自由竞争的话，则必然造成富者越富，贫者越贫，这样就需要对社会的弱小者阶层加以保护。弱小者阶层中，劳动者需要劳动保障。妇女、青少年、老人、残疾人、少数民族、宗教上少数者的利益需要特殊的保障机制。所以，社会保障法是非常重要的。

（5）审判、司法。这是一个国家司法权力如何行使、如何监督、如何约束、如何程序化的重要的法律部门。

（6）刑法，这是对犯罪行为的法律制裁。

# Ⅱ. 词汇热身 Vocabulary Warm-up

**Directions**：*Give the English equivalents of the following Chinese expressions*：

| | | |
|---|---|---|
| 法治建设 | 推进政府职能转变 | 金融研究所 |
| 国家法律制度成熟的标志 | 管理创新 | 金融管制 |
| | 依法行政 | 市场自律 |
| 全国人大及其常委 | 提请……审议法律议案 | 有市场就会有风险 |
| 享有立法权 | 向社会公开征求意见 | 经济体制转轨 |
| 非诉讼程序法 | 取消……（法令） | 金融体制的不适应 |
| 法律规范 | 行政执法责任制度 | 金融机构退出 |
| 中国特色社会主义法律体系 | 行政复议制度 | 存款保险 |
| | 上位法 | 金融控股公司 |
| 有法可依，依法治国 | "红头文件" | 资产证券化 |
| 人民当家作主的权利 | 深入人心 | 委托理财 |
| 共同的行为准则 | 中国人民银行行长 | 破产法 |
| 起支架作用的法律 | 国务院发展研究中心 | |

**Directions**：*Give the Chinese equivalents of the following English expressions*：

| | |
|---|---|
| The Bar Council of the Hong Kong Bar Association | Chief Justice |
| | Secretary for Justice |

"off piste"

Legal Aid Scheme

access to Justice

non-Permanent Judge

Kafkaesque doorkeeper

prohibitive

Billable hours

pro bono

public expense

life and limb

Convention Against Torture（CAT）

Earthly Branches

Animal zodiac

in no small measure to

separation of powers

tenure

on the bench

Continuous Profession Development
（CPD）points

# Ⅲ. 课文口译 Text for Interpreting

## ◆ *Passage 1*

**Directions：** Listen to the passage and interpret from Chinese into English at the end of each segment.

（下文节选自 2009 年 9 月 22 日全国人大常务委员会法工委副主任信春鹰题为"建国 60 年我国法治建设的成就"的演讲）

女士们，先生们，大家好，很高兴今天有这样一个机会向大家介绍建国 60 年我国法治建设的成就。//

法治建设是一个国家法律制度成熟的标志。我国社会主义法律制度建设的成就反映了我国社会主义制度发展的历程，浓缩了我国社会主义制度建设的实践。立法是法治建设的前提。//

截至 2009 年 8 月底，全国人大及其常委会共制定了现行有效的法律 229 件，涵盖宪法及宪法相关法、民商法、行政法、经济法、社会法、刑法、诉讼及非诉讼程序法 7 个法律部门；国务院共制定了现行有效的行政法规 682 件；地方人大及其常委会共制定了现行有效的地方性法规 7000 余件；民族自治地方人大共制定了现行有效的自治条例和单行条例 600 余件；5 个经济特区

共制定了现行有效的法规 200 余件；国务院部门和有立法权的地方政府共制定规章 2 万余件。//

以宪法为核心，以法律为主干，包括行政法规、地方性法规等规范性文件在内，由 7 个法律部门、3 个层次法律规范构成的中国特色社会主义法律体系已经基本形成，国家经济、政治、文化、社会生活的各个方面基本做到了有法可依，为依法治国、建设社会主义法治国家、实现国家的长治久安提供了有力的法治保障。//

法律体系不是抽象的数字或者指标体系，它是由特定国家法律制度的发展路径和社会对法律的需求所决定的。在我国社会主义制度下，法律是党的主张和人民意志的统一。立法从党和国家发展的大局和实际需要出发，把亟须法律调整、立法条件比较成熟的领域制度化、法律化，通过国家的强制力保障实施。这既是我国法律制度发展的成功经验，也是做好立法工作，发挥法律在社会生活中的作用的基本前提。//

我国法律保障了人民当家作主的权利。人民群众对立法享有知情权、参与权、表达权和监督权。立法通过制度化的渠道凝聚民意，确定共同的行为准则并保证其实施；我国法律确立和维护人民民主专政的国家制度，确立并不断完善国家的政权结构和组织形式，推进政府职能转变和管理创新，强化社会管理和社会服务；我国法律确立和维护国家的经济制度。通过引导、规范、促进保障法律支持的经济活动、禁止并制裁违法的经济活动，推动经济的发展；我国法律确立和维护和谐稳定的社会秩序。通过法律手段保障人民群众享有广泛的权利、协调社会利益关系、保护环境、保护自然资源，维护人与自然的和谐和经济可持续发展。//

为了达到于 2010 年形成中国特色社会主义法律体系的目标，今年的立法工作有两个重点：一是抓紧制定和修改在法律体系中起支架作用的法律，在继续完善经济、政治、文化领域立法的同时着力加强社会领域立法。二是完成法律清理工作。对已经明显不适应发展社会主义市场经济的需要、前法与后法不尽一致或者不够衔接、操作性不强的法律规定，通过废止、修改、解释、配套等方式进行分类处理，促进法律体系的科学、统一、和谐，保障其实施。//

政府法治建设是我国社会主义民主法治建设的重要方面，依法行政是政府法治建设的基本主题，是全面落实依法治国基本方略的基础和关键。多年来，我国政府采取了一系列有效措施切实加强政府法治建设，全面推进依法行政。经过多年来坚持不懈的努力，依法行政取得了重要进展。主要表现在以下几个方面。//

（1）各级政府行使行政权力基本做到了"有法可依"，政府立法质量显著提高。国务院始终坚持政府立法决策和改革决策的统一。从1979年到2009年8月底，国务院共提请全国人大及其常委会审议法律议案231件，制定现行有效行政法规682件，从1987年建立法规规章备案制度到2009年8月底，国务院部门和有立法权的地方政府共制定规章26 308件。更加注重科学立法、民主立法。截至今年8月底，共有53部行政法规草案向社会公开征求了意见。//

（2）政府职能进一步转变，政府自身建设切实加强。稳步推进行政审批制度改革。国务院和地方各级政府分批取消、调整行政审批项目，国务院分4批取消了1992项行政审批，地方各级政府共取消、调整77 692项行政审批。//

（3）改革行政执法体制，推行行政执法责任制，行政执法行为得到严格规范。行政执法责任制的推行有效地规范了行政执法行为。//

（4）完善行政监督制度，创新行政监督方式，对行政行为的监督不断强化。认真实施行政复议制度。各级行政复议机构积极发挥职能作用，及时妥善化解矛盾。目前，每年通过行政复议化解的行政争议超过了8万件。国务院自1987年开始从事法规规章备案工作。目前，当年制定的法规规章基本做到了全部报备，一些与上位法相抵触的法规规章能够得到及时处理，有效地维护了法治统一。各地方在国务院的指导下积极探索建立规范性文件备案审查制度，有效地解决了"红头文件""乱"和"滥"的问题。//

（5）行政机关工作人员特别是领导干部依法行政的意识和能力明显增强。各地方、各部门积极采取各种有效措施对行政机关工作人员进行依法行政培训，依法行政的理念已经深入人心。

谢谢大家！//

◆ *Passage 2*

**Directions**：*Listen to the passage and interpret from Chinese into English at the end of each segment.*

（本文节选自中国人民银行副行长 2005 年 4 月 26 日在国务院发展研究中心金融研究所举办的"2005 年中国金融改革高层论坛"上题为"金融风险的防范与法律制度的完善"的发言）

各位朋友，女士们，先生们：

非常高兴出席这次由国务院发展研究中心金融研究举办的中国金融改革高层论坛。//

金融法律制度既是对金融机构、金融业务主体和金融业务法律关系进行规范和调整的制度安排，也是对金融监督管理者自身行政行为进行规范和约束的制度安排。金融立法的最根本目的就是规范和调整金融监督管理者、金融机构、金融机构客户之间的法律关系，强调对金融机构客户合法权益的保护，通过在政府失灵的领域强化监督管理，发挥市场在金融发展中的主导作用，实现金融管制与市场自律间的平衡和协调发展。有市场就会有风险，有金融市场就会有金融风险。因此，金融立法的主旨并不是要消灭所有的金融风险，而是要将金融风险控制在金融监督管理者可容忍的范围和金融机构可承受的区间内。正是在这个意义上，金融风险的防范、控制和化解离不开金融法律制度的建立健全和有效执行。这里我想在金融创新这个大背景下，从完善金融立法这一侧面，谈一谈我国金融风险的防范问题。希望得到与会代表的指正。//

我国金融体系中的各种高风险是多年积累起来的，是国民经济运行中各种矛盾的综合反映。经济体制的转轨、社会环境的变化、金融体制的不适应、监管手段的落后，以及金融法律制度的不完善等都是造成我国金融体系中存在高风险的原因。对此，理论界和实际部门都有过很多研究和分析。//

我们知道，金融法律制度在本质上是一种工具，调整着金融监督管理者、金融机构、金融产品当事人之间的各种关系。金融法律制度除了规范法律关系这一功能外，还具有惩罚、鼓励或禁止、引导等多种功能，从经济学意义上讲就是一种可期待的利益或可预期的损失。改革开放以来，我国的金融法治建设取得了很大的成绩，建立了以《中国人民银行法》《商业银行法》《银行业监督管理法》《证券法》《保险法》等以规范金融监督管理行为、规范金融经营主体和经营行为为主要内容的基本金融法律制度。而在行政法层面上，又有《行政处罚法》《行政复议法》《行政许可法》等法律约束金融监督管理

者的行政行为。在民商法律层面，也有《票据法》《担保法》《公司法》等法律规范民商事行为。//

但是，也应当看到，目前的金融法律制度是在发展新兴市场和经济体制转轨过程中制定的。面对我国金融体制改革的深入、金融业对外开放进程的加快以及金融业自身创新动力的日益增强，现行的金融法律制度安排已经难以适应变化着的金融业的需要。尤其是需要跳出金融的框架全面审视我国金融业赖以生存和发展的基础法律生态环境，同时强化对金融创新（包括体制创新、机构创新和产品创新等）的法律关系研究。

当前我国的金融改革和发展正向前加速推进，同时防范金融风险的任务也变得越来越重要和艰巨。由于金融行业固有的风险性质，金融立法尽管不能从根本上消灭金融风险，但完善的法律法规却是缓解金融机构过度冒险、减少制度性风险的一个重要手段；一个良好的法律环境也是金融体系稳定运行的必要基础。//

目前，中国人民银行正按照科学发展观的要求，加快推动有关金融立法工作。包括：尽快促成《征信管理条例》的出台；积极参与并关注《企业破产法》和《刑法》条文的修改；认真配合做好《证券法》的修订；抓紧起草《反洗钱法》；进一步研究金融机构退出、存款保险、金融控股公司立法、资产证券化、委托理财等方面的法律关系问题。尽早出台这些法律法规以及实施细则，改善金融市场重要法律法规不健全、某些重要金融活动无法可依的现象。并结合我国实际情况，彻底清理我国金融法律制度，该立法的立法、该修改的修改、该废止的废止。//

从长远来看，我国的金融法治建设既要在金融立法方面下功夫，也要在金融执法方面强化执法的严肃性，真正做到"两手都要抓、两手都要硬"。就金融立法而言，我认为核心的问题是树立科学的立法价值取向。不同的金融发展阶段有不同的金融立法价值取向。现阶段的金融立法价值取向应当是：以"三个代表"重要思想为指导，按照科学发展观的要求，全面体现加强执政能力建设的要求，把金融立法工作的重点放在推动金融市场基础设施建设、规范金融创新法律关系、提高金融监督管理的协调性和有效性以及充分利用市场自律监管上来。具体而言：//

第一，金融立法要有统筹、科学和全局的眼光。目前我国的经济体制改革和金融体制改革都已经进入了改革攻坚阶段，原来采取的单独推进的改革策略已经难以适应当前改革开放的需要。金融立法也应当围绕这一转变，确立统筹规划、科学立法的思维。具体而言，对于金融市场应当通过立法手段逐步推进金融市场的统一和整合，对于同质的金融产品按照相同的监督管理规则约束市场主体的交易行为，保证不同的市场在其基础设施方面，如发行、登记、托管、结算和清算规则方面的基本统一。对于金融机构而言，要按照功能监管的思想，用统一的规则去规范其机构创新、业务创新和产品创新行为，同时要强化金融风险信息在金融监督管理部门间的共享和流转；而对于支撑金融发展和改革的其他法律制度，则应当按照既保护债权人又保护债务人的原则进行系统修改，《刑法》的修改则应当与时俱进，强调对单位犯罪的刑事制裁和对个人刑事责任的追究。//

第二，要坚持保护存款人和投资者利益、保护债权人利益的取向。保护金融机构存款人、金融产品投资人的利益永远是维护金融机构信誉的重要因素。当前应当强调对基础金融法律关系的研究，同时做好金融创新产品的法律关系的规范，金融监督管理部门在许可金融机构推出创新产品的过程中应当重视对于投资者知情权、收益权等合法权益的保护。要尽快完善《企业破产法》，根据《企业破产法》的基本原则，考虑金融机构破产的特殊性，尽快制定《金融机构破产条例》，同时应当尽快建立健全金融安全网制度，制定包括《存款保险条例》《证券投资者保护基金管理办法》在内的金融法律制度。//

第三，要坚持自律和他律相结合的取向。在调整金融监管关系的立法方面，要强化商业银行、券商和上市公司等经济主体在建立完善的、良好的法人治理结构方面的机制，强调金融机构的自律作用，保障金融机构在经营中的自主权，并注意为金融机构的发展留下足够的空间。//

第四，要坚持培养全社会金融风险意识和金融法治意识的取向。防范金融风险、保障金融安全的重要措施之一就是在全社会大力普及宣传金融法律知识，并在全社会真正树立金融法治观念。在加强金融法治意识的过程中，要重视全社会信用观念的建立，要培养公众和投资者的风险防范意识和合法投资观念。

谢谢大家！//

# Ⅳ. 参考译文 Reference versions

## ◆ *Passage 1*

(*The following is an excerpt from the speech "Achievements of China in rule of law in the past* 60 *years since the founding of the People's Republic" by Ms. Xin Chunying, deputy director of the Legal Work Committee of the NPC Standing Committee on Sept.* 22, 2009)

Ladies and gentlemen:

Good morning. I am very happy today to have the opportunity to brief you on the achievements China has made in rule of law in the past 60 years since the founding of the People's Republic. //

"Rule of law" is the symbol of a politically civilized society. One of the important components of the great cause of building Chinese-style socialism is the achievements in striving to make China a state of rule of law in the past 60 years since the founding of the People's Republic of China. The successes in developing a socialist legal system not only reflect the course of China's socialist progress but have enriched its experience in building the socialist system. Legislation is the premise for rule of law. //

By the end of August, 2009, the National People's Congress and its Standing Committee have enacted 229 laws in effect, covering seven branches, i. e., Constitution and constitutional law, civil and commercial law, administrative law, economic law, social law, criminal law, and law of procedure and extrajudicial procedure; the State Council has formulated 682 administrative regulations in effect; the local people's congresses and their standing committees, more than 7,000 local regulations; the local congresses of the national autonomous areas, more than 600 autonomous regulations and separate regulations; the legislatures of the five special economic zones, more than 200 regulations in total; in addition, the departments under the State Council and the local governments vested with the power of legislation have formulated over 20,000 pieces of rules. //

So far, a Chinese-style socialist legal system is basically in shape, which takes the Constitution as the heart and the laws the backbone, contains administrative regulations, local regulations and other regulatory documents, and comprises seven legal branches and three levels of legal norms. It ensures there are laws to go by for almost every aspect of the nation's economic, political, cultural and social life. And it provides the legal guaranty for governing the country according to law, making China a socialist country of rule of law, and ultimately attaining long-lasting peace and order. //

Legal system is not a system of abstract numbers or indexes; on the contrary, it is decided by the way of development of a country's legal system and by the society's need for law. Under China's socialist legal system, the law integrates the Party's standing and the people's will. Proceeding from both the future of the Party and the Nation in a larger picture and the practical need, we institutionalize and legalize through legislation the fields where prompt regulation is wanted and where the conditions for legislation are considerably mature; and implementation of these legislations are guaranteed by the mandatory power of the State. This is not only the successful experience in the development of China's legal system but the essential prerequisite for making good laws and bringing them into full play. //

The law of China ensures the power of the people to run the country as the masters. The masses of people enjoy the right of information, participation, expression and supervision in the process of legislation. Through institutionalized channel, legislation embodies the willpower of the people, defines the common code of conduct and ensures the enforcement of such code. The law of China establishes China as a socialist state under the people's democratic dictatorship and protects it as such, establishes and keeps improving the political structure and organization of the state, carries forward functional transformation of the government and administrative innovation, and enhances public administration and service. The law of China establishes and protects the economic system of the state, promoting economic progress through guiding, regulating, encouraging and supporting the economic activities protected by law and banning and punish those in violation of law. The law of China establishes and maintains a social order of harmony and stability, ensuring that the masses of people enjoy their rights extensively, balancing the relations and interests among various social groups, protecting environment, conserving natural resources, harmonizing the relation between man and nature, and maintaining sustainable development of the economy. //

To attain the goal of forming the Chinese-style socialist legal system by the year 2010, we focus on two major tasks in this year's legislative work. One task is to pay close attention to enacting and revising laws that are supportive in the legal system, and enhance legislation in the field of social law while keeping improving legislation in the economic, political and cultural fields. The other is to sort out the existing laws, categorizing the laws that are obviously unable to adapt to the need for development of the socialist economy, or are not completely consistent with one another, or are not coherent with each other, or are not sufficiently enforceable, and disposing them respectively by abolishing, revising or interpreting them or by enacting complementary laws, in order to make a more scientific, consistent and harmonious legal system to ensure implementation. //

Legal construction within the government is an important aspect of China's socialist democratic and legal development. Administration according to law is the essential subject of governmental legal construction and the foundation and key for fully implementing the basic policy of governing the country according to law. For many years the Chinese Government has adopted a series of effective measures to enhance legal construction within the government, to promote administration according to law in an all-round way. With all these years' unremitting efforts, great progress has been made in promoting administration according to law, which is mainly reflected in the following aspects: //

Governments at various levels on the whole abide by law when exercising their administrative power and the quality of legislations formulated by them has definitely improved. The State Council from beginning to end has been adhering to complying legislative decisions with policies of reform. From 1979 to the end of August, 2009, the State Council has made 231 legislative proposals to the National People's Congress and its Standing Committee for deliberation, formulated 682 administrative regulations in effect. From 1987 when the recording system for regulations and rules was established to the end of August, 2009, the departments under the State Council and the local governments vested with the power of legislation have formulated 26,308 pieces of rules. More emphasis is attached to legislation in a scientific and democratic way. By the end of last August, the drafts of 53 administrative regulations were published for soliciting opinions from the general public. //

The government further transforms its functions and enhances internal construction. Reforming of the system of administrative review and approval is going steadily. The State Council and the local governments at various levels rescind and adjust in groups the items previously subject to administrative review and approval so far, the State Council has rescinded 1,992 items in four groups and the local governments at various levels have rescinded or adjusted 77,692 items in total. //

Administrative law-enforcement system is reformed and an accountability system for administrative law-enforcement is applied, therefore law enforcement is strictly regulated. The aforesaid accountability system effectively regulates acts of administrative law-enforcement. //

The system of administrative supervision is improved and new methods of administrative supervision are introduced, which enhance supervision over administrative acts. Administrative reconsideration system is earnestly implemented. The authorities for administrative reconsideration at various levels have brought their role into active play when performing their functions to settle disputes in a timely manner. Now more than 80,000 cases in dispute are settled through administrative reconsideration each year. The State Council has initiated recording of regulations and rules in 1987. At present, almost all the regulations and rules formulated are reported and recorded in the year, and those contravening upper-level laws are handled in time, which helps maintain the consistency of the legal system. Under direction of the State Council, local governments have been actively exploring ways to establish their own recording and review system for regulatory documents and effectively tackled the problem of issuing official documents in an abusive and excessive way. //

Awareness and capability of administration according to law of the staff members, especially the leaders, of administrative organs has obviously increased. Localities and departments have taken various measures to train their staff members in administration according to law, the idea of administration according to law has taken root in their hearts.

Thank you all. //

## ◆ *Passage 2*

*( The following is an excerpt from the speech " Improving the Legal System to Prevent Financial Risks" , by the Deputy Governor of the People's Bank of China delivered at the "2005 High-level Forum of China's Financial Reform" on April 26, 2005)*

Ladies and Gentlemen:

It's a pleasure to attend this high-level forum of China's financial reform, sponsored by the Financial Research Institute, Development Research Center of the State Council. //

Financial legal system not only provides regulation for financial institutions, financial business participants and their legal relationship, but also improves the self-discipline of financial supervisors. The main target of financial legislation is to adjust the legal relationship among financial supervisors, institutions and customers, protect customers' legitimate rights, and strengthen the supervision on those areas where market plays a leading role in coordinating financial supervision and market self-discipline. Where there is market, there is risk, which is also the same for the financial sector. Thus, the purpose of financial legislation is not to wipe out all risks, but to control it in a certain scale that can be handled by the supervisors and absorbed by the financial institutions. Viewing from this aspect, the establishment and enforcement of financial legal system are indispensable for preventing, controlling and dissolving financial risks. On today's occasion, I would like to share with you my observations about the prevention of financial risks in China in the broad context of financial innovation from the aspect of financial legislation. //

The high risks embedded in China's financial system are the result of various problems in the national economy over a protracted period. The transition of the economic system, the change of the social environment, the rigidity of the financial system, the inadequacy of financial supervision and the defects in the legal framework for the financial sector are among the causes of the high risks in China's financial system. Scholars and government officials have done numerous studies in those regards. //

As is known to all, the legal framework is in essence a tool to regulate the relationship among financial supervisors, financial institutions and investors in financial products. In addition to regulating the legal relationship, the legal framework for the financial sector has many other functions, including punishment, encouragement, inhibition and guidance. In economic terms, it could be translated into predictable interest or loss. A large number of rules and regulations for the financial sector have been formulated since 1979, when China adopted the reform and opening-up policy. Such rules as the Law of the People's Republic of China on the People's Bank of China, the Commercial Banking Law of the People's Republic of China, the Law of the People's Republic of China on Banking Regulation and Supervision, the Securities Law of the People's Republic of China, and the Insurance Law of the People's Republic of China which regulate financial supervision, financial institutions and their behaviors, have formed the fundamental legal framework for the financial sector. The Law on Administrative Penalty, the Law on Administrative Appeal, and the Law on Administrative License are designed to regulate the administrative behavior of financial supervisors. In addition, the Law on Negotiable Instruments, the Guarantee Law, and the Company Law are designed to regulate civil and commercial relations. //

However, we should be aware that the existing financial legal rules were established in the development of emerging markets and the transitional period of economy. With the deepening reform of China's financial system, the accelerating opening-up and the enhancing innovation of the financial sector, the existing legal framework can hardly satisfy the changing requirement of the financial sector. Especially, we need to make an overview of the basic legal environment that our financial sector relies on and improve the research on laws for financial innovation (including system innovation, institution innovation and product innovation) . //

As China's financial reform is accelerating, the task of preventing financial risks has become more important and challenging. Given the innate risks associated with the financial sector, the legal framework for the sector cannot eliminate all financial risks once and for all. However, a sound legal framework may help deter imprudent risk-taking activities of financial institutions and reduce systemic risks. Furthermore, a favorable legal environment is the precondition for the steady performance of the financial system. //

The People's Bank of China is stepping up its efforts in improving the legal framework for the financial sector. More specifically, it is facilitating the formulation of the Regulations on Credit Information Management; it is actively involved in the amendment of the Enterprise Insolvency Law and the Criminal Law; it is offering suggestions for the amendment of the Securities Law of the People's Republic of China; it is drafting the Law on Anti-Money Laundering; and it is doing research on the legal issues concerning the market exit of financial institutions, deposit insurance, legislation for financial holding companies, asset securitization, and entrusted wealth management. We hope to promulgate these laws, regulations and implementary rules as soon as possible so as to effectively regulate certain important financial activities. In a word, China's legal framework for the financial sector should be overhauled necessary new laws should be drafted, existing laws should be amended as appropriate, and outdated laws should be invalidated. //

In the long run, we should not only focus on legislation but also on the enforcement of existing laws. In my view, the core issue of financial legislation lies in a scientific approach. Different stages of the financial sector call for different approaches. At present, financial legislation should focus on improving infrastructure of the financial market, regulating legal relationship concerning financial innovation, advancing the coordination and effectiveness of financial supervision, and making the best use of market self-discipline. //

First, we shall approach financial legislation in a coordinated, scientific and comprehensive manner. China's economic reform and financial reform are at a critical period, when the stand-alone strategy no longer meets the requirement. Therefore, coordinated planning and rational thinking should prevail in financial legislation. Specifically, we should gradually promote the integration and consolidation of the financial market through legislation; regulate the trading of homogenous financial products through identical supervisory rules; and ensure the consistency of the infrastructure (such as the rules on issuance, registration, custody, settlement and liquidation) in different markets. We should apply uniform rules in regulating the institutional innovation, business innovation and product innovation of financial institutions. We should also work on the sharing and transmission of financial-risk-related information among financial regulatory bodies. Other laws that support financial development and reform should be amended so as to protect both the creditor and the debtor. The revision of the Criminal Law should also reflect the current social environment so as to highlight criminal sanctions on corporate crime and the investigation of individual criminal liability. //

Second, we should stick to the protection of the interest of the depositor, investor and creditor. Protecting the interest of depositors of financial institutions and the interest of investors in financial products is always an important factor in the maintenance of the reputation of financial institutions. Our present task is to study the fundamental legal relationship in the financial sector and to standardize the legal relationship concerning financial innovation products. While approving innovation products, financial supervisory bodies should work hard to protect such lawful rights of the investors as the right to know and the right to receive due return. We should step up our efforts in improving the Enterprise Bankruptcy Law. Under the basic principles of the Enterprise Bankruptcy Law, we should formulate, while taking into consideration the unique features of bankruptcy of financial institutions, the Regulations on the Bankruptcy of Financial Institutions. We should also establish and improve the financial safety network and formulate a series of supporting laws and regulations such as the Regulations on Deposit Insurance and the Rules on Administration of the Securities Investor Protection Fund. //

Third, we should stress both self-discipline and external discipline. In drafting laws concerning financial supervision, we should stress the importance of a sound and complete mechanism for corporate governance by such players as commercial banks, brokers and listed companies. While emphasizing the self-discipline of financial institutions, we should also guarantee the autonomy of these institutions in their operation and leave sufficient room for their future development. //

Fourth, we should raise the public awareness of financial risks and rules, which is one of the most effective methods for preventing financial risks and ensuring financial safety. During the process, we should foster the extensive publicity of credit culture, increase the awareness of risk prevention among the public and investors, and preach the virtues of lawful investment. //

Thank you very much! //

# Ⅳ. 句子精炼 Sentences in Focus

**Directions**: *Interpret the following sentences alternatively into English or Chinese*:

1. 截至 2009 年 8 月底，全国人大及其常委会共制定了现行有效的法律 229 件，涵盖宪法及宪法相关法、民商法、行政法、经济法、社会法、刑法、诉讼及非诉讼程序法 7 个法律部门。

2. 在我国社会主义制度下，法律是党的主张和人民意志的统一。立法从党和国家发展的大局和实际需要出发，把亟须法律调整、立法条件比较成熟的领域制度化、法律化，通过国家的强制力保障实施。

3. 立法通过制度化的渠道凝聚民意，确定共同的行为准则并保证其实施；我国法律确立和维护人民民主专政的国家制度，确立并不断完善国家的政权结构和组织形式，推进政府职能转变和管理创新，强化社会管理和社会服务；我国法律确立和维护国家的经济制度。

4. 对已经明显不适应发展社会主义市场经济的需要、前法与后法不尽一致或者不够衔接、操作性不强的法律规定，通过废止、修改、解释、配套等方式进行分类处理，促进法律体系的科学、统一、和谐，保障其实施。

5. 从 1979 年到 2009 年 8 月底，国务院共提请全国人大及其常委会审议法律议案 231 件，制定现行有效行政法规 682 件，从 1987 年建立法规规章备案制度到 2009 年 8 月底，国务院部门和有立法权的地方政府共制定规章 26 308 件。

6. 金融立法的最根本目的就是规范和调整金融监督管理者、金融机构、金融机构客户之间的法律关系，强调对金融机构客户合法权益的保护，通过在政府失灵的领域强化监督管理，发挥市场在金融发展中的主导作用，实现金融管制与市场自律间的平衡和协调发展。

7. 经济体制的转轨、社会环境的变化、金融体制的不适应、监管手段的落后，以及金融法律制度的不完善等都是造成我国金融体系中存在高风险的原因。

8. 改革开放以来，我国的金融法治建设取得了很大的成绩，建立了以《中国人民银行法》《商业银行法》《银行业监督管理法》《证券法》《保险法》等以规范金融监督管理行为、规范金融经营主体和经营行为为主要内容的基本金融法律制度。

9. 从长远来看，我国的金融法治建设既要在金融立法方面下功夫，也要在金融执法方面强化执法的严肃性，真正做到"两手都要抓、两手都要硬"。

10. 要尽快完善《企业破产法》，根据《企业破产法》的基本原则，考虑金融机构破产的特殊性，尽快制定《金融机构破产条例》，同时应当尽快建立健全金融安全网制度，制定包括《存款保险条例》《证券投资者保护基金管理办法》在内的金融法律制度。

## 第五单元 大陆法系及普通法系

**Unit 5  Civil Law System & Common Law System**

# Ⅰ. 专题知识 Legal Knowledge

西方学者根据各国法律的特点、历史传统及其源流关系，把世界大部分国家的法分为了大陆法系与普通法系（又称英美法系）两大法系。但需要注意的是，大陆法系和英美法系原是对西方主要国家法律的一种划分，并不涵盖所有国家。例如，中东的部分伊斯兰国家，其法律具有相当的独特性，很难归到大陆法系或英美法系里面。

## 一、大陆法系

大陆法系是以古代罗马法以及 19 世纪《法国民法典》和《德国民法典》为传统发展起来的各国和地区法律的总称。由于这一法系源于欧洲大陆并仍在欧洲大陆居于主导地位，因此被称为大陆法系，又因为这一法系的民法传统非常深厚，所以也常被称为民法法系。

除了法国、德国、意大利、西班牙、葡萄牙等欧洲大陆国家，大陆法系还包括以下两类国家和地区：一是曾被上述欧洲国家殖民的国家和地区，如巴西、阿根廷和加拿大的魁北克地区等；二是通过变法革新，主动向西方学习的国家，典型的有日本、土耳其等国。

从清末开始到中华人民共和国成立之前，中国的法律基本可以被划到大陆法系。新中国成立后，先是师从苏联，改革开放后又开始博采众长，兼采英美法系和大陆法系，法律的精神实质和具体内容不断发生变化，但法律的形式、司法体系，法律推理和法学研究的方法依然具有显著的大陆法系特点。

## 二、英美法系

英美法系是以英国中世纪至资本主义时期的法为传统而产生和发展的各国和地区的法律的统称。由于这个法系以英国和美国为最主要的代表，因此被称为英美法系；又因为该法系推崇以普通法为代表的判例法，所以也常被称作普通法。其中，判例法指英国在审判活动中逐渐确立了"遵循先例"（stare decisis）原则，法院判决中所形成的法律原则不仅适用于该案，而且适用于以后的案件审理，并具有法律约束力。

属于英美法系的国家，除英国、美国之外，主要是曾经属于英国殖民地、附属国的国家和地区，如印度、巴基斯坦、加拿大、澳大利亚、新西兰、新加坡等。

## 三、两大法系的主要区别

（1）立法权归属不同。在大陆法系国家，立法权主要由立法机关（制定基本法律）和行政机关（制定行政法规、规章）行使，法院不参与立法，有关判决对于之后的审判仅具有参考价值，不具有法律约束力。而在英美法系国家，由于"遵循先例"原则的存在，司法机关与立法机关、行政机关一样，享有制定法律规则的权力。

（2）法律体系不同。大陆法系国家的法律体系比较完整、清晰，理论化程度较高。一般而言，这些国家的法律体系由宪法、行政法、民法、刑法、诉讼法、经济法等构成。英美法系国家更注重实用主义，法律的系统性不强，许多法律是根据当时的紧迫需要制定的。

（3）法典化程度不同。大陆法系沿袭了罗马法以来的传统，注重成文法典的编撰。各国一般都有《民法典》《刑法典》等基本法典，而英美法系则不存在这样的法典。

（4）司法组织不同。大陆法系国家的司法体系比较清楚，一般都由法院、检察院和司法行政机关三者构成。英美法系则有不同，英国不设司法部，也没有完整意义上的最高法院（上议院履行最高法院职能）。美国虽设有司法部，但其部长同时又兼任总检察长。从法院系统来看，英美法系国家一般只有一套法院系统，审理各种类型的案件。而大陆法系国家则对应不同性质的案件设立不同种类的法院，一般常见的有普通法院、行政法院、宪法法院等。

（5）陪审方式不同。基于民主的原则，两大法系都采用了陪审制，但其运行有较大的差异。在英美法系国家，陪审员不是合议庭的组成人员，陪审团只负责认定案件的事实部分，至于法律适用和最终作出判决则是法官的职责。在大陆法系国家，陪审员直接参加合议庭，并享有和法官大致相同的权力。

（6）诉讼活动不同。大陆法系国家的法官主导整个庭审活动，通过询问当事人、询问证人等方式查清案情，具有较强的主动性；而英美法系的法官则比较"消极"，只负责引导案审进行，案件事实主要靠当事人双方及其代理律师和辩护律师通过言词辩论逐步澄清。

# Ⅱ. 词汇热身 Vocabulary Warm-up

**Directions**：*Give the English equivalents of the following Chinese expressions*：

| | | |
|---|---|---|
| 具有里程碑意义的 | 澳门特别行政区 | 动荡和纷乱 |
| 两百周年 | （香港）在英国管治 | 保障人民民主 |
| 《法国民法典》 | 时期 | 加强法制 |
| 香港城市大学 | 香港特别行政区 | 为……奠下根基 |
| 盛事 | 动荡的年代 | 傲人的经济增长 |
| 从大局/宏观层面思考 | 风云变幻的年代 | 中国入世 |
| 大中华地区 | 可见一斑 | 回归 |
| 民法法系制度 | 苏维埃模式的法律 | 司法管辖区 |
| 大陆法系制度 | 制度 | 美国路易斯安那州 |
| 普通法系制度 | 沿用下来的法律原则 | 加拿大魁北克省 |
| 英美法系制度 | 废除 | 履行欧盟所订下的众 |
| 屹立不倒 | 反右运动 | 多义务 越来越多人认 |
| 欧洲大陆 | 荡然无存 | 同 |
| 综合性法典 | 取而代之 | 加强沟通 |

**Directions**：*Give the Chinese equivalents of the following English expressions*

| | |
|---|---|
| inaugural lecture | Justice IT |
| the Bar | CPS（Crown Prosecution Service） |
| the then director-general of Criminal | the Lord Chancellor's Department |

investment on the margins

a back office system called CREST

Crown Courts

computerized bulk claims centre

Northampton

legal aid MP (Member of Parliament)

the House of Commons

civil justice

Lord Woolf

Woolf Day

to cause an uproar

to remain unscathed

pilot schemes

Digital audio recording

electronic presentation of evidence

bungalow

the civil and family courts

on pragmatic grounds

to spearhead

CBE (Commander of the British Empire)

OBE (Officer of the Order of the British Empire)

Money ClaimsOnline system

the Home Office

the Law Officers' Department

in due course

a national roll-out

freestanding laptops

Snaresbrook Crown Court

the Old Bailey

judicial liaison

odd hiccup

jury in retirement

Essex

Holloway Prison

criminal proceedings

to plead guilty

Blackfriars

a VAT fraud trial

the Treasury

Tasmania

"whispering witness" technology

to take the initiative

wireless amplification

one-off experiment

Manchester

the preliminary stages of a criminal trial

magistrates' courts

police escorts

the Court Service

to pay a heart felt tribute to

coherent chronological order

on circuit as a High Court judge

to grind to a halt

high staff turnover

to enthuse about/over sth.

to pull the plug

to disband

long snake close to the top of the Snakes and Ladders Board

"jam tomorrow"

to adjourn the trial

provide a panacea to all ills

in arrears

the sky fell on St Swithin's Day

Bangor University

Magna Carta

# III. 课文口译 Text for Interpreting

## ◆ *Passage 1*

**Directions**：Listen to the passage and interpret from Chinese into English at the end of each segment.

（*以下为 2004 年 11 月 9 日香港律政司司长梁爱诗当日出席香港城市大学〈法国民法典〉200 周年纪念研讨会就"大中华区大陆法的现况与未来"致辞全文*）

张信刚校长、孟嗣德先生、马培德院长、各位嘉宾：//

这个研讨会意义重大，承蒙邀请在会上发言，本人深感荣幸。《法国民法典》200 周年纪念，以及香港城市大学 20 周年纪念，都是值得热烈庆贺的盛事。//

这两大盛事推动我们从更广的层面去考虑现实的法律问题，也就是要求我们从宏观的角度来思考。我们的法律制度是如何演变成现有模式的呢？其中主要受到什么影响？未来我们应把握什么方向？我们的法律制度最终的目标是什么？//

这两天的研讨会，让我们有机会从中国整体的情况，探讨这些基本的问题。世界各国之中，没有几个拥有如此丰富的法律传统。中国同时受惠于现代世界最主要的三种法律制度：大陆法制度、普通法制度和社会主义制度。//

大家都知道，大陆法源于《法国民法典》。《法国民法典》在整个欧洲大陆乃至其余各大洲广泛传播，经过 200 年仍屹立不倒，而且日益稳固。19 纪日本进行的法制维新，以及 1928 年至 1935 年间中国颁布的综合性法律，无不受到《法国民法典》的影响。以葡萄牙的模式为蓝本的大陆法制度也在澳门特别行政区确立和发展。1999 年澳门回归祖国之后，这个制度根据《澳门特别行政区基本法》的规定被保留下来。//

香港的普通法制度为市民、商人和投资者提供了可靠的法律环境。回归后普通法制度根据《香港特别行政区基本法》的规定继续在香港实行。//

中华人民共和国在 1949 年成立之后，废除了旧有的法律制度，并着手建

设全新的社会主义法律制度。20 世纪 50 年代，苏维埃模式的法律制度建立起来。//

邓小平先生在 1978 年的中央工作会议上宣布："为了保障人民民主，必须加强法制。"自此，中国的法律制度迅速发展，步伐令人瞩目，为中国骄人的经济增长奠下根基。《宪法》强调，中华人民共和国实行法治，保障公民的法定私有财产，并尊重和维护人权。而加入世贸组织，无疑进一步加快了中国法制改革的步伐。//

刚才我概述了我们的法律制度的发展进程。日后的发展又会怎样？4 个法域的情况可能各有不同，但就我国的利益来说，不同的法律制度仍可共同合作。//

这次研讨会所讨论的多个议题中，包括探讨各种合作形式，例如判决和仲裁裁决的相互承认和执行。尽管法律制度不同，但这些范围的合作是可以达成的。了解彼此的法律制度，对于彼此的合作，无疑会有裨益。自回归以来，各个司法管辖区一直采取积极的措施，加深彼此的了解，这实在叫人欣慰。可以肯定的是，这些措施将会继续下去。//

一国之内，不同的法律制度也可以并存。美国和加拿大主体上是普通法司法管辖区，但路易斯安那州和魁北克省却采用大陆法制度。欧盟证明了实行普通法和大陆法的国家都可以在商业和人权等范畴履行欧盟所订立的不同义务。事实上，成为欧盟的成员，有助于各具不同法律传统的国家协调其所实施的法律。//

全球一体化是另一个影响跨国商法发展的因素，越来越多新颁布的国际公约，在奉行不同法律制度的国家实施。//

法律制度的存在有其目的。我相信在中国越来越多的人会认同法律制度的目的就是协助维持政治稳定和社会秩序，以及保障市民的基本权利。在中国领土内，不同地方可能采用不同的方式，以达至上述目的，但若我们朝着这个相同目标共同努力，我们定能克服种种障碍，为我国的经济和社会发展作出贡献。//

因此，我们必须加强沟通。这次研讨会是沟通过程的重要部分。主办机构举办这次研讨会，内容丰富，饶有意义，实在值得我们嘉许。//

我谨祝这两天的研讨会圆满举行，各位都取得丰硕成果。//

◆ *Passage 2*

**Directions**：Listen to the passage and interpret from English into Chinese at the end of each segment.

[ *The following is an excerpt from the speech "modernization and the crisis facing our civil courts" made by Lord Justice Brooke, Vice-President of the Court of Appeal (Civil Division) Court, Society of Advanced Legal Studies, London, 24 November 2004* ]

I have been asked to talk to you tonight about the modernization of the courts. I do not know what the opposite of an inaugural lecture is called. Perhaps I should call it "Good-bye to All That". At the end of last June I finished 19 years of promoting the use of technology in the legal system. I started it by being a member of the first committee ever set up to give advice to the Bar about computers. I ended it by being for four years a member of the small Board which has been taking forward the £260 million court modernization program. Tonight I have come to tell you something of the story. //

I have written elsewhere about the reasons why there was such chronic under-investment in IT in support of the courts during the 1990s. Two years ago I was at a presentation given by the then director-general of Criminal Justice IT. This showed how far the courts had lagged behind the police, the CPS and all the other agencies which make up our criminal justice system. I lived through the lean years in which investment in IT was regarded by the Lord Chancellor's Department as investment on the margins, and they never had any money to spend on the margins. They could afford to install IT networks in their own headquarters offices. But the courts, and particularly the front offices in the courts, where the judges work, were an IT desert. //

I must mention four developments in the 1990s. The first was a back office system called CREST. This was installed in the Crown Courts 13 years ago. It enabled court staff to produce common form documents without having to type each of them out one by one. It also helped them to perform some other fairly basic back office tasks. Similar arrangements, called CASEMAN and FAMILYMAN, were installed in the back offices in the county courts about seven years ago. There was also an excellent computerized bulk claims centre at Northampton which processed straightforward debt collection claims by their thousands. This process led up to a computerized default judgment which never went anywhere near a court. And a small amount of money was set aside to allow 400 judges to have their first direct experience of using a PC in their work. //

A large part of the difficulty was that the Lord Chancellor's Department was chronically overwhelmed, year after year, by unbudgeted overspends on legal aid. MPs are good at encouraging ministers to devote more resources to causes they are interested in. But they never seemed to have much interest in what was needed to keep the courts functioning effectively. In those 19 years I was only ever asked once to speak to a group of parliamentarians. That was a delegation from the state of Victoria, which had crossed the world to learn about best practice in court modernization. Later on I will tell you what I saw when I visited Melbourne last year. //

It was about six years ago that things started to wake up. A team of civil servants examined what might be done to improve the efficiency of the Crown Courts. Among other things, they looked at the possibilities of investment in technology. On the civil justice side, Lord Woolf delivered his final report in 1996, and it was unthinkable that his reforms could ever be put into effect without heavy investment in IT to help judges and court staff. This was because huge new burdens were being placed upon the judges to enable them to control civil litigation from the centre. In 1988 a Government inquiry team had strongly recommended investment in court based IT to help the judges. Nothing was then done, and things stood still for ten years. //

On the Crown Court side the team produced a report called "Transforming the Crown Court". This report caused an uproar, but its uncontroversial elements remained unscathed. Money was allocated immediately, and also in the Government spending review in 2000, to the start of a modernization program in the Crown Court. The idea was to produce a specification for wiring and cabling every Crown Court in the country. As a result each would have a modern networked IT infrastructure fit for the next thirty years. There was also to be investment in pilot schemes at a few Crown Courts to test the possibilities of different technologies. Digital audio recording（"DAR"）, electronic presentation of evidence（"EPE"）, and an electronic public information system which the politicians fancied were at the front of the list. On the civil justice side valiant efforts were made in 1997 and 1998 to try and make plans for IT systems to support the Woolf reforms. These plans were always doomed. The rule-makers went on changing the rules right up to Woolf Day on 26 April 1999, and nobody can design complex IT systems under those conditions. Those of us who knew a little about IT were worried that yet another set of inadequate systems were to be rushed out with no prospect of leading anywhere afterwards. Professor Richard Susskind, who advised us, kept on saying that we should now be building the foundations for a twelve-storey office block, and not another bungalow. //

Eventually it was decided to call the whole thing off. We needed to do some really hard thinking about what had to be done to save our system of justice in the civil and family courts from falling apart for lack of investment. In the meantime the Lord Chancellor decided to go ahead with the civil justice reforms without the IT support they needed. The Head of Civil Justice, Sir Richard Scott, was known to disagree with that decision, because he really did not know how the courts would be able to cope. But Lord Woolf supported it on pragmatic grounds, and a fairly rudimentary system called High Court Forms was rushed out to support the High Court Masters who had never had to manage court files before. The judges received then what we thought was a very firm promise that we would receive the IT back-up we needed as soon as it was ready. //

The boards responsible for modernizing the Crown Courts and the civil and family courts were amalgamated in 2001 because there were so many points of similarity. But I think it would be better if I treated these two topics separately since the differences in their treatment have been so striking. What is common to both, however, is the professionalism of the team that has been driving the program forward. During the last four years two of the civil servants and three of the judges who have been spearheading this work have been awarded the CBE or the OBE for public services. Two years ago the team running the £160 million project concerned with installing IT infrastructure in the courts won an award from the Cabinet Office for the best managed IT project within Government that year. Some of the team's projects, like the Money Claims Online system, have won international praise. And the Court Service has won awards from US judges in two separate years for producing one of the best designed "foreign" court websites. It will be an important theme of this lecture that in this team, with whom I worked closely for four years, we had a resource of international quality. It is a tragedy that it is now being broken up because funding is simply not available to take their work the next logical step forward. //

Four years ago the team was allocated enough money to start implementing their plans in the Crown Courts during the three years which began in April 2001. Two years later the Government made a massive investment in criminal justice IT for the three year period starting in April 2003. By this time Government had absorbed a message Sir Brian Neill and I started trying to teach it in 1986. This was that the different players in the court system are inter-dependent. It is foolish for one part of the system, whether it is the police or the CPS or the Court Service, to design its IT systems as if they are in an oasis, totally isolated in its private patch of desert from anyone else. In 1986 we founded the IT and the Courts Committee ("ITAC") to take forward this message, but nobody listened. In the same year we were very critical of the designers of the CREST system, because they were making no provision at all for the flow of information electronically into the courts from other court users. We had to wait for 15 years for that mistake to be put right. //

What was arranged two years ago was that there was to be a £1. 1 billion investment in criminal justice IT over the next three year period. This was not all new money, because a lot of it had already been allotted from 2003 to 2004, but it was much more than had ever been provided before. The money was to be held by a new organization called Criminal Justice IT. None of it could be allocated without the agreement of a minister from each department and also the Director-General of Criminal Justice IT. //

Most of the main spending allocations were made early on. Because our basic IT infrastructure was so far behind everyone else, we were allotted the funding to install it in all our Crown Courts by April 2006. But that was about it, so far as the criminal courts were concerned, with one exception. There was no new money for DAR. No new money for EPE. No money at all for the case handling systems we so badly needed. No new money for video-conferencing, either, although in due course money was secured from a different budget to provide 30 Crown Courts with video links with prisons. //

The one exception to all this was the XHIBIT project. This project had always been a political favorite. It provided very few benefits for judges and court staff, and we would have greatly preferred to invest the money elsewhere. But the project was perceived to benefit the public, and to be a good example of a "joined up" project in which investment in one part of the criminal justice system would benefit people in other parts of it. So a green light was given to it, and although it then ran into serious delays, approval has now been given for a national roll-out. This will start in two weeks' time with courts in the North-East. //

In last year's book I described how after all that careful planning we appeared to have struck that long snake close to the top of the Snakes and Ladders Board. We were all sent back a very long way, and the morale of judges and court staff was badly shaken. On the evening of the spending review announcement in July 2002 the Treasury published a description of the objectives of the Lord Chancellor's Department. The modernization of the civil and family courts did not rate a mention. It was obvious that most of the relief we hoped that technology would bring to civil and family court judges and their staff would not be forthcoming. Whether "jam tomorrow" would ever turn into "jam today" was back in the lap of the gods. //

I have spent over forty years of my life in the world of civil justice. Two and a half years ago I really thought we were on the way to creating new arrangements for civil and family justice of which this country could be proud. Now I see no light on the horizon at all. I do not even see any evidence that the scale of the problem is being properly addressed because there are so many other initiatives currently being pursued, which are distracting the attention of our policy-makers. And so long as the Treasury insists on its full cost recovery regime, things can only get worse, much worse. //

# IV. 参考译文 Reference versions:

## ◆ *Passage 1*

(*The following is an Opening Statement by the Secretary for Justice, Ms Elsie Leung, on "The Present and Future of Civil Law in Greater China" at a conference on the Bicentenary of the French Civil Code at the City University of Hong Kong.*)

President Zhang, Mr. Mostura, Dean Malanczuk, ladies and gentlemen, //

It is a great honor for me to say a few words at this landmark conference. The bicentenary of the French Civil Code, and the 20th anniversary of the City University of Hong Kong, are proud events that are worth celebrating. //

They prompt us to look at current legal issues from a broader perspective — to look at the big picture. How did our legal system develop in the way it did? What were the major influences? What direction should we take in future? What is the ultimate goal of our legal system? //

This two-day conference gives us an opportunity to explore these fundamental questions in the context of China. There can be few, if any, countries which have within them such a rich legal heritage. China has benefited from all three major legal systems of the modern world : the civil law system, the common law system, and the socialist system. //

The civil law system originated, of course, from the great French Civil Code. That Code now stands tall after 200 years, having spread throughout continental Europe and to other continents. It influenced the modernization of the Japanese legal system in the 19th century, and the promulgation of comprehensive codes in China between 1928 and 1935. In its Portuguese form, the civil law took hold in Macau. After the Reunification of Macau and the Mainland in 1999, that system remains in force by virtue of the Basic Law of the Macau SAR. //

The common law system in Hong Kong contributed to Hong Kong's development by providing a secure legal environment for residents, businessmen and investors. That common law system continues here after Reunification by virtue of the Basic

Law of the Hong Kong SAR. //

After the establishment of the People's Republic of China in 1949, the previous legal system was abolished and steps taken to construct a new socialist one. In the 1950s, a Soviet-style legal system was being developed. //

Fortunately, in 1978, Deng Xiaoping declared, "in order to safeguard people's democracy, the legal system must be strengthened". Since then, the Chinese legal system has developed at an impressive pace, and is underpinning China's incredible economic growth. The Chinese Constitution now emphasizes that the PRC exercises the rule of law, protects citizens' lawful private property, and shall respect and safeguard human rights. China's accession to the WTO will undoubtedly further speed up the process of modernizing its legal system. //

That, in a nutshell, is how we got where we are now. But what about the future? The four legal systems within Greater China may differ, but they can still work together for the good of the country. //

Among the topics to be discussed at this conference are various types of co-operation, such as the recognition and enforcement of judgments and arbitral awards. Co-operation in these areas can be achieved despite the differing legal systems. But it undoubtedly helps if we understand each others' systems first. Since Reunification, it is gratifying to see the positive steps that have been taken by the various legal jurisdictions to understand each other better. I am sure that these steps will continue. //

There is no reason why different legal systems cannot happily co-exist within one country. The USA and Canada are largely common law jurisdictions, and yet Louisiana and Quebec operate under the civil law. The European Union has demonstrated that both common law and civil law countries can give effect to the multitude of EU obligations, in areas such as commerce and human rights. Indeed, membership of the EU is helping to harmonize the laws in countries with different legal traditions. //

Globalization is another factor at work in the development of transnational commercial laws. And an increasing number of international conventions are being promulgated, and implemented in countries regardless of the system of law they practice. //

Legal systems exist for a purpose. Within Greater China I believe there is a growing consensus on what that purpose should be to contribute to political stability and social order, and to protect the basic rights of the citizen. The way in which this is done may vary in the various parts of Greater China. But, if we are working towards the same goal, we can overcome obstacles and contribute to the economic and social development of our country. //

We must therefore keep up our dialogue. This conference is an important part of that process, and the organizers are to be commended for the excellent programme they have put together. //

I wish all of you a fruitful and enjoyable two days. //

## ◆ *Passage 2*

[节选自英国上诉法院（民事分庭）副院长布鲁克勋爵大法官 2004 年 11 月 24 日于高级法律研究协会（伦敦）的致辞：《法院现代化与法院所面临的危机》]

今晚，我应邀与各位谈谈我对法院现代化的看法。我不知道就职演说的反义词该叫什么。也许我该称之为"告别演说"吧。截至去年 6 月底，我结束了 19 年来在司法系统中对科技运用的推广。我是首个给大律师公会提供有关电脑方面意见的委员会的成员。随后的 4 年，我成了另一个小型委员会的成员。该委员会一直在推动一个价值 2.6 亿英镑的法院现代化计划。今晚我想和各位分享一下我的故事。//

我曾在其他地方发表过 20 世纪 90 年代支持法院的 IT 投资为何会又慢又少的看法。2 年前，我去听了刑事司法 IT 处时任处长的讲座。通过这个讲座，我发现法院在 IT 方面远远落后于警察局、皇家检察署（CPS）及组成刑事司法系统的其他机构。我们对法院 IT 的投资可以说是捉襟见肘，因为大法官部认为对 IT 的投资是最无谓的，他们从来不会在无谓的东西上花钱。他们若有钱可以在自己的总部办公室安装网络。但是，在法院，尤其是法官工作的法院行政办公室，可以说曾是 IT 的"沙漠"。//

我必须说一说 20 世纪 90 年代的四个发展。第一个是名为 CREST 的后勤办公室系统，英国刑事法庭 13 年前安装了这个系统。该系统让法院工作人员能够不用一个个字地打出来就可以制作出一般的表格文件，还可以帮助他们执行一些其他相当基本的后台工作。县法院在 7 年前，也在后勤办公室安装了类似的系统，名为 CASEMAN 和 FAMILYMAN。在北安普敦（英国南部城市）也安装了性能优秀的电脑批量索赔处理中心系统，该系统能直接处理数以千计的债务回收索赔。该系统催生了电脑化缺席判决的出现，在此之前法院从未出现过这种状况。同时，另外划出的一小部分资金使 400 名法官在工作中首次直接使用了电脑。//

造成资金困难的很大一部分原因在于，大法官部年复一年地被未编入预算的法律援助超出开支压得喘不过气。国会议员都善于鼓动部长向他们感兴趣的事业投入更多资源，但他们对于保持法院的有效运作所需的资源似乎没什么太大的兴趣。在这 19 年里，我只应邀发表过一次对法院现代化的演讲，对象是来自澳大利亚维多利亚州的议员代表团，他们横跨大西洋来学习法院现代化的最佳实践。稍后我想跟大家分享一下，去年我访问墨尔本的见闻。//

大约 6 年前开始，情况渐渐出现转变，一公务员小组对可以采取何种措施以改善英国刑事法庭的效率进行了审查。其中，他们还研究了对科技进行投资的可能性。在民事司法方面，伍尔夫勋爵在 1996 年发表了最后的报告，如果不大量投资 IT 以帮助法官和法院工作人员，很难想象他的改革可以生效。这是因为法官被赋予了沉重的新责任，使他们能够从中心控制民事诉讼。1988 年，政府调查小组曾强烈建议对法院进行 IT 投资，以帮助法官。但当时并没有采取实际的行为，且此后 10 年没有任何新进展。//

在英国刑事法庭方面，该调查组提交了一份名为《改变英国刑事法庭》的报告。这份报告引起了轩然大波，但其引起争议的问题最后还是没有得到解决。当时有关当局立即划出资金，并在 2000 年审查政府开支时启动了英国刑事法庭现代化计划。当时的想法是，为国内每一个刑事法庭提供一套相同规格的电缆和有线网络。这样一来，每个刑事法庭都会有一套可以用 30 年的现代化网络 IT 基础设施。当时还投资了若干个作为试点计划的刑事法庭，以测试不同技术的可能性。当时上层领导想象的清单，包括了数码录音（DAR）、证据呈现电子化（EPE）以及电子化公共信息系统。在民事审判方面，在 1997 年和 1998 年曾付出过巨大的努力，计划制作一个 IT 系统以支持上述伍尔夫勋爵的改革。但这些计划总是无疾而终。后来，决策者继续改革规则，直到 1999 年 4 月 26 日伍尔夫勋爵改革纪念日，仍没有人能在那种条件下设计出复杂的 IT 系统。因为我们并不精通 IT，担心匆忙制作出来的系统会有缺陷，导致日后没有任何领先前景可言。我们的顾问理查德·萨斯坎德教授，以前总是说我们现在应该建设一个 12 层的办公大楼作为日后发展的基础，而不是再建另一座平房。//

但整个计划最终还是被取消了。我们需要三思，如何拯救民事和家庭法院的司法制度，使之不因缺少投资而分崩离析。在此期间，大法官决定，在缺乏所需 IT 支持的情况下，继续开展民事司法制度的改革。民事司法处处长理查德·斯科特爵士对此决定并不赞同，因为他认为没有 IT 的支持，法院很难应对改革所带来的挑战。但是伍尔夫勋爵以务实的理由支持这一决定，然后一套名为"高等法院制表器"的简单系统被匆匆赶制出来，以支持从来没有管理过法庭文件的"高等法院管理器"系统。当时法官们都得到了非常坚定的承诺，表示会尽快为他们准备好所需的 IT 支持。//

负责刑事法庭、民事和家庭法庭现代化的两个委员会在 2001 年进行了合并，因为这两个委员会有许多相似点。不过，我还是把刑事和民事这两个领域分开来讲，因为针对两个领域所采取的措施的差异性非常之大。但两者有一个共同点，那就是两个团队都以高度的专业素质推动着计划的前进。在过去 4 年中，共有 2 名公务员和 3 名法官在这项工作中发挥了先锋的作用，为公共服务事业作出了杰出贡献，并因此被授予了大英帝国司令勋章（CBE）和大英帝国勋章（OBE）。2 年前，该团队负责高达 1.6 亿英镑的法庭 IT 基础设施安装项目，并获得了内阁办公室授予的年度最佳管理 IT 项目奖。该团队的一些项目，如金钱索赔网上系统，赢得了国际赞誉。此外，法院服务处因设计了最佳的"外国"法院网站，连续 2 年获得了美国司法部的奖项。这个讲座的一个重要主题就是，这支我曾与之密切工作了 4 年的团队，曾拥有达到国际水准的资源。但可惜的是，由于缺乏能使之进一步合理发展的足够资金，该团队被迫解散了。//

4 年前，该团队获得了足够的资金，于 2001 年 4 月开始执行为期 3 年的在刑事法庭开展的计划。2 年后，政府对刑事司法的 IT 进行了大规模投资，该投资为期 3 年，从 2003 年 4 月开始。至此，政府采纳了布赖恩·奥尼尔爵士和我自 1986 年就开始努力传播的理念。法院体系中不同的参与者都是互相关联的。因此，司法体系中的任何一方，无论是警察还是皇家检察院抑或法院服务处，如果自以为身处绿洲，将自己与周围的沙漠完全隔离开来，自顾自地设计自己的 IT 系统，那是非常愚蠢的。1986 年，我们成立了 IT 及法院委员会（ITAC），希望能让大家明白这一点，但没有人听。在同年，我们对 CREST 系统设计者提出了不少批评，因为在使法院之间形成电子信息流通这一点上，他们毫无建树。我们不得不等待了 15 年，才让这个错误才得以纠正。//

2 年前，根据安排，接下来 3 年将有 11 亿英镑会被投资到刑事司法的 IT 发展上。其实并非所有资金都是新的，因为大部分是早在 2003 至 2004 年就已拨出的，但这已是迄今为止最大金额的拨款了。这笔资金将由一个名为刑事司法 IT 处的新机构负责管理。只有取得上述所有部门的部长及刑事司法 IT 处处长的同意，方可支配资金。//

大部分资金很早就分配下去了。因为我们的 IT 基础设施远远落后于其他机构，我们在 2006 年 4 月就把资金用于在所有的刑事法庭安装 IT 基础设施。但迄今为止，我们就只顾及了刑事法庭，它可以说是例外。之前提到的 DAR、EPE 系统，完全没有获得新的资金，而它们正是最需要资金来更新系统的软设备。尽管后来我们适时地从其他预算中拨出资金，给 30 个刑事法庭安装了与监狱相连的摄像机，但还是没有获得新的资金安装视频会议设备。//

唯一的例外是 XHIBIT 信息系统。这个项目一直是上层领导的最爱。但该项目给法官和法院工作人员所带来的益处却非常少，因此我们更希望能把资金投入其他地方。可该项目被认为能使市民受惠，并且被认为是"桥梁"项目的典范。所谓"桥梁"项目是指在刑事司法系统某一部分投资也将使系统的其他部分受益的项目。因此，该项目一路"绿灯"，尽管该项目曾一度陷入严重的延误，但现在已获得批准在全国推广。东北部的法庭将在 2 周内启动该项目。//

我在去年出版的书中描述道，在经过认真的规划后，我们在快要达成目标之时却突然失败了。我们不得不重新来过，法官和法院工作人员的士气也被严重动摇。2002 年 7 月发表政府开支报告的那个晚上，财政部公布了大法官部的工作目标说明，其中并没有提及民事和家庭法院的现代化目标。显然，我们原本希望会给民事和家庭法院法官及其工作人员带来便利的 IT 技术支持没有得到兑现。"打包票"是否会变成"空头支票"？我们的前路再次变得难以预料。//

我生命中的 40 多年都是在民事司法中度过的。两年半前我真的以为，我们即将为民事和家庭法院带来能让国家感到骄傲的全新变革。然而现在，我完全看不到水平线尽头的希望之光。我甚至看不到问题得到适当解决的迹象，因为目前司法体系中正在推行那么多其他项目，分散了决策者对我们的关注。而且，只要财政部依然坚持其"回收全部成本"的制度，我们的情况只会变得更糟，越来越糟。//

# IV. 句子精炼 Sentences in Focus

**Directions**：*Interpret the following sentences alternatively into English or Chinese*：

1. 中国同时受惠于现代世界最主要的三种法律制度：大陆法制度、普通法制度和社会主义制度。

2. 香港特别行政区的普通法制度为市民、商人和投资者提供了可靠的法律环境。回归后普通法制度根据《香港特别行政区基本法》的规定继续在港实行。

3. 《宪法》强调，中华人民共和国实行法治，保障公民的法定私有财产，并尊重和维护人权。加入世贸组织，无疑进一步加快中国法制改革的步伐。

4. 美国和加拿大主体上是普通法司法管辖区，但路易斯安那州和魁北克省却采用大陆法制度。欧盟证明了实行普通法和大陆法的国家，都可以在商业和人权等范畴，履行欧盟所订立的不同义务。

5. 全球一体化是另一个影响跨国商法发展的因素，越来越多新颁布的国际公约，在奉行不同法律制度的国家实施。

6. 在中国，不同地方可能采用不同的方式，以达至上述目的，但若我们朝着这个相同目标共同努力，我们定能克服种种障碍，为我国的经济和社会发展作出贡献。

7. I started it by being a member of the first committee ever set up to give advice to the Bar about computers. I ended it by being for four years a member of the small Board which has been taking forward the £260 million court modernization program.

8. I lived through the lean years in which investment in IT wasregarded by the

Lord Chancellor's Department as investment on the margins, and they never had any money to spend on the margins.

9. On the civil justice side valiant efforts were made in 1997 and 1998 to try and make plans for IT systems to support the Woolf reforms. These plans were always doomed. The rule-makers went on changing the rules right up to Woolf Day on 26 April 1999, and nobody can design complex IT systems under those conditions.

10. But Lord Woolf supported it on pragmatic grounds, and a fairly rudimentary system called High Court Forms was rushed out to support the High Court Masters who had never had to manage court files before. The judges received then what we thought was a very firm promise that we would receive the IT back-up we needed as soon as it was ready.

11. During the last four years two of the civil servants and three of the judges who have been spearheading this work have been awarded the CBE or the OBE for public services.

12. It is foolish for one part of the system, whether it is the police or the CPS or the Court Service, to design its IT systems as if they are in an oasis, totally isolated in its private patch of desert from anyone else.

第六单元 庭审前奏

Unit 6 Pre–trial Procedure

# Ⅰ. 专题知识 Legal Knowledge

在参加庭审口译之前，译员必须充分熟悉庭审之前的各种司法文书，在绝大部分情况下要进行大量的相关笔译工作。根据中国法庭审理案件的需要，当事人和律师在开庭前的准备工作包括以下主要内容：

（1）向当事人发送起诉状、答辩状副本。

（2）确定审判组织。

（3）告知当事人合议庭组成人员。

（4）确定审判人员是否自行回避。

（5）审查并确定案由。

（6）确定当事人范围、通知遗漏的当事人参加诉讼。

（7）审核诉讼材料。

（8）认真调查和收集证据。主要方法有：询问当事人、第三人；要求当事人、第三人提供证据；询问证人、鉴定人；提取物证、书证、视听资料为证据；勘验物证、现场。

（9）查清是否需要采取证据保全措施。

（10）查清是否需要采取财产保全措施。

（11）查清是否有需要合并审理的情况。

（12）查清是否有分开审理的情况。

（13）查清是否有法定不公开审理的情况。

（14）制定庭审提纲。

（15）开庭通知及公告。起诉时应提交的材料。

在向法院提起诉讼时，当事人应当依照法院的要求提交相关文件，这些文件包括：民事起诉状（在提交起诉状时，应当按照对方当事人的人数提交副本，也就是说，对方当事人有几人就应当另外再提交几份副本）；提起诉讼所依据的证据（在有些情况下还需要对证据有关情况进行说明或者提供证据清单）；原告是公民的还应当提供原告的身份证复印件，是法人的应当提供加盖本单位印章的法人营业执照复印件和法定代表人身份证明；当事人委托亲戚、朋友或者其他人代理的还应当提供经原告签名的授权委托书以及受委托人的身份证复印件。

答辩是指在原告起诉后，被告人针对原告人起诉的理由和依据进行的回答、辩解或反驳。民事诉讼中的被告，在收到原告的起诉状副本后，在法定期限内，针对原告在诉状中提出的事实、理由及诉讼请求，进行回答和辩驳的书状，被称为第一审民事答辩状。第一审民事答辩状具有下列特征：首先，必须是民事案件的被告向法院提出的。其次，必须在法定期限内提出。《民事诉讼法》第 128 条第 1 款规定："人民法院应当在立案之日起五日内将起诉状副本发送被告，被告应当在收到之日起十五日内提出答辩状……"第 2 款又规定："被告不提出答辩状的，不影响人民法院审理。"由此可见，提出答辩状，对于民事被告来说既是义务又是权利，但主要的还是权利。最后，必须针对起诉状的内容进行答辩，也就是被告的答辩状应当紧紧围绕原告的诉讼请求、事实和理由进行。书写、递交答辩状是当事人的一项诉讼权利。但有的当事人怕打输官司，不写答辩状，认为这样"法院不能审理"。其实，这样做恰恰是放弃了自己的诉讼权利，放弃了自己向法院提出解释或者辩解的机会。民事答辩状的重要特性就在于其辩解性，被告或被上诉人在答辩状中应针对原告或上诉人的诉讼请求、事实和理由进行具体的答复，有力地驳斥和有理地辩解。当然，被告的答辩也不能无理取闹、空口无凭地去辩解，答辩状在坚持辩解性的同时还必须坚持其客观性，答辩应尊重客观事实，所述事实应有相应证据材料予以证明。

## Ⅱ．词汇热身 Vocabulary Warm-up

**Directions**：*Give the English equivalents of the following Chinese expressions*：

| | |
|---|---|
| 案由 | 必要 |
| 律师见证书 | 共同诉讼人 |
| 律师意见书 | 传票 |
| 委托辩护 | 变通管辖 |
| 答辩状 | 基层人民法院 |
| 本诉 | |

# Ⅲ. 课文口译 Text for Interpreting

## ◆ *Passage 1*

**Directions**：Listen to the passage and interpret from Chinese into English at the end of each segment.

下面宣读律师行委托信：

本律师行受 ABC 管理公司委托。

根据委托人的指示，你/贵公司拖欠管理费、利息及催收费用，总额达251 800元，详见附页文件。根据委托人的指示，依照本物业大厦公契的规定，委托人有权并在此向你/贵公司追收因此而引起的律师费，现计为 43 260 元。尽管委托人多次要求你/贵公司清还欠款，你/贵公司至今仍然没有清缴上述款项。//

现委托人指示，你/贵公司必须于本信件发出的 7 天内缴付本行总数 295 060元（即上述 251 800 元 + 43 260 元），否则委托人将别无他法，唯有在土地注册处登记一份物业押记令，或采取其认为适当的其他行动，不予另行通知。而且，到时你/贵公司得支付因此增加的律师费、登记物业押记令及其后解除有关物业押记令引致的额外律师费及杂费，现估计为 357 800 元。//

某某律师行<br>副本送：管理公司 //

## ◆ *Passage 2*

**Directions**：*Listen to the passage and interpret from Chinese into English at the end of each segment.*

I am informed by therelevant news reports that the "bank card charge" plan formulated or under formulation by your bank is very similar to those by the above mentioned two banks involved in a lawsuit. Its hasty enforcement may restart a similar lawsuit which is a possible threat to your bank's business reputation. In view of this, I, the lawyer, hereby send this attorney opinion letter to your bank, hoping that you will consider cautiously the charge plan which you have formulated or are formulating, and reanalyze and re-estimate its legitimacy. If such legitimacy cannot be confirmed, I suggest that you hold such a responsible attitude towards your customers and your bank's reputation as to delay enforcing the charge plan while waiting for the final judgment from the People's Court. All the above advice and suggestions are for your reference. //

◆ *Passage 3*

**Directions**: *Listen to the passage and interpret from Chinese into English at the end of each segment.*

下面宣读答辩状：
答辩状
答辩人名称：ABC 有限公司
所在机构：删略
主要负责人姓名：删略
职务：删略
电话：删略
对 CYD 公司诉 DOC 公司和本公司广告合同纠纷一案，现提出答辩如下：//
我们认为：该案与本公司无关，请法院撤销原告对我方的诉讼请求。//
我方与被告 DOC 公司或原告 CYD 公司没有发生过接触或其他交易行为，也没有跟 DOC 公司或 CYD 公司或其他任何机构签订有关在《全球经济报道》播放任何广告的协议，更没有授权 DOC 公司或 CYD 公司作为我方的广告代理人，因此与本案无关。//
至于 DOC 公司与原告的种种行为及活动，给原告造成的损失，我方表示遗憾，并且保留对 DOC 公司影响我方商誉的追诉权利。但我方在此郑重声明：DOC 公司的行为及活动在事前事后均没有得到我方的明示或暗示的允许、同意和授权。这是一种单方面、无效的行为，是没有法律效力、得不到法律保护的。//

因此，原告将我方也列入被告是错误的。我方不承担与 DOC 公司的连带责任。//

此致

北京市朝阳区人民法院

附：本答辩状副本三份

答辩人：ABC 有限公司//

## ◆ *Passage 4*

**Directions**：*Listen to the passage and interpret from English into Chinese at the end of each segment.*

Application for Re-opening of A Court Session for Arbitration Case Concerning the Dispute over YEDG as Supply Agreement //

Secretariat of China International Economic and Trade Arbitration Commission Shanghai Commission, //

Concerning the arbitration case relating to the SDG2009247 Gas Supply Agreement (the claimant is AA Shanghai Co. Ltd. and the respondent is BB Co. Ltd.), the claimant hereby confirms its receipt from you on March 29, 2010 two written notices numbered (2010) China Mao Zhong Hu Zi No. 1816 and (2010) China Mao Zhong Hu Zi No. 1818 respectively. //

After opening of the first court session of the arbitration tribunal and upon subsequent exchange of opinions in writing, the claimant has found that some facts in this case are yet to be identified. For instance, the claimant's failure to complete all renewal procedures for the work safety license before the designated date results from omission of the respondent. In addition, concerning the new arbitration request made by the claimant, the detailed calculation basis and grounds therefore are yet to be presented to the arbitration tribunal. In this regard, the claimant is currently preparing new evidences and supporting documents so that the arbitration tribunal may have a full knowledge of the facts before rendering a decision regarding this case. //

The claimant hereby entreats the arbitration tribunal to re-open a court session for the arbitration case concerning the YED Gas Supply Agreement. //

Best Regards,

Claimant：AA Shanghai Co. , Ltd. //

◆ *Passage 5*

下面宣读民事诉状：

民事诉状

诉讼请求：

1. 判令被告立即支付货款人民币伍拾壹万捌仟肆佰元整（RMB 518,400）。

2. 判令被告立即支付约定违约金人民币伍万壹仟捌佰肆拾元整（RMB 51,840）。//

事实与理由：

2009 年 8 月 9 日，原被告双方签订了一份《梅捷亚产品买卖合同》，合同约定原告卖给被告梅捷亚产品，合同总价款为人民币 518 400 元，交货地在广州市白云区新市二街××号；货款在被告收货后 2 个月内一次性付清。合同还约定，如被告未能履行付款义务，须支付未付款部分 10% 的违约金。合同还对双方的其他权利义务作了约定。合同生效后，原告按约将货物供给被告，但被告收货后却没有按期支付原告货款，拖欠至今。被告的违约行为已违背了诚实信用原则，给原告造成了直接经济损失。//

现原告为维护自身的合法权益，根据《民事诉讼法》第 25 条的规定，特向人民法院提起诉讼，请判决如下诉讼请求。//

此致

广州市中级人民法院

具状人：ABC 有限公司

二〇〇一年七月七日

## ◆ *Passage 6*

Dear Sirs,

Re: Seepage of water/sewage to Abamor Plaza ("the Premises")

We act for the owner of the Premises and understand that you are the owner of the premises above the Premises ("the Above Premises"). //

We are instructed that water/sewage seeped from the Above Premises to the Premises causing seepage and rusting at the ceiling of the toilet of the Premises. //

Such seepage is at law a nuisance caused to our client and is in breach of the Deed of Mutual Convent of the Estate. We are instructed that despite repeated complaints by our client either directly or through the Manager of the Estate, you have not caused the nuisance to stop. //

We are instructed that unless you do within 14 days cause the nuisance to stop and agree to indemnify our client the loss and damages caused thereby including but not limited to the costs for the repair of the ceiling at the toilet now estimated at HK $2,083, our client shall institute proceedings in Court without further notice. //

Yours faithfully //

## ◆ *Passage 7*

### The People's Procuratorate of Guangzhou, Guangdong
### The People's Republic of China
### Indictment

*Suijiangongyisu* No. 165 of 2008 //

The accused Andoh Paul, male, born on August 17, 1970, is a citizen of the Republic of Ghana, holding passport No. H1857×××. He was put into investigative detention on December 12, 2007 and was arrested on January 17, 2008 upon approval by the People's Procuratorate of Guangzhou, Guangdong, the People's Republic of China on January 16, 2008. //

Upon completion of investigation of the illegal confinement case against Andoh Paul by the Public Security Bureau of Guangzhou, Guangdong, the People's Republic of China, the case was transferred on June 2, 2008, to the People's Procuratorate of Guangzhou, Guangdong, the People's Republic of China for examination and prosecution. The facts are ascertained as follows:

In November 2007, the accused Andoh Paul had a dispute with the employer of Victim Martins Ekemezie (hereinafter referred to as Martins) Collins arising from payment for goods. On the evening of December 10, 2007, the accused Andoh Paul found Victim Martins in the vicinity of Yixin Building in Baiyun District, Guangzhou, Guangdong, the People's Republic of China, requesting the latter to call Collins and ask Collins to come over to discuss the payment for goods. However, Collins failed to show up. The accused Andoh Paul, in collusion with others, took Victim Martins to a rented apartment, to wit, Apartment ×××, 2 No. 25 Lane, Taoyuan St (W), Shima Village, Junhe St, Baiyun District, Guangzhou, requested such victim again to contact Collins for payment. During that period, the accused Andoh Paul and others battered Victim Martins and tied up his hands and feet with wires and other articles. Not until at around 7: 00 on December 11, 2007 did Victim Martins, taking the opportunity when the accused Andoh Paul was off guard, called passengers downstairs for help. Thereafter, the police who heard about the incident rescued Victim Martins and captured the accused Andoh Paul in the meantime. //

The aforesaid criminal facts are ascertained as true and correct upon investigation and verification and supported by reliable, sufficient and conclusive evidence. //

The Procuratorate holds that the accused Andoh Paul, disregarding the law of the People's Republic of China, illegally confined another person for the purpose of getting payment of a debt, all in violation of Paragraph 3 Article 238 of *the Criminal Law of the People's Republic of China*, and that his acts constitute the crime of illegal confinement. For the purpose of enforcing the law of the People's Republic of China, protecting the right of the person of foreign citizens from infringement, maintaining the administration of public order, and ensuring smooth progress of socialist construction, we hereby initiate public prosecution in accordance with Article 141 of *the Criminal Procedure Law of the People's Republic of China* and make a plea for judgment in compliance with the law. //

To: the Intermediate People's Court of Guangzhou, Guangdong, the People's

Republic of China

Prosecutor: Song Yonghong

This twenty-third day of June two thousand and eight (2008)

(Seal of the Procuratorate)

This duplicate is verified as identical to the original. //

Appendics:

1. The accused Andoh Paul isnow detained in the Third Detention House of Guangzhou, Guangdong, the People's Republic of China.

2. One list of evidence;

3. One volume of photocopies of main evidence;

4. One name list of witnesses;

5. One volume of dossier marked with "A".

In case of any discrepancy between the original and the translated version, the original shall prevail. //

# IV. 参考译文 Reference versions

## ◆ *Passage 1*

Name of Owner

Address

Dear Sirs:

Re: address

We act for ABC management company. //

We are instructed that you have failed to settle the outstanding management charges as well as interest and collection charges in the sum of 251,800 RMB as per copy statement enclosed. We are also instructed that pursuant to the terms of the Deed of Mutual Covenant, our client is entitled to and does hereby demand from you for the reimbursement of the costs incurred by our client in this matter, now in the sum of 43,260 RMB. Despite repeated requests and demands of our client, you failed and still fail to pay the aforesaid sum to our client. //

We are instructed that unless you do pay to us on behalf of our client the sum of 295,060 RMB (the aggregate of 251,800 RMB and aforesaid 43,260 RMB) within 7 calendar days from today, our client shall have no alternative but to register a Memorandum of Charge in the Land Registry or take other actions it deems appropriate without further notice and in such circumstances you shall be held fully liable for any additional legal costs incurred as a result thereof: the additional legal costs and disbursements for filing a Memorandum of Charge and for the discharge thereof is now estimated to be 357,800 RMB. //

Yours faithfully. //

c. c. ABC management company

## ◆ *Passage 2*

从相关新闻报道得知：贵行制定或正在制定的"银行卡收费方案"与上述两家涉案银行非常相似，一旦贸然实施，很可能再次引发新的诉讼并对贵行的商誉造成不好的影响。有鉴于此，本律师向贵行发出律师公开函，希望审慎考虑原定的或正在制定的收费方案，对该方案的合法性重新进行分析和评估。如不能确认收费行为的合法性，建议持对客户负责、对企业商誉负责的严谨态度，推迟收费方案的实施，等待法院对上述案件的最终判决。以上意见及建议供参考。//

## ◆ *Passage 3*

Answer

Defendant：ABC Co. Ltd.

Address：(Deleted)

Principal：(Deleted)

Position：(Deleted)

Telephone：(Deleted)

By reason of the contract dispute based on which CYD Co. Ltd. Sued DOC Co. and this company, the defense hereby answers as follows：//

We believe that this case is of no relevance of this company and request that the plaintiff's claims against this company be dismissed. //

This company has never had any contact or other dealings with either DOC Co. or CYD Co. . Neither have we entered into any advertisement broadcasting agreements in the World Economy Report program with either DOC Co. or CYD Co. , nor have we authorized either DOC Co. and CYD Co. as our advertising agent. We therefore are not a relevant party in this case. //

In relation to the acts and conduct between DOC Co. and the plaintiff and the injuries thus caused to the plaintiff, we are sorry and reserve our rights to pursue DOC Co. for the negative impact on our good will. We hereby solemnly declare that the acts or conduct of DOC Co. have not been permitted, consented to or authorized by this company, either expressed or implied, either before or after fact. This is a unilateral and invalid act with no legal force and is not protected by law. //

Therefore, the plaintiff erroneously included this company as a defendant in this case. We should not be held jointly and severably liable with DOC Co. //

Respectfully submitted to:

Beijing Chaoyang District People's Court

Attachments: three copies of the Answer

Defendant: ABC Co. Ltd. //

## ◆ *Passage 4*

关于 YED 气体供应协议书争议仲裁案<br>再次开庭的申请

中国国际经济贸易仲裁委员会上海分会秘书处: //

在此确认, YED 气体供应协议书仲裁案件中 (申请人 AA 上海有限公司, 被申请人 BB 有限公司), 申请人已于 2010 年 3 月 29 日收到贵局发来的书面通知 2 份, 编号分别为 [2010] 中国贸仲沪字第 1816 号和 [2010] 中国贸仲沪字第 1818 号。//

经过第一次仲裁庭开庭以及之后的书面意见交换, 申请人发现案件中的部分事实尚不明晰。如申请人无法在指定的日期之前办理完安全生产许可证的所有延期手续是由被申请人的不作为所致。此外, 对于申请人提出的新仲裁请求, 尚未就计算的基础和理由向仲裁庭作出说明。就上述情况, 申请人

目前正在准备新的证据和说明文件，以便仲裁庭全面了解事实，对于本案作出裁定。//

特此，申请人恳请仲裁庭就 YED 气体供应协议书仲裁案件再次开庭。//
此致

申请人：AA 上海有限公司 //

## ◆ *Passage 5*

Legal Representative：

Remedies Sought：

1. Judgment be entered against the Defendant for immediate payment of the sum of RMB 518,400 being the price of goods sold and delivered；//

2. Judgment be entered against the Defendant for immediate payment of the sum of RMB 51,840 being the agreed liquidated damages. //

Facts and Basis of Claim：

On Aug. 9, 2009, the Plaintiff and the Defendant entered into a "Contract for Sale and Purchase of Meijieya Products" by which the Plaintiff agreed to sell to the Defendant Meijieya Cosmetics at a total contract price of RMB 518,400. It was agreed that the Plaintiff was to make delivery of the goods at #24, Xinshi Street Ⅱ, Baiyun, Guangzhgou, and that the Defendant was to settle the contract price of the goods in full by way of a lumpsum payment within two months of the receipt of the goods. It was also provided in the contract that in case the Defendant failed to discharge its payment obligation under the contract, the Defendant would be liable to pay liquidated damages equivalent to 10% of the unpaid portion of the contract price. At the same time, the contract also contained express provisions as to the other rights and obligations of the parties. After the contract takes effect, the Plaintiff made delivery of the goods to the Defendant in accordance with the terms of the contract. The Defendant, however, failed to make payment for the goods as scheduled up to the date hereof. By reason of the Defendant's breaches, the Defendant has contravened the principle of good faith and caused direct economic loss to the Plaintiff. //

In order to protect its legitimate interests, the Plaintiff hereby commences legal proceedings in accordance with Article 25 of the PRC Civil Procedure Law and the

Plaintiff respectfully prays that a judgment be entered in terms of the remedies sought. //

> To：
>
> People's Intermediate Court of Guangzhou
>
> Plaintiff：ABC Co. Ltd.
>
> July 7, 2010 //

◆ *Passage 6*

律师函

业主

地址

业主先生/女士：//

事由：委托人物业地址

（"楼下物业"）漏水事

本律师行受楼下物业业主委托，经查证土地注册处记录，确认你是楼上物业的业主。//

我们接到委托处理此事，水从上述房屋渗入楼下物业业主房屋，导致该房屋的厕所天花板渗漏和生锈。//

上述行为在法律上属滋扰行为（nuisance），并违反了物业所属小区之管理公约。尽管委托人多次直接或通过物业公司向你提出投诉，但你仍未终止上述滋扰行为。//

现委托人指示，你应在本信函发出后 14 天内终止上述滋扰行为，并因上述滋扰行为，同意赔偿委托人因该滋扰行为所引致的损失，包括但不限于维修厕所天花板的费用，现计为 2083 元港币。如你在上述时限内不履行以上要求，委托人唯有直接向法院提出申诉，不会向你另行通知。//

某某律师行启 //

◆ *Passage 7*

中华人民共和国

广东省广州市人民检察院

起诉书

穗检公一诉〔2008〕165号

被告人 Andoh Paul，中文译名安多·保罗（以下使用中文译名），男，1970年8月17日出生。国籍：加纳共和国。护照号码：H1857×××。2007年12月12日被刑事拘留。2008年1月16日经中华人民共和国广东省广州市人民检察院批准逮捕，同年1月17日被逮捕。

被告人安多·保罗非法拘禁一案，经中华人民共和国广东省广州市公安局侦查终结，于2008年6月2日依法移送中华人民共和国广东省广州市人民检察院审查起诉，现查明：//

2007年11月被告人安多·保罗因货款问题与被害人 Martins Ekemezie（中文译名马提斯，以下使用中文译名）的雇主 Collins（中文译名柯林斯，以下使用中文译名）产生纠纷。同年12月10日晚上，被告人安多·保罗在中华人民共和国广东省广州市白云区壹心大厦附近找到被害人马提斯，遂要求其打电话让柯林斯过来商讨货款的返还事宜，后柯林斯没有过来，被告人安多·保罗即伙同他人将被害人马提斯带至租住处广州市白云区均禾街石马村桃源西街25巷2号×××房，继续要求被害人马提斯联系柯林斯还钱。其间，被告人安多·保罗等人对被害人马提斯实施殴打，并用电线等物品捆绑其手脚。至2007年12月11日7时许，被害人马提斯趁被告人安多·保罗不备之机向楼下的路人求救。其后，闻讯赶至的警察解救了被害人马提斯，并将被告人安多·保罗抓获。//

以上犯罪事实，经查证属实，证据确实充分，足以认定。//

本院认为，被告人安多·保罗无视中华人民共和国法律，为索取债务非法拘禁他人，其行为触犯了《刑法》第238条第3款的规定，构成非法拘禁罪。为严肃我国法律，保护外国公民的人身权利不受侵犯，维护我国社会治安秩序，保障我国社会主义建设事业的顺利进行，依照《刑事诉讼法》第141条的规定，特提起公诉，请依法判处。//

此致
中华人民共和国广东省广州市中级人民法院 ∥

检察员：宋永红

二〇〇八年六月二十三日

本件与原本核对无异。

附：

1. 被告人安多·保罗现羁押于中华人民共和国广东省广州市第三看守所。

2. 证据目录 1 份。

3. 主要证据复印件 1 册。

4. 证人名单 1 份。

5. 本案 A 卷材料 1 册。∥

原文与翻译不一致的，以原文为准。

# 法庭交锋
## Unit 7 Courtroom Debate

# I . 专题知识 Legal Knowledge

法庭口译（Court Interpreting）主要指的是在法庭上发生的传译，有时也涵盖在其他法律场所进行的传译活动，比如监狱和警察局等。[1]英美法系也称之为庭审口译（forensic interpreting）、法律口译（legal interpreting）或司法口译（judiciary interpreting）。从言语交际的角度来看，法庭口译是操不同语言、有不同文化背景的诉讼各方以及庭审法官、合议庭或陪审团成员之间互相理解沟通的桥梁与中介。从法律沟通的角度讲，法庭译员经常肩负沟通不同法系之间差异性的重任。与此同时，法庭口译也是维护和保障法律赋予诉讼各方的公民权和法律平等的必要条件。[2]法庭口译的客户通常是操不同语言的被告或证人。这种传译的基本目的是使客户能够参与法庭诉讼，因此传译工作需要双向进行。按工作方式，法庭口译可被分为同声传译、连续传译/交替传译、联络口译、视译和耳语翻译等。

法庭口译因在历史上口语的不可记录性而无法准确追溯，但有史记载的法庭口译最早可以追溯到17世纪在南非的殖民时期。[3]柯林和莫里斯（1996年）则比较详细地记录了1682年和1820年在英国进行的有口译服务的庭审。[4]1682年的那次庭审涉及一起凶杀案，诉讼各方有多种语言背景。而当时法庭在决定哪一方诉讼人有权享有法庭口译服务时，依据的不是各方的语言需求

---

〔1〕 Mark Shuttleworth, Moira Cowie, *Dictionary of Translation Studies*, Shanghai Foreign Language Education Press, 2004.

〔2〕 李克兴、张新红：《法律文本与法律翻译》，中国对外翻译出版公司2006年版，第426~427页。

〔3〕 Holly Mikkelson, *Introduction to Court Interpreting*, St. Jerome Publishing, 2000.

〔4〕 Holly Mikkelson, *Introduction to Court Interpreting*, St. Jerome Publishing, 2000.

而是阶级，即说英语的贵族才有权享有口译服务。1820 年的庭审则是一场涉及卡罗琳王后的通奸案。该案的庭审口译不仅翻译了证人证言的语言内容，而且还解释了其中的文化差异。[1]

第一次世界大战后，由于签订《巴黎和约》的缘故，产生了英语与法语之间互译的口译需求，这是现代连续传译（consecutive interpreting）的开始。而同声传译（simultaneous interpreting）则诞生于 1945 年，即第二次世界大战之后的纽伦堡（Nuremberg）二战战犯大审判，这也是第一次开始使用电子设备的口译活动。受此启发，联合国也于 1946 年开始大量使用同声传译。

欧洲大陆很早就意识到了法庭口译的重要性，而直到 1978 年美国才开始为法庭口译立法。此前审判时使用口译人员的依据只有《联邦刑事诉讼程序法规》（Federal Rules of Criminal Procedure）第 28（b）条、《联邦证据规则》（Federal Rules of Evidence）第 604 条、《刑事审判法》（Criminal Justice Act 1964）以及《联邦民事诉讼程序规则》（Federal Rules of Civil Procedure）第 43（f）条等，其中以前两者为主。

《联邦刑事诉讼程序法规》第 28（b）条规定，法院有权自行指定口译人员，其劳务费用从法律规定或政府提供的经费中支出。但是，其中存在着两个主要问题：一是口译人员的指派与否完全由法院决定，这说明法院也有权不为母语是非英语的被告提供法庭口译服务；二是法院如何自行指定法庭口译人员。《联邦证据规则》第 604 条规定，法庭口译人员在提供口译服务时必须以专家证人的身份出庭，受有关专家证人的规定制约，并须发誓一定会照实翻译，以确保当事各方的宪法和法律赋予的其他权利。但是，在美国司法历史上，却有不少法院公然忽视被告因英语交际能力不足而需要口译帮助的例子。

由于上述原因，美国联邦法院于 1978 年制订了《庭审口译员法案》（Court Interpreters Act of 1978），并于 1988 年进行了修正，要求法庭口译员必须完整准确、一字不差地（verbatim）翻译源语信息，不得修饰和省略源语信息，不得更改源语的语体和语域。[2]该法案为联邦地方法院在民事和刑事诉讼中使用庭审口译服务提供了依据，也为颁发庭审口译员证书提供了依据，

---

〔1〕 Holly Mikkelson, *Introduction to Court Interpreting*, St. Jerome Publishing, 2000.
〔2〕 李克兴、张新红：《法律文本与法律翻译》，中国对外翻译出版公司 2006 年版。

标志着美国议会对庭审口译这一专业性很强的职业的认可。从此，法庭口译成了一个独立的职业，专门为英语水平较差者提供语言服务。该法案规定的两类服务对象是：只会说或主要说除英语以外的其他语言的人、有听力障碍的人。

在机构性话语的大背景下，法庭口译受法庭言语行为的构成性规则的严格约束，要求译员严守秘密、公正无私，同时还需要宣誓在传译时做到准确、忠实。尼克尔森（2000 年）认为法庭译员的道德规范包括忠诚性、保密性、公正性和个人规范。然而，法庭译员常处于司法公正所要求的规范和实际操作主观介入的冲突之中。法律界指望传译过程应该以一种透明的方式机械地进行，不允许译员提供解释。传译的结果几乎总是在法律上被当作原话语的有效对等形式。记录在案的并不是原话语，而是传译过来的话语。因此，法庭译员一方面需要尽可能照字面直译话语信息（甚至包括照直传递诸如说话犹豫之类的韵律特征），而另一方面又知道由于客户与法庭在语言和文化上存在着差异，坚持直译会导致所传译的意义被曲解。[1]

无论是对于法官、律师、公诉人，还是对于原告、被告、证人来说，法庭译员的出现都将一个正常的诉讼程序变成了一种双语的言语交际行为。处于法庭话语交锋风口浪尖之上的法庭译员常常面临进退维谷的尴尬，而且总是受到来自控辩各方的怀疑和不信任。Berg-Seligson（1990 年）指出，法庭译员的难堪处境源自以下言语行为中的几个矛盾：

实际上的介入与法官和律师所期望的"不多嘴"（unobtrusive roles）；带有个人偏见的打断与法庭权力结构所要求的"不偏不倚"（impartiality）；直译与语用延伸（pragmatic extensions）。

因此，法庭口译中的首要问题不在于语言本身词汇和句法上的传译，而在于对语用细节方面的延伸之义的关注。比如，译员常常有意识或无意识地改变证人的证词语气，或使得控辩律师的问题比实际上更加尖刻和充满敌意，或者在相反的情形下使得控辩律师的问题更加柔和、更富有合作性，或者比源语本身具有较弱的挑战性。如此一来，译员的言语行为不仅会影响到法庭当事人的语用意图，也会影响司法人员的判决，从而改变诉讼程序中言语行为的真正意图。

---

[1]　Mark Shuttleworth, Moira Cowie, *Dictionary of Translation Studies*, Shanghai Foreign Language Education Press, 2004.

# II. 词汇热身 Vocabulary Warm-up

**Directions**: *Give the English equivalents of the following Chinese expressions*:

| | | |
|---|---|---|
| 审判长 | 书证 | 看守所 |
| 法警 | 物证 | 盐酸海洛因 |
| 刑事诉讼法 | 法庭辩论 | 亚的斯亚贝巴 |
| 合议庭 | 无申报通道 | 走私毒品 |
| 书记员 | 海关缉私局 | 行为犯从轻判处 |
| 公诉人 | 旅检处 | 从犯 |
| 举证 | 扣押物品清单 | 现在休庭 |

**Directions**: *Give the Chinese equivalents of the following English expressions*:

| | |
|---|---|
| Domicile | the Collegiate Bench |
| had no objection about | the Clerk |
| Statement of Defense | the Public Prosecutor |
| People's Procuratorate | adducing evidence |
| the accused | luggage declaration form |
| Bill of Indictment | intentional crime |
| public prosecution | adjudicatio |

# III. 课文口译 Texts for Interpreting

**Directions**: *Interpret the following courtroom debate alternatively into English or Chinese.*

审：广州市中级人民法院刑事审判第一庭，今天依法对广州市人民检察院提起公诉的被告人清耐都·奥格邦纳（Chinedu Ogbanna）走私毒品一案进行公开开庭审理，法警带被告人到庭。//

审：被告人姓名、曾用名、化名、绰号、出生年月、民族、籍贯、文化

程度、工作单位、职务、户籍地、居住地？//

**被**：My name is Chinedu Ogbanna. I was born on Dec 22nd, 1982. I am a primary school graduate. And my passport number is A2942×××, and my Nationality is the People's Republic of Nigeria. My domicile is in city ABA, state abia, east of Nigeria. //

**审**：被告人何时被拘留？何时被逮捕？//

**被**：I was detained on Oct, 9th, 2006 and I was arrested on Nov 14th, 2006. //

**审**：被告人以前有无受过刑事处分？//

**被**：No. //

**审**：被告人有无收到起诉书副本？何时收到？//

**被**：I received it on Feb 14th, 2006. //

**审**：下面宣布有关事项：今天负责审理本案的合议庭由审判员庄灵、代理审判员何炯、钟强组成，由审判员庄灵担任审判长。书记员陈枝负责法庭记录，书记员梁华为负责法庭其他工作。广东省广州市人民检察院检察员侯东为出庭支持公诉。担任法庭翻译的是广东外语外贸大学教师杜清平。依照《刑事诉讼法》第 32 条的规定，被告人对上述人员有申请回避的权利，也就是说，如果你认为上述人员与本案有利害关系可能影响本案公正审理，可以申请换人。申请回避的理由有：1. 是本案的当事人或者是当事人的近亲属；2. 本人或者他的近亲属和本案有利害关系的；3. 担任过本案的证人、鉴定人、辩护人、诉讼代理人的；4. 与本案当事人有其他关系，可能影响公正处理的；5. 上述人员曾经接受当事人及其委托的人的请客送礼或违反规定会见当事人及其委托的人。被告人对以上合议庭、书记员以及公诉人是否听清楚了？被告人是否有这种要求？//

**被**：I am clear. I don't have such claims. //

**审**：依照法律规定，被告人有权获得辩护。除自己辩护外，还可以委托辩护人为自己辩护。受本院指定，由广州市法律援助中心委派广东恒益律师事务所周清华律师担任被告人的辩护人，被告人你是否同意？//

**被**：Yes. //

**审**：被告人在法庭审理过程中，可以提出新的证据，申请通知新的证人到庭，调取新的证据，重新鉴定或者勘查、检查，被告人听清楚了吗？//

**被**：Yes。//

审：控辩双方在申请举证时，应说明所举证据的来源及所要证明的内容。控辩双方向法庭提交证据，应当提供原件、原物。不能提交原件、原物的，应当说明理由，经法庭同意并核实后可以提交副本或者复印件。被告人在法庭辩论后有最后陈述的权利。被告人听清楚了吗？//

被：Yes。//

审：公诉人，有无新的证据向法庭提交？//

公：没有。//

审：被告人及辩护人有无新的证据向法庭提交？//

被：No。//

辩：没有。//

审：今天的庭审分三个阶段：法庭调查、法庭辩论、被告人最后陈述。现在开始法庭调查，先由公诉人宣读起诉书。//

公：（宣读起诉书略）//

审：被告人，有无听清公诉人刚才宣读起诉书的内容？对起诉书指控的内容有无异议？//

被：Yes, I heard it clearly. I had no objection about it. //

审：下面由公诉机关就指控的事实对被告人进行发问。//

公：被告人，你必须如实地回答公诉人向你提出的问题，清楚吗？//

被：Yes。//

公：被告人清耐都·奥格邦纳，你乘坐哪一班机到达广州机场？//

被：I arrived in Guangzhou by Flight ET on Oct 9th, 2006, but I cannot recall the number of the flight.

公：是从哪里上机，在哪里转机到达广州？//

被：I boarded in Nigeria, then transferred in Ethiopia and arrived in the Guangzhou Airport. //

公：来广州的目的？//

被：To buy mobile phones. //

公：当天海关检查的结果怎样？//

被：When I passed the Customs, the police took me to hospital. //

公：在海关查验房检验时你体内有无排出物品？//

被：Yes. //

**公**：什么物品？//

**被**：Seven pieces of solids. I did not know they are drugs and later on I began to realize it. //

**公**：到医院之后的情况？//

**被**：I exerted another seven solids after I got to the hospital. //

**公**：总共 14 粒东西是如何放进体内的？//

**被**：My friend gave them to me. He helped me put them into my body. //

**公**：你的朋友叫什么，是什么人？//

**被**：He is named Romannus. This guy is one of my clients, I buy the cellphones from him. I told Rommannus that I was going to China to buy some mobile phones. Rommannus then told me that he would offer me some help if I could do him a favor to bring something to China. //

**公**：你是何时知道你所带的东西是毒品？//

**被**：In the hospital. //

**公**：何时将 14 粒东西塞入体内？//

**被**：On the day I took the flight. //

**公**：罗马纳斯在生意上如何给你提供帮助？//

**被**：Romannus has some friends in China. He told me if I brought the 14 solids to his friends in China, they would buy the phones for me. //

**公**：将毒品带到广州之后，如何将毒品交给接应的人？//

**被**：He would wait at the entrance of the airport and recognize me by my clothes. //

**公**：你有无得到报酬，来广州的机票、路费是谁给的？//

**被**：I bought the ticket myself. Romannus did not give me the payment. But he promised me that he would offer me 500 $ if I had delivered the goods successfully. But I didn't get the payment. //

**公**：14 粒东西为何不放在行李箱，而要放在体内？//

**被**：I had thought to put them in the trunk, but Romannus said it would not work. He said the personnel on the flight would not allow it. //

**公**：你当时有无想到这是违法的？//

**被**：Romannus told me these things would not be allowed to take on flight, but if I had successfully took it on flight, it would be OK.∥

**公**：有无想过这样做违反中国法律？∥

**被**：No.∥

**公**：以前有无来过中国？∥

**被**：No.∥

**公**：公诉人对被告人的发问暂时到此。∥

**审**：辩护人对被告人有无问题提出？∥

**辩**：没有。∥

**审**：被告人，你刚才陈述将这些东西带上飞机就没事了，带上飞机有无违反你们国家的法律？∥

**被**：I had not known they were heroin. My friend told me they were something like the cigarettes. In Nigeria, cigarettes are not allowed to take abroad.∥

**审**：机票是谁出的？∥

**被**：I bought it myself.∥

**审**：机票价格是多少？∥

**被**：About 900 to 1000 U. S. dollars.∥

**审**：你自己带了多少钱来中国？∥

**被**：5000 $.∥

**审**：下面由公诉机关出示本案相关的证据。∥

**公**：下面出示本案相关的证据：

一、书证、物证：

（1）接受刑事案件登记表（B 卷 2）

接警时间：2006 年 10 月 9 日

接警地点：广州白云机场海关∥

**审**：被告人及辩护人对公诉人出示的上述证据有何意见？∥

**被**：No.∥

**辩**：没有意见。∥

**审**：公诉人继续举证。∥

**公**：（2）中华人民共和国广州白云机场海关查验记录（B 卷 5）

查验时间：2006 年 10 月 9 日 18 时 45 分至 20 时 30 分

查验地点：广州白云国际机场海关进境查验房

查验对象：奥格邦纳

查验的情况：当事人于 2006 年 10 月 9 日乘 ET6××航班从广州白云机场口岸进境，过海关时走无申报通道，并向海关递交了行李物品申报单，申报单上未申报任何物品，其行李经 X 光及开箱检查，未发现异常。在对其检查期间，当事人在海关查验房，从其体内排出 7 粒椭圆形粒状物，海关怀疑其体内藏毒，遂交广州海关缉私局做进一步处理。//

**审：**被告人及辩护人对公诉人出示的上述证据有何意见？//

**被：**No.//

**辩：**没有意见。//

**审：**公诉人继续举证。//

**公：**（3）查获经过 2 份、广州白云机场海关证明 1 份（B 卷 6~8）//

2 份查获经过证实：2006 年 10 月 9 日，广州白云机场海关旅检处非贸物品监管二科对到达的 ET6××航班（亚的斯亚贝巴—广州）进行监管。18 时 45 分左右，旅客 Chinedu Ogbonna（尼日利亚籍，男，23 岁，护照号码：A2942×××）通关时，随身仅携带 2 个手提包，选择走无申报通道通关，并向海关递交了没有申报任何物品的进境旅客行李物品申报单。选择查验岗位关员谢穗岚让其出示护照并询问相关问题，其不敢与谢穗岚对视，于是谢穗岚确定其为重点查验对象，指引其进入海关查验区接受检查。查验岗位关员胡皓对其行李进行过机及打开检查，2 件行李未发现异常。海关关员将其带入查验房作进一步检查，后在海关查验房，该嫌疑人由其体内排出 7 粒椭圆形粒状物，海关遂将其交缉私部门做进一步处理。//

1 份证明证实：谢穗岚、胡皓两位同志是广州白云机场海关旅检处非贸物品监管二科关员，2006 年 10 月 9 日执行对 ET6××航班旅客行李物品的监管任务。//

**审：**被告人及辩护人对公诉人出示的上述证据有何意见？//

**被：**No.//

**辩：**没有意见。//

**审：**公诉人继续举证。//

**公：**（4）武警广东省总队医院 CT 诊断报告书、出院证、拒绝手术志愿书（B 卷 15-17），证明被告人接受治疗的情况。//

**审：**被告人及辩护人对公诉人出示的上述证据有何意见？//

被：No.//

辩：没有意见。//

审：公诉人继续举证。

公：（5）情况说明（B卷18）//

广州海关缉私局出具证明，证实奥格邦纳在10月9日至10月13日住院期间，又从体内排出颗粒状物品7粒，其在医院的整个排毒过程，该局均有2名以上干警在场见证。//

审：被告人及辩护人对公诉人出示的上述证据有何意见？//

被：No.//

辩：没有意见。

审：公诉人继续举证。//

公：（6）扣押物品清单（B卷53），扣押奥格邦纳14粒共180克海洛因。//

审：被告人及辩护人对公诉人出示的上述证据有何意见？//

被：No.//

辩：没有意见。//

审：公诉人继续举证。//

公：（7）缴获的14粒毒品照片（B卷9~10）//

被告人奥格邦纳作了签认，证实14粒毒品是其塞入肛门，在10月9日乘坐ET6××航班从尼日利亚带到广州的。（法警出示照片）//

审：被告人及辩护人对公诉人出示的上述证据有何意见？//

被：No.//

辩：没有意见。//

审：公诉人继续举证。//

公：（8）缴获的飞机票原件和复印件（B卷11~12）//

被告人奥格邦纳作了签认，证实是其走私毒品到广州所持的机票。（法警出示机票复印件）

审：被告人及辩护人对公诉人出示的上述证据有何意见？//

被：No.//

辩：没有意见。//

审：公诉人继续举证。//

**公**：（9）海关申报单复印件（B 卷 13 ~ 14）//

被告人奥格邦纳作了签认，证实是其进境行李申报单复印件。//

**审**：被告人及辩护人对公诉人出示的上述证据有何意见？//

**被**：No. //

**辩**：没有意见。//

**审**：公诉人继续举证。//

**公**：（10）送物留存单、送物登记表（B 卷 54 ~ 55）//

缴获的护照、纸币 5000 美元、纸币 1060 尼日利亚元（大概相当于 10 美元）、储存卡等物，现存于广州市第一看守所。//

**审**：被告人及辩护人对公诉人出示的上述证据有何意见？//

**被**：No. //

**辩**：没有意见。//

**审**：公诉人继续举证。//

**公**：（11）被告人身份（B 卷 51 ~ 52）（法警出示护照复印件）//

**审**：被告人及辩护人对公诉人出示的上述证据有何意见？//

**被**：No. //

**辩**：没有意见。//

**审**：护照是否被告人的真实身份？//

**被**：Yes. //

**审**：公诉人继续举证。//

**公**：二、鉴定结论：

——穗关缉刑技验字［2006］65 号广州海关缉私局检验报告（A 卷 13）

检验结论：送检的 14 粒粉末压实而成的柱状固体（净重 180 克）中均检出盐酸海洛因（Heroin. HCL）。

——穗关缉刑技验字［2006］102 号广州海关缉私局检验报告（A 卷 15）

检验结论：检材中盐酸海洛因（Heroin. HCL）含量为 72.26%。//

**审**：被告人及辩护人对公诉人出示的上述证据有何意见？//

**被**：No. //

**辩**：没有意见。//

**审**：公诉人继续举证。//

**公**：三、被告人供述：

被告人奥格邦纳共供述 4 次，均承认携带 14 粒毒品，以体内藏毒的方式，乘坐飞机将毒品带至广州。（B 卷 24~50）//

2006 年 12 月 21 日供述：我在尼日利亚认识了一个叫罗马纳斯的人。10 月 8 日早晨，罗马纳斯叫我去拉各斯取毒品，一共给了 14 粒，我把它们放进肛门内，之后我乘坐从拉各斯飞到埃塞俄比亚的亚的斯亚贝巴的航班，又从亚的斯亚贝巴飞往广州，经过海关检查区时，被警察拦住了。在机场海关查验室内排出 7 粒，之后又在医院排出另外的 7 粒。因我在中国没有认识的人，想在中国做生意，罗马纳斯说可以帮我，如我愿意帮他带毒品到中国的话。并许诺成功将毒品交给广州接货的人，他会给我 500 元美金作报酬。接货的人会在机场等我，从我穿的衣服认出我。我知道这在我们国家是违法的。（B 卷 43~50）//

**审：** 被告人对原来在公安机关所作的供述有何意见？//

**被：** I know it illegal to carry Heroin, but I have no idea that what I carried with me was Heroin. In Nigeria it is also illegal to carry something like the cigarette. I had thought I was carrying something like cigarettes. //

**辩：** 没有意见。//

**审：** 公诉人有无其他证据出示？//

**公：** 证据出示完毕。//

**审：** 上述证据可以作为本案证据使用。//

**审：** 被告人在公安机关供述知道自己是带毒品，在法庭上为何称不知道？//

**被：** I only knew they were common drugs, but I did not know they were Heroin. //

**审：** 被告人、辩护人有无证据向法庭出示？//

**被：** No.

**辩：** 没有。//

**审：** 法庭调查到此结束。下面进行法庭辩论。先由公诉机关发表公诉词。//

**公：** 发表意见如下：（1）本案事实清楚，证据确实充分，足以认定。被告人违反海关法规，携带毒品进入中华人民共和国境内，未申报任何物品走无申报通道。在海关查验房排出 7 粒毒品，之后被送往医院，在医院又排出 7

粒毒品。被告人的行为已构成走私毒品罪。被告人也对携带毒品进入中国境内的犯罪事实供认不讳，其供认主观上也明知是毒品，在此情况下，仍然违反海关法规，实施走私毒品的行为。//（2）关于本案的定性问题。本案被告人在主观上具有明知，在明知是毒品的情况下仍然实施走私毒品的犯罪行为，因此被告人的行为触犯了《刑法》第347条第2款第1项的规定，构成走私毒品罪。//（3）本案被告人的行为具有社会危害性。被告人为牟取非法利益，在明知是毒品的情况下，仍然采用体内藏毒的方式携带毒品海洛因，企图携带进入中华人民共和国境内，没有申报任何物品，走无申报通道，被海关人员确定为怀疑对象后，当即在海关查验房内排出粉末压实而成的柱状固体7粒，随后被送至医院治疗，其间又从体内排出粉末压实而成的柱状固体7粒，海关人员从14粒固体（净重180克）中均检验出盐酸海洛因，含量为72.26%。//被告人违反中华人民共和国海关法规，非法携带中华人民共和国禁止进出口的毒品入境，其行为严重扰乱中华人民共和国社会管理秩序，其在明知是毒品的情况下，仍然违反我国海关法规，携带进入中国境内，是故意犯罪，其行为已构成走私毒品罪。请合议庭根据本案的犯罪事实、性质、情节、社会危害性及被告人的认罪态度依法作出判决。//

审：被告人，你的辩护意见？//

被：The defense makes the Statement of Defense. //

审：下面由辩护人发表辩护意见。//

辩：根据公诉人向法庭提交的有关证据，辩护人认为被告人犯罪事实清楚，证据充分。请法庭考虑以下几个方面：（1）被告人犯罪态度较好，其事先知道所携带的物品是毒品并予以承认，也认识到这是非法行为。被告人不清楚所携带的是海洛因，认为只是一般的毒品，犯罪的恶意不严重。被告人没有携带海洛因入境的故意，只认为是一般的毒品。（2）本案的主犯不是被告人，被告人只是走私毒品的工具，真正的主犯没有抓到。（3）被告人以前没有犯罪记录，本案是第一次犯罪。（4）被告人的文化程度是小学，对法律的认知程度比较低。综上，请法庭对被告人从轻判处。（详见辩护词）//

审：被告人，是否同意律师的辩护意见？有无补充？//

被：Agree. I appeal for a lighter punishment. //

审：下面进行第二轮法庭辩论。公诉人就本案还有无补充？//

公：（1）关于被告人的主观认知方面，辩护人认为被告人的主观恶意不严重。公诉人认为被告人明知所携带的物品是毒品，毒品对人身体毒害是很大的，毒品也包括海洛因，说明被告人主观上是明知的。(2) 主从犯的问题。只要携带的物品属于毒品，都属于走私毒品罪。走私毒品罪是行为犯，所以被告人不属于从犯。//

审：辩护人有何意见？//

辩：没有意见。//

审：被告人有何意见？//

被：No. If I had known the harmfulness the drug does, I would not have done it. //

审：对于被告人是否属于从犯的问题，法庭会根据证据予以认定。//

审：法庭辩论到此结束。下面由被告人作最后陈述。//

被：I plead for a lighter punishment. //

审：今日的庭审至此结束。何时宣判等候法院通知。现在休庭。//

# Ⅳ. 参考译文 Reference Versions

**Judge**：The first Court of the Guangzhou Intermediate People's Court of Guangdong now holds a public trial of the case of drug trafficking filed by the Guangzhou People's Procuratorate against the accused Chinedu Ogbanna. Would the bailiff please bring the accused to court? //

**Judge**：Will the accused tell the court your name, nickname, birthday information, nationality, educational background, work unit, professional title, domicile, and other personal information? //

**Accused**：我叫清耐都·奥格邦纳，男，1982 年 12 月 22 日出生，文化程度小学，尼日利亚联邦共和国国籍，护照号码：A2942×××，住尼日利亚东部阿比亚州阿巴市。//

**Judge**：When were you detained? When were you arrested? //

**Accused**：2006 年 10 月 9 日被刑事拘留，11 月 14 日被逮捕。//

**Judge**：Did you have the record of any criminal disposals? //

**Accused**：没有。//

**Judge**：Did you receive a copy of the Bill of Indictment? When did you receive it? //

**Accused**：于 2006 年 2 月 14 日收到起诉书副本。//

**Judge**：I will now announce some issues related to this court：The Collegiate Panel for the trial of this case comprises Judge Zhuang Ling, Representative Judge He Jiong and Representative Judge Zhong Qiang, with Judge Zhuang Ling acting as the Chief Judge. Chen Zhi will be the stenographer of the court trial, Clerk Liang Hua wei will be responsible for other issues related to this trial. Hou Dongwei, the representative prosecuting attorney form the Guangzhou People's Procuratorate of Guangdong, will appear in court to support the public prosecution. Professor Du Qiangping from the Guangdong University of Foreign Studies will be the interpreter for the trial. According to Article 32 of the Criminal Procedure Law of the People's Republic of China, the accused enjoys the right to challenge the qualification of the above listed personnel for this trial and apply for the replacement of any one of these personnel in one of the following circumstances：1. he or she is the party or the close relative of the party in the case；2. he or his close relative has conflicting interests of the case；3. he or she had once acted as the witness, forensic expert, defense counsel or legal representative of the case；4. he or she has other relations of the party and may probably affect the just trial of the case；5. the above personnel had once received gifts of the party or they had violated the related regulation to meet the parties and their representatives. Is the accused clear about the identities and qualifications of the members of the Collegiate Bench, the Clerk and the Public Prosecutor? Do you want to challenge them? //

**Accused**：听清楚了，不需要申请回避。//

**Judge**：According to the law, the accused enjoys the right to defend himself; he may also entrust counsels to defend him. Appointed by this court, Attorney Zhou Qinghua of the Hengyi Law Firm assigned by the aid center of law of Guangzhou, will be the counsel of the accused. Does the accused agree to employ the abovementioned attorney to represent and defend you? //

**Accused**：同意。//

**Judge**：In the process of the court trial, the accused may submit new evidence, summon new witnesses to court, present new evidences, and apply for new authentication, investigation and examination. Is the accused clear about this process? //

**Accused**：清楚。//

**Judge**：In the process of adducing evidence, both the prosecuting party and the defense party shall explain the source of your evidence and the points you want to make by the evidence. The exhibits you submit to the court shall be the original ones. In case you cannot submit the original, you should explain the reasons and submit the copies subject to the court's approval and examination. The accused enjoys the right to have a final statement after the court debate. Is the accused clear? //

**Accused**：清楚。//

**Judge**：Does the Public Prosecutor have any other new evidences to submit to the court? //

**Public Prosecutor**：No. //

**Judge**：Do the counsel and the accused have any new evidences to submit? //

**Accused**：没有。//

**Counsel**：No. //

**Judge**：Today's trial is composed of three stages: court investigation, court debate and the final statement of the accused. Now here begins the court investigation. Would the Public Prosecutor read the Bill of Indictment? //

**Public Prosecutor**：(The Public Prosecutor presented the Bill of Indictment. Omitted. ) //

**Judge**：Does the accused hear the Bill of Indictment clearly? Do you have any opinion about the Bill of Indictment? //

**Accused**：听清楚了，对起诉书指控的内容没有异议。//

**Judge**：Now the Public Prosecutor may inquire the accused of the facts as presented in the Bill of Indictment.

**Public Prosecutor**：The accused should answer the Public Prosecutor's questions honestly. Is that clear to you, the accused? //

**Accused**：清楚。//

**Public Prosecutor**：Which flight did you take to arrive in the Guangzhou Airport, the accused Chinedu Obgonna? //

**Accused**：2006 年 10 月 9 日乘坐 ET 的航班，不记得航班号码。//

**Public Prosecutor**：Where did you board on the flight and where did you transfer to Guangzhou?

**Accused**：从尼日利亚上机，在埃塞俄比亚转机到达广州。//

**Public Prosecutor**：What did you intend to do in Guangzhou? //

**Accused**：买手机。//

**Public Prosecutor**：What was the inspection result at the Customs on that day? //

**Accused**：入关时警察带我去医院。//

**Public Prosecutor**：Had you exerted something in the entry inspection room when receiving an examination?

**Accused**：有。//

**Public Prosecutor**：What thing? //

**Accused**：7 粒固状的物品，我之前不知道是毒品，之后才知道是毒品。//

**Public Prosecutor**：What was going on after you were sent to hospital? //

**Accused**：到医院之后再排出 7 粒东西。//

**Public Prosecutor**：How were these 14 solids put into you body? //

**Accused**：我的朋友给我的。是我的朋友帮我塞进体内的。//

**Public Prosecutor**：What is your friend's name and what does he do? //

**Accused**：叫罗马纳斯。这个人是我的一个顾客，我是从罗马纳斯处买的手机。我告诉罗马纳斯我要到中国买手机，罗马纳斯告诉我如果我帮他带一些东西到中国，他就给我提供帮助。//

**Public Prosecutor**：When did you get to know that what you took were drugs? //

**Accused**：在医院。//

**Public Prosecutor**：When did he insert the 14 solids into your body? //

**Accused**：乘坐飞机当天。//

**Public Prosecutor**：How did Romannus offer you help in business? //

**Accused**：罗马纳斯在中国有朋友，他告诉我如果将 14 粒东西交给他在中国的朋友，他在中国的朋友就会帮我买手机。//

**Public Prosecutor**：After you have brought the drugs to China, how would you give them to his friend?

**Accused**：这个人会在机场门口等，会认出我所穿的衣服。//

**Public Prosecutor**：Have you got the payment? Who paid the flight ticked to

Guangzhou?

**Accused**：我自己买的机票。罗马纳斯没有给我报酬，他说如果交货成功会给我 500 美元作报酬，但没有拿到。//

**Public Prosecutor**：Why did not you put the 14 solids in your trunk instead of your body? //

**Accused**：我本来想放进行李箱，但罗马纳斯说不行，如果放在行李箱，飞机上的人员是不允许的。//

**Public Prosecutor**：Had you ever thought your action might have break the law? //

**Accused**：罗马纳斯告诉我不能将这些东西带上机，但只要带上飞机就没事了。//

**Public Prosecutor**：Had you ever thought your action would have break the law of China? //

**Accused**：没有想过。//

**Public Prosecutor**：Have you ever been to China? //

**Accused**：没有。//

**Public Prosecutor**：There are no further questions for the accused. //

**Judge**：Does the defense counsel have any question for the accused? //

**Defense**：No. //

**Judge**：The accused, just now you mentioned that it would be OK if you had successfully took the things on flight. Does the action to bring the things on flight break the law of your country? //

**Accused**：我并不知道这是海洛因，我的朋友告诉我这是一种类似香烟的东西，在尼日利亚香烟是不能带出国的。//

**Judge**：Who paid the flight ticket? //

**Accused**：我自己买的。//

**Judge**：How much did it cost? //

**Accused**：大概 900 美元到 1000 美元。//

**Judge**：How much money have you brought to China? //

**Accused**：带了 5000 美元。//

**Judge**：Now the Procuratorate exhibits the evidence related to the case. //

**Public Prosecutor**：The Prosecutor has the following evidences to present to the court：

I. Documentary evidence and physical evidence：

1. Documentary evidence and material evidence.

the registration form for accepting criminal cases（2 in VolumnB）

Time of acceptance：Oct 9th, 2006

Spot of acceptance：the Customs of the Guangzhou Baiyun International Airport //

**Judge**：Does the accused and the defense counsel have any opinion about the foresaid evidence? //

**Accused**：没有意见。//

**Defense**：No. //

**Judge**：The Public Prosecutor continues to exhibit evidences. //

**Public Prosecutor**：2. the examination records provided by the Customs of Guangzhou Baiyun International Airport of the People's Republic of China（5 in Volumn B）

Time of examination：18：45 to 20：30 on Oct 9th, 2006

Spot of examination：inspection room at the Customs of Guangzhou Baiyun International Airport

Object of examination：Ogbanna

Situation of examination：on October 9, 2006, the party arrived in Guangzhou by Flight ET6×× and entered the territory of China via Guangzhou International Airport. When passing the inspection hall at the Customs, he chose the Nothing-to-Declare Channel and delivered the luggage declaration form to the Custom. He declared nothing on the luggage declaration form. There was nothing abnormal when the luggage received the X-ray examination and open case inspection. During the process of examination, the party excreted from his body seven pieces of column-shaped solids in the entry inspection room at the Customs of Guangzhou Baiyun International Airport. The Custom suspected he was hiding drugs in his body and handed him over to the Anti-Smuggling Bureau of Guangzhou Customs for further investigation. //

**Judge**：Does the accused and the defense counsel have any opinion about the foresaid evidence? //

**Accused**：没有意见。//

**Judge**：The Public Prosecutor continues to exhibit evidences. //

**Public Prosecutor**：3. two examination depositions, and one certificate provided by the Customs of Guangzhou Baiyun International Airport (6-8 in Volumn B) //

The depositions prove the following facts: on October 9, 2006, the Second Branch of Non-trade Goods Supervision of Passenger Inspection Division of the Customs of Guangzhou Baiyun International Airport was in charge of supervision of Flight ET6×× (from Addis Ababa to Guangzhou). At around 18:45, a passenger named Chinedu Ogbonna (a citizen of Nigeria, male, 23 years old, with passport No. A29422×××) was passing the Customs with two handbags. Passing via the Nothing-to-Declare channel, he submitted to the Customs the luggage declaration form for entry passengers, in which he failed to declare anything. The officer on duty Xie Suilan asked him to show the passport and interviewed him about relevant questions. During the interview, the accused Chinedu Ogbonna dared not look directly at the officer, so the officer latter listed him as a target for inspection and directed him into the Customs inspection zone for examination. The officer Hu Hao examined the two pieces of luggage by a machine and then opened them, finding nothing suspicious with the luggage. Then the Customs officers took him to the inspection room for further examination, where the suspect excreted seven oval grain - shaped solids from his body. Soon the Customs handed him over to the anti-smuggling organ for further investigation. //

The certificate proves the following facts: Xie Suilan and Hu Hao are the officers of the Second Branch of Non-Trade Goods Supervision of Passenger Inspection Division of the Customs of Guangzhou Baiyun International Airport. They were in charge of supervision of Flight ET6×× on October 9, 2006. //

**Judge**：Does the accused and the defense counsel have any opinion about the foresaid evidence? //

**Accused**：没有意见。//

**Defense**：No. //

**Judge**：The Public Prosecutor continues to exhibit evidences. //

**Public Prosecutor**：4. The CT diagnosis report, the discharge certificate and the personal statement on refusal of operation provided by Guangdong Provincial General Corps Hospital of the Armed Police Force prove the situation as the accused received the treatment. //

**Judge**：Does the accused and the defense counsel have any opinion about the foresaid evidence? //

**Accused**：没有意见。//

**Defense**：No. //

**Judge**：The Public Prosecutor continues to exhibit evidences. //

**Public Prosecutor**：5. Statement on Circumstances (18 in Volumn B)

The statement issued by the Anti-Smuggling Bureau of Guangzhou Customs proves the following fact that from October 9, 2006 to October 13, 2006, the accused Ogbonna excreted another seven pieces of grain-shaped solids when he was hospitalized. The whole process of the excretion of drugs was witnessed by two or more officers of the Anti-Smuggling Bureau. //

**Judge**：Does the accused and the defense counsel have any opinion about the foresaid evidence? //

**Accused**：没有意见。//

**Defense**：No. //

**Judge**：The Public Prosecutor continues to exhibit evidences. //

**Public Prosecutor**：6. The List of Detained Articles and Documents (53 in Volumn B) prove that fourteen pieces of Heroin, with a net weight of one hundred and eighty grams, were seized from the accused Chinedu Ogbonna. //

**Judge**：Does the accused and the defense counsel have any opinion about the foresaid evidence? //

**Accused**：没有意见。//

**Defense**：No. //

**Judge**：The Public Prosecutor continues to exhibit evidences. //

**Public Prosecutor**：7. The photographs of the fourteen seized pieces of drugs (9-10 in Volumn B)

The accused Ogbonna has confirmed the photographs as those were inserted in his anus and brought to Guangzhou by the Flight ET6×× from Nigeria on October, 9. (The bailiff exhibited the photographs. ) //

**Judge:** Does the accused and the defense counsel have any opinion about the foresaid evidence? //

**Accused:** 没有意见。//

**Defense:** No. //

**Judge:** The Public Prosecutor continues to exhibit evidences. //

**Public Prosecutor:** 8. The seized air ticket and its copy (11−12 in Volumn B)

The accused Ogbonna has confirmed that it was the ticket he used to smuggle drugs to Guangzhou. (The bailiff exhibited the copy of the air ticket. ) //

**Judge:** Does the accused and the defense counsel have any opinion about the foresaid evidence? //

**Accused:** 没有意见。//

**Defense:** No. //

**Judge:** The Public Prosecutor continues to exhibit evidences. //

**Public Prosecutor:** 9. The Copy of the customs declaration form ( 13 − 14 in Volumn B)

The accused Ogbonna has confirmed that it was thecopy of his entry baggage declaration form. //

**Judge:** Does the accused and the defense counsel have any opinion about the foresaid evidence? //

**Accused:** 没有意见。//

**Defense:** No. //

**Judge:** The Public Prosecutor continues to exhibit evidences. //

**Public Prosecutor:** 10. The dispatch receipt and the dispatch registration form (54−55 in Volumn B) prove that the passport, five thousand US dollars and one thousand and sixty Nigeria currency (almost equal with ten dollars), the deposit card and other articles carried by the accused are stored in Guangzhou First Detention House. //

**Judge:** Does the accused and the defense counsel have any opinion about the foresaid evidence? //

**Accused**：没有意见。//

**Defense**：No. //

**Judge**：The Public Prosecutor continues to exhibit evidences. //

**Public Prosecutor**：11. The identity of the accused. （54-55 in Volumn B） （The bailiff exhibited the copy of the passport. ） //

**Judge**：Does the accused and the defense counsel have any opinion about the foresaid evidence? //

**Accused**：没有意见。//

**Defense**：No. //

**Judge**：Does the passport prove the true identity of the accused? //

**Accused**：是的。//

**Judge**：The Public Prosecutor continues to exhibit evidences. //

**Public Prosecutor**：Ⅱ. Examination conclusion：

The examination Report Suiguanjixingjiyanzi〔2006〕No. 65 issued by the Anti-Smuggling Bureau of Guangzhou Customs（13 in Volumn A）proves that the fourteen pieces of column-shaped solids made of pressed powder（with a net weight of one hundred and eighty grams）were tested to contain Heroin HCL.

The examination Report Suiguanjixingjiyanzi〔2006〕No. 102 issued by the Anti-Smuggling Bureau ofGuangzhou Customs（15 in Volumn A）proves that the content of the Heroin HCL was seventy-two point two six percent. //

**Judge**：Does the accused and the defense counsel have any opinion about the foresaid evidence? //

**Accused**：没有意见。//

**Defense**：No. //

**Judge**：The Public Prosecutor continues to exhibit evidences. //

**Public Prosecutor**：Ⅲ. The confessions made by the accused.

The accused had made altogether four confessions all of which confessed that he had hidden fourteen pieces of drugs in his body and brought them to Guangzhou by flight. （24-50 in Volumn B） //

The confession made by the accused on December 21, 2006 is as followings：he knew a man named Romannus in Nigeria. On the morning of October 8, 2006, Rommannus asked him to go to Lagos to receive drugs. He was given fourteen pieces of drugs and inserted the drugs in his anus. The he left Lagos for Addis Ababa and left Addis Ababa for Guangzhou by air. When passing the Customs inspection zone, he was stopped by the police. He excreted seven pieces of drugs in the Customs inspection room and another seven pieces of drugs in a hospital. He helped Romannus carry drugs for the sake of setting up business in China because he didn't know anyone here. Romannus promised him a reward of five hundred US dollars if he succeeded in carrying the drugs to China and then giving them to the friend in China. The man to receive the drugs would wait him at the airport and recognize him from his clothes. He knew his action was illegal in his country, Nigeria. ( 43-50 in Volumn B) //

**Judge**: Does the accused have any opinion about your confession to the Public Security Organs? //

**Accused**: 我知道海洛因是非法的，但我不知道我所带的东西是海洛因。在尼日利亚带香烟之类的东西是非法的，我以为是香烟之类的东西。//

**Defense**: I have no opinion. //

**Judge**: Does the Public Prosecutor have other evidence to exhibit to the court? //

**Public Prosecutor**: There is no further evidence to exhibit. //

**Judge**: The foresaid evidences can be accepted as evidences in this case. //

**Judge**: In the confession made to the Public Security Organs the accused had admitted he knew what he carried were drugs. Why does the accused claim to have no idea about what it is? //

**Accused**: 我知道是毒品，不知道是海洛因。//

**Judge**: Does the accused and the defense counsel have any evidence to submit? //

**Accused**: 没有。//

**Defense**: No. //

**Judge**: This is the end of court investigation. Court debate now begins. First, will the Public Prosecutor please present the Statement of Prosecution? //

**Public Prosecutor**: The prosecutor has the following opinions to present to the court: Firstly, the facts of this case are clear and the evidence is conclusive. The accused violated the related regulations of the Custom, bringing the drugs to enter the territory of the People's Republic of China. When passing the inspection hall at the Customs, he chose the Nothing-to-Declare Channel, failing to declare anything to the Customs. The accused excreted from his body seven pieces of solid drugs in the inspection room at the Customs. Then the accused was sent to hospital for treatment and he excreted from his body seven other pieces of solid drugs. The accused's acts have constituted the crime of drug smuggling. The accused also confessed his acts of crime to smuggle the drugs into the territory of China. In his confession he admitted he had known he was carrying the drugs. Under such circumstance, the accused continued his violation of the regulation of the Customs and carried on his acts of drug smuggling. Secondly, as for the nature of this case is concerned. In this case, the accused committed the crime of drug smuggling even when he knew what he carried were drugs. The accused has violated Subparagraph 1 Paragraph 2 Article 347 of the Criminal Law of the People's Republic of China and his acts constituted the crime of drug smuggling. Thirdly, the accused's acts are harmful to the society. The accused hidden the drugs in his body to carry the Heroin for the sake of illegal interests when he realized what he carried were drugs. He attempted to bring the drugs into the territory of the People's Republic of China. When passing the inspection hall at the Customs, he chose to the Nothing-to-Declare channel, failing to declare anything to the Customs. When he was confirmed as the suspect by the Custom officers, he excreted seven pieces of column-shaped solids made of pressed powder. The accused was then sent to hospital for treatment. He excreted from his body another seven pieces of packed column - shaped solids when he was hospitalized. Upon examination, the aforesaid fourteen pieces of column-shaped solids, with a net weight of one hundred and eight grams, were tested to contain Heroin HCL, the content of which was seventy-two point two six percent. The accused has violated the regulations of the Customs of the People's Republic of China by illegally carrying the drugs which were prohibited to import and export by the People's Republic of China. His acts seriously disturbed the social order of the People's Republic of China. The accused continued his crime of drug smuggling when he knew what he carried were drugs. His act is intentional crime and has committed the crime of drug smuggling. We appeal to the

Collegiate Bench to make a just decision in consideration of the details of the crime, the harm it does to the society and the attitude of the accused toward conviction of his guilt. //

**Judge**: What is the opinion of the accused? //

**Accused**: 由我的辩护人先发言。//

**Judge**: The defense makes the Statement of Defense. //

**Defense**: Based on the evidences submitted by the Public Prosecutor to the court, the counsel holds that in this case the facts are clear and the evidence is sufficient. We appeal to court to take the following facts into consideration: 1. The accused honestly confessed the crime and admitted he had known what he carried were drugs. He was also aware it was illegal. But the accused did not know the drugs he was carrying were Heroin. He had thought they were common ones. Therefore his intent was not seriously malicious. The accused did not intend to carry the Heroin into China but the moderately toxic ones. 2. The accused was instigated by others, working as an accessory. 3. The accused does not have the crime record and he is a first offender. 4. The accused is a primary school graduate and knows little about the law. For the above-mentioned factors, the counsel appeal for a lighter punishment on the accused. //

**Judge**: Does the accused agree with the opinion of the defense? Does the accused have something to supplement? //

**Accused**: 同意。我请求从轻判决。//

**Judge**: Now begins the second round of court debate. Does the Public Prosecutor have some supplementary opinion? //

**Public Prosecutor**: 1. Regarding the subjective recognition of the accused, the public prosecutor does not think his intent is seriously malicious. The public prosecutor holds that since the accused had known what he was carrying were drugs the accused should have a clear subjective recognition. Since all the drugs do a great harm to humans and Heroin is undoubtedly one category of drugs. 2. Regarding the matter of accessory, the public prosecutor holds that as the suspect is carrying drugs, he has conducted the crime of drug smuggling. The crime of drug smuggling belongs to the behavior crime, therefore the accused can not be regarded as an accessory. //

**Judge**：Does the defense have any opinion? //

**Defense**：No. //

**Judge**：Does the accused have any opinion? //

**Accused**：我没有意见，如果我知道毒品的危害这么大，我不会这么做。//

**Judge**：As for the matter whether the accused is an accessory, the court will assert in accordance with the evidences. //

**Judge**：The court debate is over. Now the accused may make your final statement. //

**Accused**：请求从轻处罚。//

**Judge**：This is the end of the trial. The court will notify you of the time of adjudication later on. Now the court session adjourns. //

# V．句子精炼 Sentences in Focus

**Directions**：*Interpret the following sentences alternatively into English or Chinese*：

1. Will the accused tell the court your name, nickname, birthday information, nationality, educational background, work unit, professional title, domicile, and other personal information?

2. In the process of the court trial, the accused may submit new evidence, summon new witnesses to court, present new evidences, and apply for new authentication, investigation and examination. Is the accused clear about this process?

3. 控辩双方在申请举证时，应说明所举证据的来源及所要证明的内容。控辩双方向法庭提交证据，应当提供原件、原物。不能提交原件、原物的，应当说明理由，经法庭同意并核实后可以提交副本或者复印件。被告人在法庭辩论后有最后陈述的权利。被告人听清楚了吗？

4. 本案事实清楚，证据确实充分，足以认定。被告人违反海关法规，携带毒品进入中华人民共和国境内，未申报任何物品走无申报通道。在海关查验房排出 7 粒毒品，之后被送往医院，在医院又排出 7 粒毒品。被告人的行为已构成走私毒品罪。被告人也对携带毒品进入中国境内的犯罪事实供认不讳，其供认主观上也明知是毒品，在此情况下，仍然违反海关法规，实施走私毒品的行为。

5. 被告人犯罪态度较好，其事先知道所携带的物品是毒品予以承认，也认识到这是非法行为。被告人不清楚所携带的是海洛因，认为只是一般的毒品，犯罪的恶意不严重。被告人没有携带海洛因入境的故意，只认为是一般的毒品。

6. 关于被告人的主观认知方面，辩护人认为被告人的主观恶意不严重。公诉人认为被告人明知所携带的物品是毒品，毒品对人身体毒害是很大的，毒品也包括海洛因，说明被告人主观上是明知的。

7. 今日的庭审至此结束。何时宣判等候法院通知。现在休庭。

第八单元

# 法庭审判

**Unit 8 Court Judgment**

# Ⅰ. 专题知识 Legal Knowledge

根据《刑事诉讼法》的规定，法庭审判程序大致可被分为开庭、法庭调查、法庭辩论、被告人最后陈述、评议和审判五个阶段。

（1）开庭。刑事诉讼开庭程序除传唤被告人到庭、附带民事诉讼原告人和被告人外，与前述开庭程序相同。

（2）法庭调查。法庭调查的范围是人民检察院起诉书所指的犯罪事实和证实被告人有罪、无罪、罪轻、罪重的各种证据。

根据《刑事诉讼法》第 186 条至第 209 条及有关司法解释的规定，法庭调查的详细步骤和程序如下：①公诉人宣读起诉书；②被告人、被害人陈述；③讯问被告人、询问被害人和附带民事诉讼原告人；④询问证人、鉴定人；⑤出示物证宣读鉴定结论和有关笔录；⑥调取新的证据；⑦法庭调查核实证据。

附带民事诉讼部分的调查，一般在刑事诉讼部分调查结束后进行，具体程序以民事诉讼法的有关规定进行。

（3）法庭辩论。法庭辩论中控辩双方可以对案件事实是否清晰，证据是否确实、充分互相进行辩论。法庭辩论在审判长的主持下，按照下列顺序进行：①公诉人发言；②被害人及其诉讼代理人发言；③被告人自行辩护；④辩护人辩护；⑤控辩双方进行辩论。附带民事诉讼的辩论在刑事诉讼部分辩论后进行。

（4）被告人最后陈述。被告人最后陈述不仅是法庭审判的一个独立阶段，而且还是法律赋予被告人的一项重要诉讼权利。被告人最后陈述只要不超出本案范围，一般不应限制其发言时间，或随意打断其发言，而应让被告人将话尽量讲完。被告人在最后陈述中提出了新的事实、证据，合议庭认为可能影响准确裁判的，应当恢复法庭调查；如果被告人提出新的辩解理由，合议庭认为确有必要，可以恢复法庭辩论。

（5）评议和审判。合议庭应当根据已经查明的事实、证据和有关的法律规定，并在充分考虑控辩双方意见的基础上进行评议，确定被告人是否有罪，应否追究刑事责任；构成何罪，应否处以刑罚；有无从轻、从重、减轻或者免除处罚的情节；附带民事诉讼如何解决；赃款赃物如何处理等，并依法作出判决。

根据《刑事诉讼法》第 200 条及有关司法解释的规定，人民法院应当根据案件的具体情形，分别作出裁决：①案件事实清楚，证据确实充分，根据法律认定被告人有罪的，应当作出有罪判决；②根据法律认定被告人无罪的，应当作出无罪判决；③证据不足，不能认定被告人有罪的，应当作出证据不足，指控的犯罪不能成立的判决。

根据《刑事诉讼法》第 202 条的规定，宣告判决一律公开进行。当庭宣告判决的，应当在 5 日内将判决书送达当事人和提起公诉的人民检察院；定期宣告判决的，应当在宣告后立刻将判决书送达当事人和提起公诉人的人民检察院。

## Ⅱ. 词汇热身 Vocabulary Warm-up

**Directions**：*Give the English equivalents of the following Chinese expressions*：

| | | |
|---|---|---|
| 人民检察院 | 二审案件 | 合议庭审判长 |
| 认定事实 | 答辩陈述书 | 代理审判员 |
| 刑事诉讼 | 二审 | 速录员指派 |
| 上诉案件 | 辩护律师辩护人 | 指定 |
| 一审案件 | 辩论阶段 | 有利害关系 |
| 原告 | 驳回上诉 | 回避 |
| 驳回反诉 | 维持原判 | 要求回避 |
| 休庭 | 驳回请求 | 传唤（证人） |
| 宣判 | 上诉人 | 控辩双方 |
| 答辩 | 答辩状 | 原件，原物 |
| 高级人民法院 | 刑事审判庭第一庭 | 副本 |

复印件                    法庭调查                        被告人最后陈述

委托                      法庭辩论                        讯问完毕

支持公诉

**Directions**：*Give the Chinese equivalents of the following English expressions*：

dismiss a counterclaim                    appellate case

reject a counterclaim                      case of trial of second instance

deny/dismiss a motion                    petition for appeal

Higher People's Court                    keep in records

reject/dismiss the appeal                deliberation

sustain the original judgment/ruling      The court is in sessionThe court is in recess

appellant

adjourn the court                          The court is in adjournment.

pronounce judgment；determination        We are adjourned

case of trial of first instance            criminal detention

plaintiff                                  detain

determine facts                            arrest

# III. 课文口译 Text for Interpreting

## ◆ *Passage 1*

**Directions**：*Listen to the passage and interpret from Chinese into English at the end of each segment.*

（下文节选自湖北省宜昌市中级人民法院作出的李某涛诉西陵人保公司保险合同纠纷案的判决书）

宜昌市西陵区人民法院一审认为：原告李某涛在被告西陵人保公司处投保的"学生、幼儿平安保险"，属于人身保险；其附加的意外伤害医疗保险，性质亦应属人身保险。因此，被告关于附加的意外伤害医疗保险是一种财产性质的保险，应使用损失补偿原则理赔的观点无法律依据。保险事故发生后，被保险人申请理赔，应当向保险人提供所能提供的确认保险事故的性质、原因、损失程度的证明和材料，并未要求必须提供相关资料原件。因此，被告要求原告必须提供医疗费收据等资料原件方可理赔的答辩观点，缺乏法律依据。据此，宜昌市西陵区人民法院于 2004 年 9 月 1 日判决：被告西陵人保公司给付原告李某涛医疗保险金 1011.12 元。//

西陵区人保公司不服一审判决，向湖北省宜昌市中级人民法院提出上诉，理由是：本案中的意外损害医疗保险的保险标的为医疗费用，是一种财产损失，而财产保险适用损失补偿原则。被上诉人的损失已经得到补偿，被上诉人不能提供有效票据（即医疗费票据原件），因此上诉人对被上诉人的理赔申请有权拒绝。请求依法撤销原判，改判驳回被上诉人的诉讼请求。//

被上诉人李某涛答辩称：人身保险业务包括人寿保险、健康保险、意外伤害保险等保险业务。原判认定事实清楚，适用法律正确，应予维持。//

宜昌市中级人民法院二审认为：意外伤害医疗保险虽然具有一些特点，但是，其毕竟是基于人身发生意外伤害而形成的保险，属于人身保险范畴。损失补偿原则不适用于人身保险，当然也不适用于属于人身保险的意外伤害医疗保险。在处理人身保险赔偿事宜时，只要被保险人提供的有关证明和资料能够确认保险事故及相关费用已经发生，保险公司就应按照保险合同履行给付保险金的义务，而不应以被保险人出具相关费用单据原件为必备条件。对于保险责任范围内的索赔，保险公司只有在相关法律和保险合同有明确规定的情况下才能予以拒赔。综上，上诉人的上诉理由均不成立，原审判决认定事实清楚，使用法律正确，程序合法，应予维持。据此，宜昌市中级人民法院依据《民事诉讼法》第 153 条第 1 款第 1 项之规定，于 2004 年 11 月 16 日判决：驳回上诉，维持原判。//

## ◆ *Passage 2*

**Directions**：*Listen to the passage and interpret from Chinese into English at the end of each segment.*

（下文节选自南京利源公司诉金兰湾公司商标侵权纠纷案判决书）

南京利源物业发展有限公司（以下简称"利源公司"）是"百家湖"注册商标的专用权人。该商标用于服务项目第 36 类，即不动产出租、代理、中介、评估等服务。利源公司曾以"百家湖花园"加注册商标符号的使用形式，

在报纸上刊登多种售房广告。//

百家湖是南京市江宁区东山镇的一个地名。南京金兰湾房地产开发有限公司（以下简称"金兰湾公司"）在该地开发了一个被命名为"枫情家园"的住宅小区。2001 年 10 月至 11 月，金兰湾公司在报纸上多次刊登广告，预售其在"枫情家园"中新开盘的高层住宅。广告使用"百家湖 枫情国度"表述该高层住宅。//

利源公司为此提起诉讼称：百家湖花园是原告在 9 年时间里投资数亿元开发出的房地产界知名品牌，原告已取得"百家湖"注册商标专用权。被告金兰湾公司未经许可，就在不动产业使用"百家湖"字样进行广告宣传，侵犯了原告的注册商标专用权。请求判令被告立即停止侵权行为，公开赔礼道歉，给原告赔偿经济损失 100 万元，并负担本案诉讼费用。//

被告金兰湾公司辩称："百家湖"是南京市家喻户晓的地名，被告的"枫情国度"高层住宅坐落在该地区。为了使消费者了解高层住宅的坐落地点，被告在这个高层住宅的名称"枫情国度"前标注"百家湖"，是对地名的合理使用，不是想让消费者把被告开发的"枫情国度"高层住宅误认成原告的"百家湖花园"。原告的诉讼请求没有道理，应当驳回。//

## ◆ *Passage 3*

**Directions**：*Listen to the passage and interpret from English into Chinese at the end of each segment.*

（下文节选自星源公司等诉上海星巴克等商标侵权及不正当竞争纠纷案判决书）

The ruling court of first instance, Shanghai No. 2 Intermediate People's court held that: The STARBUCKS series trademarks possess a wide international reputation and the plaintiff has been using and advertising the trademark "星巴克". Therefore the trademarks have already been well known by the relevant public in Mainland China. The trademark "星巴克" and "STARBUCKS" should be recognized as well-known trademarks. The Defendant Shanghai Xing Ba Ke registered the word "星巴克" as its corporate name in bad faith and used various marks identical to the plaintiff's trademark "星巴克" in its business operation, which has infringed the plaintiff's exclusive right on its trademarks and simultaneously constituted unfair competition against the plaintiffs. In summary, the Shanghai No. 2 Intermediate People's Court made the following judgment: //

1. To order the Defendant to stop infringing the plaintiff's exclusive right on its well-known trademarks "STARBUCKS" and "星巴克" as well as its exclusive right on trademarks "STARBUCKS" and "星巴克", "STARBUCKS" word and device; and to stop infringing the plaintiff United STARBUCKS' right of using the above trademarks. //

2. To order the Defendant to stop its unfair competition against STARBUCKS Corporationand United STARBUCKS. //

3. To order the Defendant to change its corporate name within 30 days of the taking effect of this judgment and its corporate name after alternation shall not be containing the characters "星巴克". //

4. To order the Defendant to pay damages of RMB 500, 000 to the plaintiff and publish a statement on XINMIN Evening News to apologize to the plaintiffs and eliminate the negative effects. //

Shanghai XING BA KE and Shanghai XING BA KE Branch were dissatisfied with the judgment and appealed to the Shanghai Higher People's Court for its overruling the judgment of the first instance and rejecting all the claims made by the Starbucks Corporation and United STARBUCKS. The reasons of their appeal include: //

1. The procedure of the first instance is unjust; and

2. The facts found in first instance are unclear and the laws applied are inaccurate. //

Shanghai Higher People's Court considered that this case was complicated and the evidence involved was massive. Therefore it was justified for the Court in the first instance to postpone the time limit for providing evidence. There was no factual foundation for the appellants to challenge the legitimacy of the procedure of the first instance. The judgment of the first instance is based on clear verification of facts and accurate application of law. The appeal was rejected and the judgment of the first instance was affirmed. //

◆ *Passage 4*

**Directions**：*Listen to the passage and interpret from Chinese into English at the end of each segment.*

（下文节选自广东省广州市中级法院刑事判决书）

下面宣读判决书：

中华人民共和国
广东省广州市中级人民法院
刑 事 判 决 书

公诉机关：中华人民共和国广东省广州市人民检察院。//

被告人 Andoh Paul（中文译名安多·保罗，以下使用中文译名），男，1970 年 8 月 17 日出生，加纳共和国国籍，护照号码：H1857×××，案发时住中华人民共和国广东省广州市白云区均禾街石马村桃源西街 25 巷 2 号×××房。因本案于 2007 年 12 月 11 日被羁押，次日被刑事拘留。2008 年 1 月 17 日被逮捕。现被押于广东省广州市第三看守所。//

辩护人 GGG、JJJ，广东易春秋律师事务所律师。

翻译人员洪××，广州市 YY 翻译服务有限公司翻译员。//

中华人民共和国广东省广州市人民检察院以穗检公一诉［2008］165 号起诉书指控被告人安多·保罗非法拘禁一案，于 2008 年 6 月 30 日向本院提起公诉。本院受理后，依法组成合议庭公开开庭审理了本案。中华人民共和国广东省广州市人民检察院指派检察员宁永聪出庭支持公诉。广州市 YY 翻译有限公司受本院委托，指派翻译员洪××担任法庭翻译工作。被告人安多·保罗及其辩护人陈秋云、曾利霞等到庭参加诉讼。本案现已审理终结。//

公诉机关指控：2007 年 11 月，被告人安多·保罗因货款问题与被害人马提斯的雇主柯林斯产生纠纷。同年 12 月 10 日晚上，被告人安多·保罗在中华人民共和国广东省广州市白云区壹心大厦附近找到被害人马提斯，遂要求其打电话让柯林斯过来商讨货款的返还事宜，后柯林斯没有过来，被告人安多·保罗即伙同他人将被害人马提斯带至其租住处广州市白云区均禾街石马村桃源西街 25 巷 2 号×××房，继续要求被害人马提斯联系柯林斯还钱。期间，被告人安多·保罗等人对被害人马提斯实施殴打，并用电线等物品将其手脚捆绑。至 2007 年 12 月 11 日 7 时许，被害人马提斯利用被告人安多·保罗不备之机向楼下的路人求救。其后，闻讯赶至的警察解救了被害人马提斯，并将被告人安多·保罗抓获。

为证明上述事实，公诉人当庭出示或宣读了被害人马提斯的陈述、证人证言、现场勘查笔录及照片、抓获经过、报警登记表、法医鉴定结论、被告人的护照、被告人的供述等证据。据此，公诉机关认为，被告人安多·保罗为索取债务非法拘禁他人，其行为触犯了《刑法》第 238 条第 3 款的规定，构成非法拘禁罪。特提请本院依法判处。//

被告人安多·保罗对指控的事实有异议，表示其并非有意捆绑被害人。//

其辩护人提出以下辩护意见：①被告人没有非法拘禁被害人的主观故意，被害人自己同意到被告人家中商量债务解决办法；②被告人控制被害人的时间只有 2 小时，时间短，不构成犯罪；③被告人与被害人发生的只是"肢体冲突"，并非刑法意义上的殴打行为；④被告人绑被害人双手是事出有因的过激自助行为，且在绑后 1 小时就主动松绑，不应机械地认定为非法拘禁罪的"捆绑"情节。综上，被告人的行为属于《治安管理处罚法》第 40 条规定的一般非法拘禁行为，情节轻微，危害不大，不属于犯罪。//

经审理查明：2007 年 11 月，被告人安多·保罗因货款问题与被害人的雇主柯林斯产生纠纷。同年 12 月 10 日晚上，被告人安多·保罗在中华人民共和国广东省广州市白云区壹心大厦附近找到被害人马提斯，遂要求其打电话让柯林斯前来商讨货款的返还事宜。因柯林斯没有来，被告人安多·保罗即伙同他人将被害人马提斯带至其租住处广州市白云区均禾街石马村桃源西街 25 巷 2 号×××房，继续要求被害人马提斯联系柯林斯还钱。其间，被告人安多·保罗等人对被害人马提斯实施殴打，并用电线等物品将其手脚捆绑。至次日 7 时许，被害人马提斯趁被告人安多·保罗不备之机向楼下的路人求救，其后，闻讯赶至的警察解救了被害人马提斯，并将被告人安多·保罗抓获。//

上述事实，由庭审中公诉人当庭宣读或出示，并经控、辩双方质证，本院查证属实的下列证据证实：

（1）广州市公安局白云区分局出具的受理报警登记表、抓获经过、情况说明证实：2007 年 12 月 11 日 7 时 13 分，广州市公安局白云区分局接到群众的 110 报警电话，称在白云区均禾街石马村桃源西街有外国人被绑架。接报后，公安人员即赶到案发现场白云区均禾街石马村桃源西街 25 巷 2 号×××房，并叫房内的人员开门。公安人员在被告人安多·保罗开门后，解救出被害人马提斯，并抓获被告人安多·保罗。//

（2）广州市公安局白云区分局制作的穗公云刑（技勘）字［2007］2757号现场勘验检查工作记录及照片证实：现场位于广州市白云区均禾石马村桃源西街 25 巷 2 号×××房。现场提取到指纹 17 枚、皮带 2 条、电线 1 捆、刮刀 1 把、拉链 1 条、插线板 1 个等痕迹、物证。//

（3）现场提取的电线照片：经被告人安多·保罗签认，确认照片中的电线是其用来捆绑被害人马提斯的。//

（4）广州市公安局刑事警察支队刑事技术所出具的穗公刑技（法医）［2007］172 号法医学活体检验鉴定书证实：经检验，被害人马提斯的胸、背部的皮下出血和肘关节的新鲜痂皮符合被钝力作用所致，不构成重伤和轻伤。//

（5）广州市公安局白云区分局出具的调查情况说明证实：广州市白云区均禾街石马村桃源西街 25 巷 2 号房屋的业主是陈某棠，房屋的承租人是证人项某俚。项某俚租用后擅自将楼房作为旅馆业出租。案发后，项某俚因经营无牌旅业被行政拘留 15 天，现去向不明。//

（6）被告人安多·保罗的护照证实：被告人安多·保罗的国籍等身份情况。//

（7）被害人马提斯陈述证实：2007 年 12 月 10 日 20 时许，其在广州市三元里壹心大厦对面马路，这时有 5 人围过来，其中的 Obiagu 叫其打电话给柯林斯。柯林斯表示会过来，但其等了 2 个小时都没有过来。凌晨 2 时许，那 5 人将其带上出租车到他们的住处。其和 Obiagu、Emeka 同坐一辆出租车，Animal Skin 和 Ogbnugu 及一名不知名的人坐另一辆出租车。到 Obiagu 的租住处后，他们又让其打电话叫柯林斯拿钱过来，说柯林斯欠了他们 9000 美金。其被推进洗手间，Obiagu、Emeka 用电线、皮带绑其手脚，脱掉其衣服把冷水淋在其身上，还打其两巴掌。Emeka 用小刀顶住其脖子，说不还钱就捅死其，还用打火机烧其阴茎。后来其睡着了，醒来时发现 Obiagu 已经回房内睡觉，其他人不在。其听到楼下有脚步声，就大呼救命，有中国群众听到。过了 5 分钟左右，中国警察就来救他，并将其与 Obiagu 带到公安机关。因警察敲门，Obiagu 迫于无奈才去开门，并在警察进房前用小刀把电线和皮带切断了。其身上的人民币 1300 元和护照、诺基亚手机被他们抢走了。柯林斯在广州做二手手机生意。其是给柯林斯打工的，其没有欠 Obiagu 的钱。而 Obiagu 曾经和柯林斯做过一次手机生意，但具体情况其不清楚。而其被绑期间，Obiagu 告诉其柯林斯欠他 9000 美金。其是从洗手间跳到阳台上向路人呼救的，并向路人展示其被反绑的双手。路人可以看到其被反绑的情况。//

经其辨认照片，指认出被告人安多·保罗就是 Obiagu。//

（8）证人 Charles Yeboah 证实：其还有一个名字叫 Collins（即柯林斯）。其在中国广州做卖手机的生意。其档口在广州二沙头二手手机市场 233 档。马提斯在档口帮其卖手机，安多·保罗是加纳人，是其客户。一个月前，安多·保罗到其档口批发 800 部冒牌诺基亚手机，给了其 2 万美元。当安多·保罗准备把这 800 部冒牌手机带回加纳时，被白云机场的警察没收了。安多·保罗要求其退款。其退了 1 万美元，另 1 万美元迟点再退。之后安多·保罗经常打电话催其快点还款，其表示慢慢来，到时一定退。在其与安多·保罗做这笔生意时，马提斯也在场，但他只是打工的。2007 年 12 月 10 日晚，马提斯与安多·保罗发生矛盾。安多·保罗将马提斯抓住并关押起来。马提斯打电话给他，叫其过去他那里，具体是什么地方其不知道，后来其在白云均禾派出所见到他们两人。在马提斯被绑架期间，其没有接过马提斯或者安多·保罗的电话。//

经其辨认照片，指认出被告人安多·保罗就是因与其发生货款纠纷而绑架马提斯的人。//

（9）证人周某祥证实：2007 年 12 月 11 日早上 7 时许，其和工友途经白云区石马村桃源西街 25 巷 2 号时，听到 4 楼的阳台上传来叫喊声，但听不懂是什么意思。其往上看，发现在 4 楼一阳台上有一名没有穿上衣，双手反绑的外籍黑人在叫喊，旁边没有人。过几分钟后，又有一名黑人走出阳台，将叫喊的黑人带回房间。当时其等人以为有人跳楼，于是其用手机打 110 报警，并留在楼下看有什么情况。大约十分钟，有两名警察和十多名治安员来到，由其中一名治安员打开楼梯门，警察和治安员就一起上楼。大约十分钟，警察带了两个黑人下楼，其中一名黑人手上戴着手铐，之后警察离去。//

（10）证人项某佴证实：2007 年 6 月，其向业主陈某棠承租石马村桃源西街 25 巷 2 号两幢房屋，然后将房屋用于转租和住宿。2007 年 10 月，有一名外籍黑人男子租住 2 号出租屋的×××房，并提供了护照的复印件。到了

2007年12月11日早上7时，在上述×××房发生外国人打架的事情，有民警到场处理。//

（11）被告人安多·保罗的供述：大概两个星期前，其介绍 Jude 与马提斯的搭档柯林斯做手机生意，Jude 已经汇了9000美元给柯林斯，但柯林斯收款后一直没有发货，还躲了起来。为了让柯林斯还钱，其通过马提斯找柯林斯解决。2007年12月10日23时许，其见到马提斯在白云区壹心大厦和2个黑人朋友谈话，那2个黑人朋友也认识他。其就过去打听柯林斯的下落。可能双方吵得比较大声，隔壁商店的一些黑人围过来，其中有2个与其认识。于是6个人商量找柯林斯出来解决此事，由马提斯打电话。当时柯林斯答应出来，但其等人等了2个多小时都不见他过来。于是6人乘两辆出租车到其住处等柯林斯。到达住处后，柯林斯一直没有来。到了凌晨3时许，其叫马提斯再打电话给柯林斯，但马提斯不同意，并说不认识柯林斯。其打了马提斯两巴掌。马提斯的2个朋友叫其不要打他。此时马提斯想跳窗，另外2个黑人马上拉住他。为了防止马提斯跳窗逃跑，于是其找到黑色、白色两种电线将马提斯的手脚绑住，大约凌晨5时，其就回房间睡觉，其他黑人相继离开。12月11日7时许，有警察上来，将其和马提斯带回派出所处理。其没有拿马提斯任何东西。马提斯说他在壹心大厦时已经将东西交给朋友带走保管，其中包括人民币1200元。其没有泼马提斯冷水，没有用刀威胁他，也没有用打火机烧他的阴茎。//

经其辨认照片，指认出被害人马提斯。//

本院认为，被告人安多·保罗无视中华人民共和国法律，为索取债务非法拘禁他人，其行为已构成非法拘禁罪，依法应予惩处。公诉机关指控的事实清楚，罪名成立，应予支持。关于被告人安多·保罗的辩护人提出安多·保罗的犯罪情节显著轻微，属一般违法行为，不应以犯罪论处的辩护意见，经查，被告人安多·保罗为向证人柯林斯索取债务，非法拘禁被害人马提斯，在拘禁期间对被害人马提斯实施殴打、捆绑等行为。被告人安多·保罗以非法剥夺他人人身自由方式索取债务的行为，具有严重的社会危害性，依法应按非法拘禁罪追究其刑事责任，故上述辩护意见据理不足，本院不予采纳。依照《刑法》第6条第1、3款，第238条第1、3款，第35条的规定，判决如下：//

被告人安多·保罗犯非法拘禁罪，判处有期徒刑1年，附加驱逐出境

（刑期从判决执行之日起计算。判决执行以前先行羁押的，羁押一日折抵刑期一日，即自 2007 年 12 月 11 日起至 2008 年 12 月 10 日止）。//

如不服本判决，可在接到判决书的第二日起 10 日内，通过本院或者直接向中华人民共和国广东省高级人民法院提出上诉。书面上诉的，应当提交上诉状正本 1 份，副本 2 份。//

审　判　长　　DYK

代理审判员　　AAA

代理审判员　　CCC

二〇〇八年八月二十二日

本件与原本核对无异

书　记　员　　XXX //

# IV. 参考译文 Reference versions

## ◆ *Passage 1*

In the first-instance trial of the case, Xiling District People's Court in Yichang City gave the following consideration:

The "safety insurance" for students and infants that Li Moutao (the plaintiff) procured from Xiling Life Insurance Co. (the defendant) belonged to personal insurance, and the additional injury covered by it also belonged to personal insurance by nature. Therefore, there is no legal basis to support the point of view of the defendant that the additional medical insurance against accidental injury covered by the student safety insurance the plaintiff procured from the company had been an insurance of property, with indemnity payable by the principle of compensation for damage. In applying for compensation after the insured accident took place, the insurant should be required to provide the insurer with all the available documents and materials needed to determine the nature, cause, extent of damage of the insured accident that the insurant could provide, but there was no requirement that the insurant must provide the relevant documents or materials in the original. Therefore, there lacks the legal basis to support the pleading of the defendant that the plaintiff must provide it with the original copies of the invoices for medical treatment, etc. before compensation could be extended. On the basis of the foregoing consideration, Xiling District People's Court in Yichang City gave a judgment on September 1, 2004 to order the defendant to pay the insurant a separate line of compensation for medical insurance to the tune of 1,011.12 yuan. //

After the pronouncement of the first-instance judgment, Xiling Life Insurance Co. refused to accept it, and proceeded to appeal the case to Yichang City Intermediate People's Court in Hubei Province, with the pleading that the object of the medical insurance against accidental injury in this case was medical expenses, which belonged to a type of property losses, and the principle of compensation for damage is applicable to property insurance; and that as the losses sustained by the appellee was unable to provide valid documents (namely the original copies of the invoices for medical treatment), the appellant has the right to reject the application of the appellee for compensation. On the basis of this pleading, Xiling Life Insurance Co. requested the intermediate court to quash the original judgment and give a new judgment to reject the claims of the appellee. //

In response, Li Moutao (the appellee) contended that the scope of the personal insurance business covers life insurance, health insurance, insurance against accidental injury and other insurance businesses; and that as the original judgment makes clear determination of the facts in the case and was based on correct application of law, it should be upheld. //

In its second-insurance trial of the case, Yichang City Intermediate People's Court gave the following consideration: Although medical insurance against accidental injury is of some unique characteristics, it is actually an insurance business developed on the basis of occurrence of accidental personal injury, and thus belongs to the scope of occurrence of accidental personal injury, and thus belongs to the scope of personal insurance. The principle of compensation for damage is not applicable to personal insurance. Of course, it is not applicable to medical insurance against accidental injury, which belongs to the scope of personal insurance, either. In the settlement of claims of compensation for personal insurance, as long as the relevant records and materials provided by the insurant are capable of providing the occurrence of the insured accident and the incurrence of the relevant expenses, the insurance company should, in accordance with the relevant insurance contract, fulfill its obligation of extending compensation, rather than take whether the insurant is able to provide the original copies of the invoices for the relevant expenses as an indispensable condition for compensation. Where there is any claim for compensation within the scope of insurance liability, the insurance company can refuse to extend compensation only under circumstances explicitly prescribed by the relevant law and insurance contract that merit exemption of liability. To sum up, the grounds of appeal are untenable. As the original judgment makes clear determination of the facts in the case, was based on correct application of law, and was made in accordance with the lawful procedure, it should be upheld. On the basis of this consideration, Yichang City Intermediate People's Court, in accordance with Item (1) in Clause 1 of Article 153 of the Civil Procedure Law of the People's Republic of China, gave a final judgment in the case on November 16, 2004 to reject the appeal and uphold the original judgment. //

## ◆ *Passage 2*

Nanjing Liyuan Property Management Development Co. Ltd. ("Liyuan Co.") is the owner of exclusive right to use the registered trademark "Baijiahu" on services falling under Category 36, i. e. real estate lease, agency, intermediary, appraisal, etc. Liyuan Co. has advertised in newspapers to sell homes in the form of using "Baijiahu Garden" plus registered trademark symbol. //

Baijiahu is a place in Dongshan Town, Jiangning Disrict, Nanjing. Nanjing Jinlanwan Real Estate Development Co. Ltd. ("Jinlanwan Co.") developed a residential area named "Fengqing Homeland" in this place. From October to November 2001, Jinlanwan Co. advertised in newspapers many times for the presale of a new high-rise apartment building in "Fengqing Homeland". In its advertisements, "Baijiahu Fengqing Country" was used to describe the high-rise apartment building. //

For this, Liyuan Co. filed an action by claiming that: Baijiahu Garden was a well-known real estate brand that had been developed by the plaintiff within nine years with investment of hundreds of millions of Chinese yuan, the plaintiff had acquired thc cxclusive right to use the registered trademark "Baijiahu", and the defendant Jinlanwan Co. without authorization by using the word "Baijiahu" in its advertisements in the real estate industry had infringed the plaintiff's exclusive right to use the registered trademark. It requested the court to rule that the defendant should desist from such an infringement immediately, make a public apology, compensate the plaintiff for economic losses of one million Chinese yuan, and bear solely the litigation costs of this case. //

Jianlanwan Co. contended that: "Baijiahu" was a house-hold place name in Nanjing and its "Fengqing Country" high-rise apartment building was located in this place; it added the prefix "Baijiahu" to the name "Fqngqing Country" of the high-rise building to enable the consumers to mistake the "Fengqing Country" high-rise apartment building for the plaintiff's "Baijiahu Garden"; and the plaintiff's claims should be rejected by the court for unreasonableness. //

◆ *Passage 3*

上海市第二中级人民法院一审认为：星巴克系列商标具有广泛的国际知名度，加上原告不断对"星巴克"商标的宣传、使用，"SARBUCKS""星巴克"已为中国大陆相关公众所熟知。故应当被认定为驰名商标。被告上海星巴克恶意将"星巴克"文字作为企业名称中的字号进行登记并在经营活动中使用含有与原告星源公司"星巴克"商标相同的各类标识侵犯了原告的商标专用权，同时构成对原告的不正当竞争。综上，上海市第二中级人民法院判决：

（1）被告停止侵犯原告星源公司享有的"星巴克""Starbucks"专用权，停止侵犯原告统一星巴克对上述商标的使用权；//

（2）被告停止对原告星源公司、统一星巴克的不正当竞争行为；//

（3）被告于本判决生效之日起 30 日内更改企业名称，变更后的企业名称中不得包含"星巴克"文字；//

（4）被告赔偿原告经济损失人民币 50 万元；被告在新民晚报上刊载声明，向原告赔礼道歉，消除影响。//

上海星巴克、上海星巴克分公司不服一审判决，向上海市高级人民法院提出上诉，请求撤销原判，驳回被上诉人星源公司、统一星巴克的全部诉讼请求。理由是：

（1）原审判决程序不公正；

（2）原审判决认定事实不清，适用法律错误。//

上海市高级人民法院认为：本案案情复杂。证据繁多，适当延长举证期限并无不妥。故上诉人认为一审程序违法，没有事实依据。一审判决认定事实清楚，适用法律准确，随判决驳回上诉，维持原判。//

◆ *Passage4*

## Intermediate People's Court of Guangzhou, Guangdong
## The People's Republic of China
## Criminal Judgment

Public prosecution department: the People's Procuratorate of Guangzhou, Guangdong, the People's Republic of China

Defendant

Name: Andoh Paul（"Paul"）

Sex: male

Date of birth: August 17, 1970

Nationality: the Republic of Ghana

Passport No. : H1857×××//

Temporary residence at the time of crime: Apartment ×××, 2 Alley 25, Taoyuan St（W）, Shima Village, Junhe St, Baiyun District, Guangzhou, Guangdong, the People's Republic of China//

In suspicion of his involvement in this case, he was detained on December 11, 2007 and put into investigative detention the next day. He was arrested on January 17, 2008 and is now detained in the Third Detention House of Guangzhou.

Defense counsels: GGG and JJJ, lawyers with Guangdong E-Times Law Firm

The interpreter: Hong ××, English interpreter with YY Ltd. //

The illegal confinement case of the People's Procuratorate of Guangzhou, Guangdong, the People's Republic of China vs. the defendant Paul was filed with this

Court for public prosecution with Indictment ( *Suijiangongyisu* No. 165 of 2008 ) on June 30, 2008. After accepting the case, this Court formed a collegial panel in compliance with the law and heard the case in public sessions. Prosecutor Ning Yongcong assigned by the People's Procuratorate of Guangzhou, Guangdong, the People's Republic of China appeared in court to support public prosecution. The interpreter Hong ×× entrusted by this Court and assigned by Guangzhou Talent Translation Services Co. , Ltd. worked as the court interpreter. The defendant Paul and his defense counsels Chen Qiuyun and Zeng Lixia participated in the court proceedings. The trial of the case has been concluded. //

The People's Procuratorate of Guangzhou, Guangdong, the People's Republic of China accused that: //

In November 2007, the defendant Paul had a dispute with the employer of the victim Martins Ekemezie ( hereinafter referred to as Martins ) Collins arising from payment for goods. On the evening of December 10, 2007, the defendant Paul found the victim Martins in the vicinity of Yixin Building in Baiyun District, Guangzhou, Guangdong, the People's Republic of China, requesting the latter to call and ask Collins to come over to discuss the payment for goods. However, Collins failed to make his presence. The defendant Paul, in collusion with others, took the victim Martins to a rented apartment, to wit, Apartment ×××, 2 Alley 25, Taoyuan St ( W ), Shima Village, Junhe St, Baiyun District, Guangzhou, and requested such victim again to contact Collins for payment. During that period, the defendant Paul and others battered the victim Martins and tied up his hands and feet with wires and other articles. Not until at around 7:00 on December 11, 2007 did the victim Martins, taking the opportunity when the defendant Paul was off guard, called passengers downstairs for help. Thereafter, the police who heard about the incident rescued the victim Martins and captured the defendant Paul in the meantime. //

For the purpose of proving the aforesaid facts, the public prosecution department presented or read in court the following evidence: inter alia, the statement of the victim Martins, the depositions of the witnesses, the on-the-spot inspection record and photographs, the Statement on the Process of Capture and Seizure, the Case Report Registration Form, the Forensic Medical Examination Report, the passport held by the defendant, and the confession of the defendant. Relying on the aforesaid evidence, the public prosecution department maintains that the defendant Paul illegally confined another person for the purpose for getting reimbursed for loans in violation of Paragraph 3 Article 238 of *the Criminal Law of the People's Republic of China*, and committed the crime of drug smuggling. It submitted the case to this Court for judgment in compliance with the law. //

The defendant Paul holds no objection to the charged facts but claims that he had no intent to bind and fasten the victim. //

The defense counsel defends as follows: Firstly, the defendant did not have the intent to illegally confine the victim. The victim agreed to discuss payment of the loans at the defendant's home. Secondly, the defendant had confined the victim for only two hours, so his acts do not constitute a crime due to the short period. Thirdly, the defendant and the victim had only "physical collision" which shall not be deemed as battery as defined in the criminal law. Fourthly, the defendant's binding the hands of the victim was an extreme self-defense with a probable cause, and he voluntarily loosened the victim after one hour. Such circumstance shall not be rigidly regarded as "binding and fastening" in illegal confinement. To sum up, the acts of the defendant constitute common illegal confinement under Article 40 of *the Penalty Law of Public Security Administration* and are not a crime due to slightly harmful circumstances. //

Upon examination, the facts are ascertained as follows: //

In November 2007, the defendant Paul had a dispute with the employer of the victim Martins Ekemezie (hereinafter referred to as Martins) Collins arising from payment for goods. On the evening of December 10, 2007, the defendant Paul found the victim Martins in the vicinity of Yixin Building in Baiyun District, Guangzhou, Guangdong, the People's Republic of China, requesting the latter to call and ask Collins to come over to discuss the payment for goods. However, Collins failed to make his presence. The defendant Paul, in collusion with others, took the victim Martins to a rented apartment, to wit, Apartment ×××, 2 Alley 25, Taoyuan St (W), Shima Village, Junhe St, Baiyun District, Guangzhou, and requested such victim again to contact Collins for payment. During that period, the defendant Paul and others battered the victim Martins and tied up his hands and feet with wires and other articles. Not until at around 7 : 00 on December 11, 2007 did the victim Martins, taking the opportunity when the defendant Paul was off guard, called passengers downstairs for help. Thereafter, the police who heard about the incident rescued the victim Martins and captured the defendant Paul in the meantime. //

The aforesaid facts are proved by the following evidence which was read or presented by the public prosecution department, challenged by the prosecuting and defending parties in court and confirmed to be authentic by this Court. //

1. The Registration Form on Accepting a Case Report, the Statement on the Process of Capture and Seizure, and the Statement of Facts all issued by Baiyun Branch of the Public Security Bureau of Guangzhou prove the following facts: at 7 : 13 on December 11, 2007, such Branch received a case report by 110 that a foreigner was kidnapped at Taoyuan St (W), Shima Village, Junhe St, Baiyun District. The public security officers immediately arrived at the crime scene in Apartment ×××, 2 Alley 25, Taoyuan St (W), Shima Village, Junhe St, Baiyun District and ordered the person inside such apartment to open the door. After the defendant Paul opened the door, the public security officers rescued the victim Martins and captured the defendant Paul. //

2. The On – the – Spot Inquest and Examination Record [ *Suigongyunxing* ( *jikan* ) *zi* No. 2757 of 2007] issued by and the photographs of the crime scene provided by Baiyun Branch of the Public Security Bureau of Guangzhou prove that the crime scene was located in Apartment ×××, 2 Alley 25, Taoyuan St (W), Shima Village, Junhe St, Baiyun District, Guangzhou where such imprints and physical evidence as seventeen samples of fingerprints, two leather belts, one bundle of wires, one shaver, one zipper, and one plug plate were collected.

3. The photographs of the wires collected from the crime scene were signed by the defendant Paul in confirmation that the wires therein were used by him to bind and fasten the victim Martins. //

4. The Report on Forensic Medical Examination of Living Body [ *Suigongxingji* ( *fayi* ) No. 172 of 2007] issued by the Criminal Technology Office of the Criminal Police Detachment under the Public Security Bureau of Guangzhou proves that upon

examination, the under-skin bleeding on the chest and back as well as the fresh crust on the elbow joint of the victim Martins were all caused by blunt force and do not constitute serious or minor injury. //

5. The Statement on Investigation issued by Baiyun Branch of the Public Security Bureau of Guangzhou proves the following facts: the owner of the housing at 2 Alley 25, Taoyuan St (W), Shima Village, Junhe St, Baiyun District, Guangzhou was Chen Moutang, and lessee of such apartment was the witness Xiang Mou'er who without obtaining the agreement of the owner, subleased such housing for lodging business. After the crime, Xiang Mou'er was put into administrative detention for fifteen days due to his failure to obtain a license for lodging business, but his whereabouts remain unknown at present. //

6. The passport held by the defendant proves his identity including his nationality. //

7. The statement of the victim Martins was as follows: at around 20:00 on December 10, 2007, he was on the road opposite to Yixin Building in Sanyuanli, Guangzhou when five men surrounded him. Obiagu, one of the five men, asked him to call Collins who said he would come. But Collins failed to make his presence after he had waited for him for two hours. At around 2:00, the five men took him to their residence by taxi. He, Obigagu and Emeka were in one taxi, and Animal Skin, Ogbnugu and an unknown man were in another taxi. Upon arrival in the rented residence of Obiagu, they again asked him to call Collins and ask him to bring money, saying that Collins owned them nine thousand US dollars. He was pushed into the bathroom. Obiagu and Emeka bound his hands and feet with wires and leather belts. They also took off his clothes and watered him with cold water. They slapped him in the fact twice. Emeka put a knife on his neck, saying that he would kill him if he did not return money. Emeka even burned his penis with a lighter. Later, he slept. He found that Obiagu had returned to his home and slept when he woke up, and that others were not in. He then heard someone walking downstairs, so he cried loudly for help. Some Chinese people heard his cry. About five minutes later, Chinese policemen arrived, and they rescued him and took him and Obiagu back to the public security department. When the policemen knocked at the door, Obiagu had no

choice but open the door. He cut off the wires and leather belts with a knife before the policemen came into the apartment. He was robbed of one thousand three hundred yuan, the passport and a Nokia mobile phone. Collins did business in second-hand mobile phones in Guangzhou, and he worked for Collins. He did not own Obiagu any money. Obiagu once had a transaction in mobile phones with Collins, but he did not know the details of the transaction. When he was bound, Obiagu told him that Collins owned him nine thousand US dollars. He jumped from the bathroom to the balcony and shouted to passengers for help. He showed passengers his two hands which were tied up, and the passengers saw his two hands tied up. //

Upon photograph identification, he identified the defendant Paul as Obiagu. //

8. The witness Charles Yeboah testified as follows: he was also named Collins. He did business in mobile phones in Guangzhou. He ran Shop 233, Ershatou Second-Hand Mobile Phone Market, Guangzhou. Martins helped him sell mobile phones in the shop. Paul was from Ghana and was his customer. One month before, Paul came to his shop and purchased 800 counterfeited Nokia mobile phones at wholesale price, and Paul gave him twenty thousand US dollars. Such 800 counterfeited mobile phones were confiscated by the police at Baiyun Airport when Paul was going to take them to Ghana. Paul asked him for a refund, and he returned to him ten thousand US dollars, saying that the rest ten thousand US dollars would be returned later. Afterwards, Paul frequently called him, asking for the refund, and he said it would take him some time but promised to return such money. Martins was present when he conducted such transaction with Paul, while Martins was only his employee. On the evening of December 10, 2007, Martins had a dispute with Paul. Paul caught Martins and confined the latter. Martins called him, asking him to meet them, but he did not know the exact place. Later, he saw them two at Baiyun Junhe Police Substation. When Martins was kidnapped, he did not answer any phone call from Martins or Paul. //

Upon photograph identification, he identified the defendant Paul as the one who had a dispute with him and kidnapped Martins. //

9. The witness Zhou Mouxiang testified as follows: at around 7∶00 on December 11, 2007, he and his coworker heard cry for help from the balcony on the fourth

floor when they passed 2 Alley 25, Taoyuan St (W), Shima Village, Baiyun District, but they could not understand it. He and others looked up and saw a foreign black man crying for help, without upper clothes on and with hands bound on his back, but they saw nobody beside such foreign black man. Several minutes later, another black man walked to the balcony, taking the crying black man back to the room. They thought someone wanted to jump from the building for the moment, so he called 110 with his mobile phone to report the case and remained downstairs to see what would happen. About more than ten minutes later, two policemen and more than ten security guards arrived. One of the security guards opened the door to the stairway, and the policemen and security guards went upstairs together. About more than ten minutes later, the policemen took two black men downstairs, and one of the black men wore handcuffs. The policemen then left. //

10. The witness Xiang Mou'er testified as follows: in June 2007, he rented two buildings at 2 Alley 25, Taoyuan St (W), Shima Village from the owner Chen Weitang. He then subleased and used such buildings for lodging business. In October 2007, a foreign black man rented Apartment ××× of Building 2 and provided him with the photocopy of his passport. At 7:00 on December 11, 2007, some foreigners had a fight in the aforesaid Apartment ×××, and policemen arrived at the spot to investigate the case. //

11. The confession of the defendant Paul was as follows: about two weeks before, he introduced Jude to the partner of Martins Collins for mobile phone business. Jude remitted nine thousand US dollars to Collins, but Collins failed to deliver the goods after he received the money and even hid himself from them. In order to ask Collins to return money, he asked Martins to look for Collins so as to solve the problem. At around 23:00 on December 10, 2007, he saw Martins talking to two black men in Yixin Building in Baiyun District. Those two black men also knew him. He then went up to them to find out the whereabouts of Collins. Probably because the two sides quarreled with each other loudly, some black men from the next store came out and surrounded them. Two of such black men knew him, so they six discussed how to find Collins and solve the problem. Martins called Collins, and the latter agreed to meet them. However, they did not see Collins show up after wait-

ing for more than two hours, so they six took two taxis to his residence to wait for Collins. Collins did not come after they arrived at his residence. At around 3：00, he asked Martins to call Collins again, but Martins did not agree to do so, saying that he did not know Collins. He slapped Martins in his face twice. Martins' two friends asked him not to batter him. At that moment, Martins attempted to jump from the window, and the other two black men held him immediately. In order to prevent Martins from jumping, he found two types of wires in black and white color and bound the hands and feet of Martins with them. At around 5：00, he went back to his bedroom to sleep, and the other black men left in succession. At around 7：00 on December 11, policemen came upstairs and took him and Martins back to the police station for investigation. He did not take anything away from Martins. Martins said that he had given his belongs to his friends for safekeeping in Yixin Building, and such belongs included one thousand two hundred yuan. He did not water Martins with cold water, nor did he threaten him with a knife. He did not burn Martins' penis with a lighter, either. //

Upon photograph identification, he identified the victim Martins. //

This Court holds that the defendant Paul, disregarding the law of the People's Republic of China, illegally confined anther person for the purpose of getting reimbursed for loans, and that his acts constitute the crime of illegal confinement, so he shall be punished by the law. This Court finds the defendant guilty of the crime charged by the public prosecution department with clearly ascertained facts. The defense counsel of the defendant Paul opines that the criminal circumstances were obviously slight, and the acts of the defendant shall be deemed as a common offence but not a crime. As to such opinion, this Court, upon examination, holds as follows: the defendant, for the purpose of getting reimbursed by the witness Collins for loans, illegally confined the victim Martins. During confinement, he battered and bound the victim. The defendant asked for payment of loans with the method of depriving another person of his personal freedom, causing serious harm to society, so he shall be found guilty of illegal confinement and investigated for criminal liability. Therefore, the aforesaid defense is groundless and dismissed by the Court. In accordance with Paragraphs 1 and 3 of Article 6, Paragraphs 1 and 3 of Article 238, and Article 35 of *the Criminal Law of the People's Republic of China*, the judgment is hereby entered as follows: //

The defendant Paul is guilty of illegal confinement and is sentenced to a fixed term imprisonment of one year, and concurrently to deportation upon expiration of the sentence. (The term of imprisonment is counted from and upon the enforcement date of the judgment. In the case of detention prior to execution, one day in detention is deemed as one day in prison. To wit, the term commences as of December 11, 2007 and expires on December 10, 2008.) //

Where the defendant refuses to accept the present judgment as final and binding, he or she may appeal to the Higher People's Court of Guangdong directly or though this Court within ten days commencing on but not including the date when the judgment is received. The original petition for appeal together with two duplicates thereof is required to be turned in the case of a written appeal. //

Presiding Judge: DYK

Acting Judge: AAA

Acting Judge: CCC

This twenty-second day of August two thousand and eight (2008)

(Seal of the Court)

This duplicate is verified as identical to the original.

Clerks: ×××//

In case of any discrepancy between the original and the translated version, the original shall prevail. //

# V. 句子精炼 Sentences in Focus

**Directions**: *Interpret the following sentences alternatively into English or Chinese*:

1. Where there is any claim for compensation within the scope of insurance liability, the insurance company can refuse to extend compensation only under circumstances explicitly prescribed by the relevant law and insurance contract that merit exemption of liability.

2. The confession of the defendant Paul was as follows: about two weeks before, he introduced Jude to the partner of Martins Collins for mobile phone business. Jude remitted nine thousand US dollars to Collins, but Collins failed to deliver the goods after he received the money and even hid himself from them. In order to ask Collins to return money, he asked Martins to look for Collins so as to solve the problem.

3. This Court holds that the defendant Paul, disregarding the law of the People's Republic of China, illegally confined anther person for the purpose of getting reimbursed for loans, and that his acts constitute the crime of illegal confinement, so he shall be punished by the law.

4. This Court finds the defendant guilty of the crime charged by the public prosecution department with clearly ascertained facts. The defense counsel of the defendant Paul opines that the criminal circumstances were obviously slight, and the acts of the defendant shall be deemed as a common offence but not a crime.

5. As to such opinion, this Court, upon examination, holds as follows: the defendant, for the purpose of getting reimbursed by the witness Collins for loans, illegally confined the victim Martins. During confinement, he battered and bound the victim.

6. The defendant asked for payment of loans with the method of depriving another person of his personal freedom, causing serious harm to society, so he shall be found guilty of illegal confinement and investigated for criminal liability.

7. Therefore, the aforesaid defense is groundless and dismissed by the Court. In accordance with Paragraphs 1 and 3 of Article 6, Paragraphs 1 and 3 of Article 238, and Article 35 of *the Criminal Law of the People's Republic of China*, the judgment is hereby entered as follows:

8. Where the defendant refuses to accept the present judgment as final and binding, he or she may appeal to the Higher People's Court of Guangdong directly or though this Court within ten days commencing on but not including the date when the judgment is received. The original petition for appeal together with two duplicates thereof is required to be turned in the case of a written appeal.

# 法庭调查（英美法系）

**Unit 9 Court Examination
(The Common–law System)**

# Ⅰ. 专题知识 Legal Knowledge

英美法系国家法庭审判的主要活动是法庭调查。此调查程序不同于大陆法系国家，不由法官直接询问当事人或证人，而是在法官的主持下由双方当事人的律师通过直接调查、证据出示和交叉调查等方式来完成。法庭调查的程序，首先是由原告（或刑事案件的检察官）传唤自己一方的证人出庭，并对其询问，由其提供证人证言，即直接调查（Direct Examination）。在直接调查中，有时为了加强证人证言的说服力，律师还会出示其他证据材料（Exhibit），并就此向证人发问。对于原告一方（或刑事案件的检察官），直接调查完毕后，请求法院允许其向证人提问，以削弱其已提供的证据的证明力。这种询问方式被称为交叉调查（Cross Examination）。在原告对其所有证人进行调查、所有证据材料出示完毕后，被告可以开始其直接调查程序，就自己一方的证人进行询问，并出示相关证据材料。如果原告认为有必要，可以请求交叉调查。在民事案件中，如果律师进行直接调查，那么第一位接受询问的是被告本人，然后是其他证人。直接调查和交叉调查充分体现了英美法系国家抗辩式审判方式的特点。

## 一、直接调查（Direct Examination）

直接调查是律师对本方证人提问的程序。证人证言是此诉讼程序的核心。使自己一方的证人证言更加可信，就是律师诉前准备的主要工作。经过充分准备的直接调查可以起到良好的抗辩效果，使陪审团对证人证言产生深刻印象和高度信任。为了提高证人证言的可信度，在询问中须注意以下问题：提问要简单明确，因为陪审团并不是法律专业人士。比如，在向陪审团介绍证人的背景时，律师就不会提问："请您介绍一下您的姓名、住址、工作背景、教育背景和家庭情况。"而是就每个问题逐个提问，个别问题与本案有密切关系的，还可以详细追问。

提问要有逻辑性。询问证人的过程也是向陪审团复原案件的过程，为了使案件复原的效果更加贴近真实的案情，使陪审员内心确信自己一方证人对案件事实的陈述，证人出场顺序的安排同样关系重大。证人出场的顺序一定要讲求逻辑性。一般来讲，从介绍背景开始，顺次安排证人介绍案发现场情景、案发经过、案发结果、损害的补救等情况。

在询问证人时，要注重于解决陪审团脑海中的疑问。面对一个证人，陪审团首先会有疑问："他是谁？""他为什么在现场？""我为什么要相信他？"所以，介绍证人背景可以主要从这几个方面入手。从证人自我介绍入手，转入介绍证人在现场及其在场的原因，最后结合案情询问一些问题，以增加陪审团对证人的信任度。

在介绍案发现场情景时，最好首先通过询问证人来进行，而不是首先展示照片等资料。证人的描述可以加深陪审团的印象。资料、图片等使用的目的在于加强、补充证人证言的可信度。在直接调查完毕后展示这些资料不但不会打断证人询问，还可以起到总结和重述的作用。

禁止使用诱导性问题（leading questions）提问。虽然律师希望证人按照自己的期望回答问题，但是证人有自由作证的权利，律师的提问如果带有诱导性，就会限制证人的自由度。比如，律师问道："你在案发现场看到的人是一个身高 1.7 米左右，25 岁左右的男士吗？"对这个问题，证人只能回答是或不是，陪审团不能从中得到更多的信息。所以，正确的提问方式为："你在案发现场看到了什么样的人，请你描述一下。"

在询问过程中，为了使陪审团的注意力集中于证人身上，律师的站位非常重要。为了突出证人的重要性，律师一般不在法庭上来回走动，转移陪审团的注意力，而是要么站在律师席上提问，要么站在陪审席的尾部提问。

在介绍证人出场时，常用的表达方式为："Your Honor, we'll call Mr. X as our first（or next）witness."接着，法庭工作人员就会在大厅外传唤证人 X 出台作证。

## 二、证据出示（Exhibit）

### 1. 证据材料的准备

在对证人的直接调查完毕后，律师可以出示其他证据材料，以加强证据的说服力。证据材料要提交给法庭书记员，由书记员做标记，表明提供方、证据号和提供时间。证据一般按照组编号，一组为一号，一组中有数份证据材料的，可以再细分为 1A、1B、1C 等。比如，如果是原告提供的证据则表明："Plaintiff's Exhibit # 1"；如果是被告提供的则表明："Defendant's Exhibit # 1"等。

### 2. 出示证据材料

（1）向对方律师出示。当事人任何一方在庭审中出示的证据都必须事先向对方出示，以便对方提出反驳意见。如果证据事先没有向对方出示过，则有必要在阐明证据的内容和所要证明的事实之前，首先将此份证据材料送交对方律师，使其有机会检查或阅读。同时，出示的每一份证据都要说明所要证明的事实，以便对方了解证据材料的用途，也便于法庭记录。通常来讲，律师在出示每一份证据材料时，都要首先告知对方律师其要出示的证据的编号。

（2）向证人出示。Exhibit 的法律含义不同于 Evidence，在法官确认其为证据（Evidence）之前，Exhibit 不是法律意义上的证据。由于陪审团只对证据进行审查，在审查证据的基础上根据举证责任和证明规则的有关规定作出判决，所以在 Exhibit 被认定为证据之前，不可以向陪审团出示。律师根据 Exhibit 向证人提问时，最好不要让陪审团看见，以免扰乱陪审团的视听。向证人出示 Exhibit 时可以作如下表述：

**Counsel**：Mr. X, I am handing you Plaintiff's Exhibit # 1. (walk to the witness and hand it to him or place it in front of him)

律师向证人出示完有关材料之后，为了证明所出示的证据具有证据效力，要向证人提问。一份材料是否具有证据效力主要看其所提供的证据与所要证明的问题之间是否有关联性和真实性。此时，为了使陪审团的注意力集中于证人，律师一般会站在陪审席的尾部提问。

（3）向陪审团出示。如果 Exhibit 经法官认可可以被作为证据使用，那么就要出示给陪审团，由陪审团进行审核。如果 Exhibit 的篇幅不长，律师可以读给陪审团，如果篇幅很长，可以在出示的同时简要归纳一下其主要内容。将 Exhibit 交付陪审团之后，律师可以站在证人席的旁边，面对陪审团向证人提问。陪审团出示证据材料的常见表达方式为：

**Counsel**：Your Honor, we offer Plaintiff Exhibit # 1 in evidence.

**Court**：Any objects, counsel?

**Opposing Counsel**：Yes, your Honor. It's Hearsay.

**Court**：The objection is overruled. Plaintiff Exhibit #1 is admitted.

**Counsel**：Your Honor, may we show Plaintiff's Exhibit # 1 in evidence to the jury at this time?

**Court**：You may.

**Counsel**：Ladies and Gentlemen, Plaintiff Exhibit # 1 reads as follows：（then read）

### 三、直接调查（Direct Examination）

交叉调查是指在律师对自己一方证人进行调查后，如果对方律师认为有必要，经法官允许对该证人进行的调查程序。交叉调查的目的：一方面在于使对方证人承认一些对自己有利的事实，另一方面在于削弱对方证人在直接询问中提供的证言的证明力。所以，律师在启动交叉调查程序时必须有的放矢，起到"以其人之矛，攻其人之盾"的效果。

虽然交叉调查可以起到极强的对抗效果，但是如果考虑不周，也可能会弄巧成拙，使陪审团增强对对方的信任度而丧失对本方的信心。所以，如果对方证人证言没有危及本方立场，不要交叉调查，以免给其补救的机会；如果对方证人证言证明力极强，自己一方无法战胜，也不要交叉调查。

与直接调查不同，交叉调查要多使用诱导性问题（leading questions），使对方证人的回答朝着本方期待的方向发展，而不能给其太多的自由度。在证人的回答实现了本方的目的，证实了本方需要其说明的问题后，律师要适时结束提问，并向陪审团总结本方通过此轮交叉提问得出的主要结论。

在交叉调查中，律师最好站在陪审团的正前方，使陪审团的注意力集中到自己身上，因为律师在此程序中要起到主角的作用，要控制整个局面，尤其是控制住证人的思维。

### 四、提出反驳（Objection）

在法庭调查过程中，如果律师认为对方律师的提问不适当或者带有偏见，可以随时向法官提出反驳。法官对该项反驳审核后，如果认为提问是不正当的，则要告知陪审团对律师刚材的提问不予考虑或对证人刚才的回答不予考虑；如果认为律师的提问是正当的，则驳回反驳。

提出反驳的方式。反驳的提出必须及时。如果律师一发现对方的提问违法或不当，就应当在对方问题结束后及时提出反驳。不过，如果对方的问题明显带有偏见或不当，则可以在其提问结束之前就打断其提问并表示反驳。此外，反驳的表述须明确，首先说明有反驳，然后再简要解释反驳的理由和根据。而不是先讲理由，然后才表示反驳。比如：

**Opposing counsel**：Objection，Your Honor. The question calls for a hearsay answer.

或：

**Opposing counsel**：Your Honor，we object to the hearsay answer.

或：

**Opposing counsel**：Objection，hearsay.

如果法官认为反驳理由合理，法官会说："Objection sustained."或"Sustained."如果法官认为反驳不合理，则会说："Objection overruled."

对反驳的理由应当进行简要陈述，以便陪审团清晰掌握。比如，对于传来证据的反驳，只要讲"Objection，hearsay"即足矣。对于明显的理由，法官当即就可以作出判断。如果反驳的理由在问题中体现得不明显，需要作详细的解释，则律师可以走到法官跟前，低声向法官陈述，以免陪审团听到，因为这是法律问题而非事实问题，无须陪审团裁决。这种方式被称为"side-bar conference"。必要时，法官还可以宣布陪审团暂时退庭，然后听取律师的意见。

## II．词汇热身 Vocabulary Warm-up

**Directions**：*Give the English equivalents of the following Chinese expressions*：

Acquittal                                              Challenge for cause

Closing argument                    Overrule

Cross-examination                   Parole

Guilty plea                         Peremptory challenge

Alford Jury                         Plea agreement

Jury selection                      Presumption of innocence

Leading question                    Subpoena

Motion for judgment of acquittal    Sustain

Objection                           Voir dire

# Ⅲ. 课文口译 Text for Interpreting

## ◆ *Passage 1*

**Directions**: *Listen to the passage and interpret from English into Chinese at the end of each segment.*

（案情简介：这是一起谋杀案的法庭辩论，在圣诞前夜兴冲冲地跑回家想给丈夫惊喜的被告人却发现丈夫偷情。当晚警察就接到被告人的报案，丈夫和情妇双双被射杀在床上，种种证据表明是谋杀，系被告人所为，而被告人却仿佛真的不相关，对当晚发生之事的记忆仿佛被抹平了。真相到底是什么？）

**ADA John Shubert**: She came home that evening at 9:30, catching an early flight to surprise her husband. But it was the defendant who was surprised. Susan May discovered her husband Ralph making love to a business associate, Marie Holcomb—and it was more than she could bear. The evidence will show that the defendant retrieved a handgun from the kitchen, returned to the bedroom and fired six shots—three into her husband, three into Marie Holcomb. This is the holiday season. You people should be home with your families right now. I apologize for that. Marie Holcomb's mother and father fly here every December from the West Coast. This time, it's to attend the trial of their daughter's killer. Susan May destroyed a lot of happy plans with that gun. //

**Brad Chase**: Get in Christmas. //

**Lori Colson**: Sorry? //

**Brad Chase**: Christmas is ours and Susan's. Don't let him claim it. //

**Lori Colson**: I, too, would like to apologize for taking you away from your families during this holiday season. That's Susan's family seated over there. They would dearly love to be home with her. She would dearly love to be home with them. Imagine, if you can as you prepare for your Christmas, having a loved one murdered. Add to that the horror that the police can't figure out who did it. And then, if you can possibly fathom, imagine they decide to arrest you. That's your defendant, ladies and gentlemen. A law-abiding, loving, faithful advertising executive—an innocent woman whose whole life was just suddenly and wrongly destroyed. That's your defendant, and that's what the evidence will show. //

◆ *Passage 2*

**Directions**: *Listen to the passage and interpret from English into Chinese at the end of each segment.*

（案情简介：律师通过交叉询问，削弱检察官的证据证明力度，加强自身证据的证明力度，引导陪审团朝着有利于自己代理人利益的方向去思考。在"如山铁证"面前，布拉德避实就虚，寻求突破，将公诉人的有利证据各个击破。）

**Detective Wayne Farley**: Her story didn't check out. It's as simple as that. //

**ADA John Shubert**: That story she gave you was? //

**Detective Wayne Farley**: She came home, found them dead in bed. //

**ADA John Shubert**: Was there evidence of anyone other than the victims or the defendant being in the house that night? //

**Detective Wayne Farley**: None. //

**ADA John Shubert**: And, Detective, describe for the jury if you can, the defendant's demeanor when you arrived at the scene that night. //

**Detective Wayne Farley**: She seemed pretty shook up. There was blood all over her. She claimed she got the blood on her when she went to her husband's side to see if she could revive him. //

**ADA John Shubert**：And you don't believe that? //

**Lori Colson**：I'm sorry. It seems the detective is more than willing to give testimony against my client. You don't really need to lead him. //

**Judge Phillips Stevens**：Sustained. //

**ADA John Shubert**：Did you believe the defendant's claim? //

**Detective Wayne Farley**：No. It was determined that she was standing approximately five feet away when she fired the gun. //

**Lori Colson**：I'm sorry. I hate to be a nuisance. But did I miss the point where you said she fired the gun? //

**Judge Phillip Stevens**：Sustained. //

**ADA John Shubert**：Detective, what, if anything led you to believe that the defendant fired the gun? //

**Detective Wayne Farley**：We did a trace metal test, which revealed she held the gun and her fingerprints were on the gun. //

**ADA John Shubert**：Hm. Anything else? //

**Detective Wayne Farley**：We know her driver dropped her off at 21：30. She called the police at 23：07. She told us she discovered the bodies soon after she entered the house. If so, why did she wait an hour and a half to call the police? As I said, her story just didn't add up. //

**Brad Chase**：Seems from your tone, Detective, you consider this, ah, kind of a no-brainer. //

**Detective Wayne Farley**：We applied all our mental faculties just the same and concluded your client committed the crime. //

**Brad Chase**：Oh, you concluded pretty quickly, I might add. You placed her under arrest the next day. By the way, was the spatter analysis done in a day? //

**Detective Wayne Farley**：No. That came in later. //

**Brad Chase**：I see. So when you placed Susan May under arrest, you were going on ... //

**Detective Wayne Farley**：Her fingerprints were on the gun, for starters. //

**Brad Chase**：It was her gun, was it not? //

**Detective Wayne Farley**：The fingerprints were fresh. //

**Brad Chase:** Got there, perhaps, when she picked the gun up after? //

**Detective Wayne Farley:** We also had motive, her evasive demeanor. //

**Brad Chase:** She called the police, did she not? //

**Detective Wayne Farley:** Yes, but she wasn't truthful. //

**Brad Chase:** Wasn't truthful when she said she didn't shoot them? //

**Detective Wayne Farley:** That, and she obviously wasn't truthful about calling the police immediately after finding the bodies. //

**Brad Chase:** You had her examined by a psychiatrist that night? //

**Detective Wayne Farley:** Yes. //

**Brad Chase:** The psychiatrist said she was in shock? //

**Detective Wayne Farley:** Yes. //

**Brad Chase:** Possible the shock of discovering her murdered husband caused the delay in calling the police? //

**Detective Wayne Farley:** I doubt that's what happened. //

**Brad Chase:** This doubt is based on your psychiatric training? //

**Detective Wayne Farley:** It's based on 30 years of experience as a homicide detective. //

**Brad Chase:** Thirty years as a homicide detective told you that the delay in calling the police could not have been caused by shock? Picks up a large photograph mounted on a board. Let's turn back to the blood spatter evidence. This is the blouse my client was wearing that evening, is it not? //

**Detective Wayne Farley:** Yes. //

**Brad Chase:** Lot of blood. That's all spattering? //

**Detective Wayne Farley:** Most of that blood came from handling the bodies. //

**Brad Chase:** So where's the spatter you spoke of, Detective? //

**Detective Wayne Farley:** There are two elongated markings on the left shoulder. //

**Brad Chase:** Right here? These tiny marks here? //

**Detective Wayne Farley:** Yes. //

**Brad Chase:** She supposedly fired six shots. There's only two tiny marks? //

**Detective Wayne Farley:** The other marks are likely covered up with the blood from when she handled the bodies. //

**Brad Chase**：Did you analyze these marks yourself, Detective? //

**Detective Wayne Farley**：I did. //

**Brad Chase**：Are you the person in the Boston Police Department who does this? //

**Detective Wayne Farley**：Well, there are others, obviously, but I started in the lab, so I'm trained as well. //

**Brad Chase**：Was there anyone else in the lab who analyzed this shirt? //

**Detective Wayne Farley**：Yes. We have a junior member ... //

**Brad Chase**：Junior member? It's a high-profile case. It went to a junior member? //

**Detective Wayne Farley**：As I said, I analyzed the clothes with my 30 years ... //

**Brad Chase**：Thirty years in the lab? //

**Detective Wayne Farley**：No. //

**Brad Chase**：How many years in the lab? //

**Detective Wayne Farley**：Five. //

**Brad Chase**：How about the junior member? How many years did he have? //

**Detective Wayne Farley**：I'm not sure. //

**Brad Chase**：More than five? //

**Detective Wayne Farley**：I believe so. //

**Brad Chase**：Just out of curiosity, what was his finding? //

**Detective Wayne Farley**：Inconclusive. //

**Brad Chase**：He could not determine that my client fired a gun? //

**Detective Wayne Farley**：Nor could he rule it out. //

**Brad Chase**：He could not determine that my client fired a gun. //

**Detective Wayne Farley**：Correct. But I determined she did. //

**Brad Chase**：You trace-metalled my client. Did you test for powder residue on her hand? //

**Detective Wayne Farley**：Yes. She tested negative. //

**Brad Chase**：Gee, how could that be?

**Detective Wayne Farley**：We determined that she likely wore gloves when she fired the gun. //

**Brad Chase**: So she was careful to wear gloves when she shot them, then afterwards, she took the gloves off and handled the gun? //

**Detective Wayne Farley**: If she went into shock, as you say, she probably made a mistake. Murderers often do. //

**Brad Chase**: So for the purpose of explaining the delay in calling the police, you don't buy shock. But to explain why she picked up the murder weapon barehanded after firing with gloves, you do buy shock; in fact, you seem to be selling it. //

**ADA John Shubert**: Objection. //

**Brad Chase**: Withdrawn. Did you find the gloves? //

**Detective Wayne Farley**: No. //

**Brad Chase**: You searched the entire house? I'm asking. I don't want to presume. //

**Detective Wayne Farley**: We searched the house. We did not find the gloves. //

**Brad Chase**: Any evidence of her leaving the house after she came home that night? //

**Detective Wayne Farley**: No. //

**Brad Chase**: Any unsolved burglaries in this neighborhood in the last year? //

**Detective Wayne Farley**: A couple. //

### ◆ *Passage 3*

**Directions**: *Listen to the passage and interpret from English into Chinese at the end of each segment.*

（案情简介：某大型制药公司为研制某种特效药而招募了一些志愿者接受药物测试，其中有一名中年妇女因为公司指责她没有遵守服药规则而被排除，勒令禁止再参加测试。而这位妇女却十分依赖这种药物，并且声称自己完全遵守了服药准则。）

**Marybeth Hewitt**: I've had type II diabetes since I was 25. It's been the same medicines pretty much the whole time. //

**Atty. Greg Montero**：And when you were invited to participate in a clinical trial of SV113, what did your daily regimen become? //

**Marybeth Hewitt**：I took one pill in the morning when I woke up. //

**Atty. Greg Montero**：That's all? //

**Marybeth Hewitt**：That was it. I had more energy. I was even losing weight. And no more needles. It was a godsend, until they took it away. //

**Atty. Greg Montero**：And how did that happen? //

**Marybeth Hewitt**：My doctor told me that the company had kicked me off the test. He said that I had broken the rules of the trial, but I didn't. I didn't do anything wrong. //

**Atty. Greg Montero**：And after you were taken off the test? //

**Marybeth Hewitt**：My health deteriorated again rapidly. //

**Atty. Greg Montero**：Can you tell us your prognosis today? //

**Marybeth Hewitt**：I'm dying. I've got probably five to six years, unless something changes drastically. //

**Alan Shore**：What reason did the company give for removing you from the SV113 study? //

**Marybeth Hewitt**：Noncompliance. But I complied. //

**Alan Shore**：You're a heavy smoker. Is that correct, Mrs. Hewitt? //

**Marybeth Hewitt**：I quit. //

**Alan Shore**：When did you quit, if I may ask? //

**Marybeth Hewitt**：A week before the study. //

**Alan Shore**：Just like that? Two packs a day, cold turkey? //

**Marybeth Hewitt**：My life depended on it. //

**Alan Shore**：Some of the doctors and clinicians, uh, smelled cigarette smoke on you during your exams. //

**Marybeth Hewitt**：My husband's a chain smoker. It was his smoke they smelled on my clothes. //

**Alan Shore**：Amazing. You smoked two packs a day, you live with a chain smoker, and you're able to just quit, cold turkey. //

**Atty. Greg Montero**：Objection. //

**Judge Dale Wallace**: Sustained. //

**Alan Shore**: Mrs. Hewitt, 177 million people in the world have diabetes. This drug study is the only way to get SV113—the drug you yourself called a godsend—approved for sale. 177 million people are counting on you to follow the rules, Mrs. Hewitt. //

**Marybeth Hewitt**: Which I did. //

**Alan Shore**: With the stakes being so enormously high, with some 70 thousand people dying every year from diabetes, with a desperate need to develop a drug that can save those lives, you realize how important it is for my client not to take any chances, don't you? //

**Marybeth Hewitt**: I followed all the rules. //

◆ *Passage 4*

**Directions**: *Listen to the passage and interpret from English into Chinese at the end of each segment.*

(案情简介：控辩双方围绕警官在特殊情形下能否采用"私刑"讯问犯罪嫌疑人这个主题，展开辩论。)

**Officer Joe Garrett**: We had received a tip that the suspect, Damon Harris, was visiting his brother Paul. So we went to the brother's house. //

**A. D. A. Nicholas Preston**: And did you find the suspect? //

**Alan Shore**: Excuse me. I'm new to this case as is the jury of course. To help us track the facts, I was wondering if you could refer to him as the kidnapping suspect so we're clear that we're talking about the man who snatched a six-year-old child. The boy sitting right over here. //

**A. D. A. Nicholas Preston**: Was the kidnapping suspect there, Officer? //

**Officer Joe Garrett**: No. //

**A. D. A. Nicholas Preston**: The brother was there? //

**Officer Joe Garrett**: Yes. //

**A. D. A. Nicholas Preston**: Could you tell us what happened? //

**Officer Joe Garrett**: Well, we searched the premises. Uh, couldn't find the kidnapping suspect. We asked the brother if he knew his whereabouts. He claimed he did not. //

**A. D. A. Nicholas Preston**: And then what happened? //

**Officer Joe Garrett**: What happened is basically what you saw on the tape. My partner began to interrogate the brother. More coercively. //

**A. D. A. Nicholas Preston**: At any time was the victim of this attack considered a suspect himself in the kidnapping? //

**Officer Joe Garrett**: No. //

**A. D. A. Nicholas Preston**: You never considered him connected to the crime? //

**Officer Joe Garrett**: No. //

**Shirley Schmidt**: As Mr. Shore noted, you were trying to find the six-year-old boy seated over here? //

**Officer Joe Garrett**: Yes. //

**Shirley Schmidt**: He was kidnapped how long before this incident? //

**Officer Joe Garrett**: The day before. //

**Shirley Schmidt**: As time goes by what are the chances of finding a kidnapped child alive? //

**Officer Joe Garrett**: After 48 hours, we consider it extremely remote. //

**Shirley Schmidt**: In fact, the kidnapper we're talking about is suspected in the kidnapping of another boy, correct? //

**Officer Joe Garrett**: Yes. //

**Shirley Schmidt**: Did you every find that boy? //

**Officer Joe Garrett**: We found his remains. //

**Shirley Schmidt**: While my client was committing his coercive acts against the brother, what did you do? //

**Officer Joe Garrett**: I stood back. //

**Shirley Schmidt**: You never intervened? //

**Officer Joe Garrett**: No. //

**Shirley Schmidt**: Did you report it? //

**Officer Joe Garrett**: Not at first. Uh, eventually. //

**Shirley Schmidt**: By the way, as a result of my client's physical coercive acts, did the brother tell you anything? //

    **Officer Joe Garrett**：He gave us a list of places his brother would frequent. //

    **Shirley Schmidt**：And did you search those places? //

    **Officer Joe Garrett**：Yes. //

    **Shirley Schmidt**：And? //

    **Officer Joe Garrett**：We found the suspect. And the child. //

# Ⅳ. 参考译文 Reference versions

## ◆ *Passage 1*

    **阿达·约翰·舒伯特（检察官）**：那天晚上她9点半回到家，搭早班飞机来给她丈夫一个惊喜，但是得到"惊喜"的却是被告本人。苏珊·梅发现她的丈夫拉尔夫正和一个生意伙伴马里·浩寇做爱，她一瞬间崩溃了。证据表明被告从厨房拿了一把手枪回到卧室，连开6枪，3枪击中她丈夫，3枪击中马里·浩寇。现在是节日期间，你们应该陪在家人身边，对此我深感抱歉，马里·浩寇的父母每年12月从西海岸飞过来。这次，他们只能参加杀女凶手的审判，因为那把枪，苏珊·梅破坏了太多圣诞节的快乐！//

    **布拉德·蔡斯（律师）**：把重点放到圣诞节。//

    **罗瑞·考森**：什么？//

    **布拉德·蔡斯**：圣诞节是我们，也是苏珊的，别让他一个人抢了。//

    **罗瑞·考森**：我也想道歉，在节日里让你们远离家人，苏珊一家坐在那里，他们本该在家里相亲相爱地陪着她，她也本该在家里相亲相爱地陪着他们！如果可以，请想象一下当你在准备圣诞节时，一个你深爱的人被谋杀了，加上由警察无法找出凶手带来的恐惧，紧接着，如果你能猜到再想象，他们决定来逮捕你！那就是被告的处境。女士们，先生们，一位守法、温柔、诚实的广告部经理，一位生活突遭横祸、被错误指控的无辜女士，那就是你们的被告！这也是证据将会表明的。//

## ◆ *Passage 2*

    **珐里探长**：她的说法不合理，就这么简单。//

阿达·约翰·舒伯特：她告诉你的说法是……∥

珐里探长：她回到家发现他们死在床上。∥

阿达·约翰·舒伯特：有任何证据表明那晚除了被害人和被告，还有其他人在那房子里吗？∥

珐里探长：没有。∥

阿达·约翰·舒伯特：探员先生，可以的话请向陪审团详细描述那晚当你抵达现场时被告的举动。∥

珐里探长：她看上去很震惊，全身都是血，她说是在她到丈夫身边查看他是否还有救时沾上的。∥

阿达·约翰·舒伯特：而你并不相信这一点吗？∥

罗瑞·考森：抱歉，看起来探员先生已经不只是给我当事人做不利证言了，你不需要再误导他。∥

斯蒂文斯法官：反对有效。∥

阿达·约翰·舒伯特：你相信被告的说法吗？∥

珐里探长：不，证据显示当她开枪的时候，大约站在 5 英尺之外。∥

罗瑞·考森：很抱歉，我不想讨人厌，但我是不是漏听了你宣称被告开了枪？∥

斯蒂文斯法官：反对有效。∥

阿达·约翰·舒伯特：探员先生，有什么东西让你相信是被告开的枪吗？∥

珐里探长：我们做过金属痕迹追踪，显示她曾拿过枪，而且枪上也有她的指纹。∥

阿达·约翰·舒伯特：还有别的吗？∥

珐里探长：我们知道司机大约在晚上 9 点 30 分让她下了车，11 点 07 分她报了警，告诉我们她发现了尸体，就在她刚进门不久，如果真是这样为什么她要等上一个半小时才报警？就像我说的，她的故事根本说不通。∥

布拉德·蔡斯：照你所说，探员先生，这故事很没有头脑。∥

珐里探长：我们绞尽脑汁结论还是一样。结论就是：你的当事人就是凶手。∥

布拉德·蔡斯：你们的结论也下得太快了点，第二天就将她拘捕，顺便一问，血液飞溅测试也是同一天进行的？∥

珐里探长：不，那是之后了。//

布拉德·蔡斯：了解，那么当你逮捕苏珊·梅的时候，依据是……//

珐里探长：最开始是因为枪上有她的指纹。

布拉德·蔡斯：枪是她的，不是吗？

珐里探长：枪上的指纹很新。

布拉德·蔡斯：也许是她之后拿枪时留下的？//

珐里探长：我们知道她的动机，还有她掩盖事实的举动。//

布拉德·蔡斯：她报了警，不是吗？//

珐里探长：是的，但是她撒谎了。

布拉德·蔡斯：撒谎说她没有开枪？

珐里探长：还有一发现尸体马上报警，这点她也明显没有说实话。//

布拉德·蔡斯：你那晚让她接受精神科医生的检查了？//

珐里探长：是的。

布拉德·蔡斯：精神科医生说她受了惊吓？

珐里探长：是的。

布拉德·蔡斯：有否可能是发现丈夫尸体的惊吓使她没能及时报警？

珐里探长：我表示怀疑。//

布拉德·蔡斯：这种怀疑是基于你精神科的受训课程？//

珐里探长：是基于30年凶杀案探员的经验。//

布拉德·蔡斯：30年凶杀案探员的经验告诉你，没及时报警不可能是惊吓造成的，那么我们回到血液飞溅实验证据，这是案发时我当事人所穿的衬衫吗？//

珐里探长：是的。//

布拉德·蔡斯：好多血，全是溅开的？//

珐里探长：大部分是因为接触尸体。//

布拉德·蔡斯：那么你说的"飞溅"在哪呢，探员先生？//

珐里探长：左肩有两处变长的血迹。//

布拉德·蔡斯：这里，这些微小的血迹？//

珐里探长：是的。//

布拉德·蔡斯：连开6枪，只有2处小小的血迹？//

珐里探长：其他的痕迹也许是在她抱住丈夫时，被粘到的血迹覆盖了。//

**布拉德·蔡斯：** 是你自己做的痕迹分析吗，探员先生？//

**珐里探长：** 是我。//

**布拉德·蔡斯：** 波士顿警局负责这些的是你吗？//

**珐里探长：** 当然还有其他人，不过我是实验室出身，我也受训过。//

**布拉德·蔡斯：** 还有其他实验室人员检测过这件衬衫吗？//

**珐里探长：** 是的，还有一个初级检验员……//

**布拉德·蔡斯：** 一个新手？这可是重案！让一个新手来操作？//

**珐里探长：** 正如我说，以我30年凶杀案探员的经验来检测。//

**布拉德·蔡斯：** 30年的实验室经验？//

**珐里探长：** 不。//

**布拉德·蔡斯：** 那在实验室的经验有多少年？//

**珐里探长：** 5年。//

**布拉德·蔡斯：** 那个新手呢？他又有几年经验？//

**珐里探长：** 我不确定。//

**布拉德·蔡斯：** 多于5年？//

**珐里探长：** 我想是的。//

**布拉德·蔡斯：** 只是出于好奇，他发现了什么？//

**珐里探长：** 没什么结论。//

**布拉德·蔡斯：** 他不能证实我当事人开枪？//

**珐里探长：** 他也不能排除这个可能。//

**布拉德·蔡斯：** 他不能证实我的当事人开了枪。//

**珐里探长：** 是，但是我能证实。//

**布拉德·蔡斯：** 你对我的当事人做过金属痕迹检测，是为了测试她手上的火药残余吗？//

**珐里探长：** 是的，结果是否定的。//

**布拉德·蔡斯：** 哇，那怎么可能？//

**珐里探长：** 我们推断她可能开枪时戴着手套。//

**布拉德·蔡斯：** 所以开枪时，她非常小心地戴上手套。然后她脱下手套，再伸手拿枪。//

**珐里探长：** 如果她像你说的惊吓过度，那她也许犯了个错误，杀人犯常常这样。//

**布拉德·蔡斯：** 所以关于延误报警的解释，你认为不是惊吓所致，但在解释她戴着手套开枪之后，再用空手拿枪，你又认为是惊吓所致，事实上，你更像是在推销这个解释。//

**阿达·约翰·舒伯特：** 反对。//

**布拉德·蔡斯：** 我收回。你找到手套了吗？//

**珐里探长：** 没有。//

**布拉德·蔡斯：** 你彻底搜查过整幢房子了吗？我可不想擅自揣测。//

**珐里探长：** 搜查过，没有找到手套。//

**布拉德·蔡斯：** 有证据表明她当晚回到家后又离开了？//

**珐里探长：** 没有。//

**布拉德·蔡斯：** 去年这社区有过未结的入室盗窃案吗？//

**珐里探长：** 有一些。//

◆ *Passage 3*

**当事人：** 我 25 岁就得了 Ⅱ 型糖尿病，从此整天与药物为伍。//

**控方律师：** 在你被邀请参加 SV－113 临床试验后，你每天是如何吃药的？//

**当事人：** 一早起来吞服一粒药。//

**控方律师：** 就这些？//

**当事人：** 就这些！我更有精力了，甚至体重还减下来了，不再需要打针，就像上天的恩赐，直到他们不再给我药。//

**控方律师：** 为什么呢？//

**当事人：** 我的医生告诉我，那个公司把我从试验中剔除了，他说我违反了试验规则，可是我没有！我没有做错任何事！//

**控方律师：** 那在你离开那个试验之后呢？//

**当事人：** 我的身体马上又开始恶化了。//

**控方律师：** 你会怎样预计自己以后的情况？//

**当事人：** 我会死掉，我大概还能活 5 年到 6 年，除非有翻天覆地的转机。//

**辩方律师：** 这家公司拿什么理由把你从 SV－113 试验中剔除？//

**当事人：** 不合作，但是我一直很合作的。//

**辩方律师**：休伊特夫人，你是个烟鬼吧？//

**当事人**：我戒了。//

**辩方律师**：冒昧问下，你什么时候戒的？//

**当事人**：实验前一周。//

**辩方律师**：原本一天两包，忽然就能戒掉？//

**当事人**：我要活下去。//

**辩方律师**：几个临床医生在检查时闻到你身上有烟味。//

**当事人**：我丈夫烟不离口，烟味会留在我衣服上。//

**辩方律师**：真厉害！你曾经每天 2 包烟，还和个烟鬼住一起，但你却能说戒就戒掉。//

**控方律师**：反对！//

**华莱士法官**：反对有效。//

**辩方律师**：休伊特夫人，世界上有 1.77 亿的人患有糖尿病，这次药物试验是 SV-113 唯一，也就是你所说的天赐之物，能被获准出售的途径，1.77 亿的人指望着你能遵守规定，休伊特夫人！//

**当事人**：我是这么做的。//

**辩方律师**：想到这样的生死攸关，想到每年 7 万人口因糖尿病而丧命，想到对研制药物的迫切渴望，以便挽救那些生命，你能理解，对我的当事人来说，不能冒任何风险，对吗？//

**当事人**：我遵守了所有的规则。//

◆ *Passage 4*

**格瑞特警官**：我们收到线报，呃，关于疑犯达蒙·哈里斯，线报说他去见他哥哥保罗，所以我们就去了他哥哥家。//

**检察官**：那么你们在那找到疑犯了吗？//

**辩方律师**：对不起，我是刚刚做这个案子的，这里的陪审团，当然了，是帮助我们寻找真相的。我想知道你是否能指认他就是绑架疑犯，这样我们就能弄清我们在讨论的事，关于一个劫持了 6 岁儿童的男人，那孩子就坐在这。//

**检察官**：绑架疑犯在那吗，警官？//

**格瑞特警官**：不。//

**检察官：**他的哥哥在那吗？//

**格瑞特警官：**在。

**检察官：**你能告诉我们发生过什么吗？//

**格瑞特警官：**好，我们搜查了那所房子，没有找到疑犯，我们询问他的哥哥是否知道些什么，他说他不知道。//

**检察官：**那么接下来发生了什么？//

**格瑞特警官：**接下来发生的就是你在那录像带上看到的，我的同事开始……呃，对他哥哥的询问更强硬。//

**检察官：**在任何时间，这案子的受害人，被错认作绑架疑犯了吗？//

**格瑞特警官：**没有。//

**检察官：**你从没认为他和那案子有关吗？//

**格瑞特警官：**是的，没有。//

**舒米特律师：**正如肖尔先生的陈述，你们试图寻找现在坐在那儿的那位6岁的男孩吗？//

**格瑞特警官：**是的。//

**舒米特律师：**这案子发生前，他已经被绑架多久了？//

**格瑞特警官：**这事发生的前天。//

**舒米特律师：**时间越来越少，你们找到活着被绑架孩子的机会有多大？//

**格瑞特警官：**48小时之后，我们就认为很难再有希望了。//

**舒米特律师：**实际上，我们讨论的那位绑架疑犯，曾经有过绑架另一个男孩的案底，是吗？//

**格瑞特警官：**是的。//

**舒米特律师：**你们找到那个男孩了吗？//

**格瑞特警官：**我们只找到了他的尸体。//

**舒米特律师：**那么，当我的当事人正对他的哥哥实施强硬行为时，你做了什么？//

**格瑞特警官：**我退后了。//

**舒米特律师：**你没有干预吗？//

**格瑞特警官：**没有。//

**舒米特律师：**你报告了这件事吗？//

**格瑞特警官：**一开始没有，呃，后来有。//

舒米特律师：顺便问一下，我的当事人实施完强硬行为之后，疑犯的哥哥告诉你们什么了？//

格瑞特警官：他给了我们一张他弟弟可能会出现的地方的单子。//

舒米特律师：那么，你们搜查了这些地方吗？//

格瑞特警官：是的。//

舒米特律师：有收获吗？//

格瑞特警官：我们找到了疑犯，还有那孩子。//

# V. 句子精炼 Sentences in Focus

**Directions**：*Interpret the following sentences alternatively into English or Chinese*：

*Exercise 1*
*Direct Examination*

**Q**：BY MR. CUMMINGS：Thank you, Your Honor. Sir, what's your occupation?

**A**：Correctional officer.

**Q**：How long have you been a correctional officer?

**A**：Six years.

**Q**：Where are you currently employed?

**A**：Pelican Bay State Prison.

**Q**：How long have you worked at Pelican Bay?

**A**：Since November 1989.

**Q**：Was that basically the opening date for the prison?

**A**：Yes.

**Q.** So you are part of the original team that started out at the institution?

**A**：Yes, sir.

**Q**：Sir, were you working in the capacity of a correctional officer on March the 28th, 1992?

**A**：Yes.

**Q**：Did you have occasion to come into contact with an inmate by the name of Johnson seated at the other end of this table?

**A**：Yes.

**Q**：Do you recognize him today?

**A**：Yes, I do.

**Q**：What facility was he housed in, do you know?

**A**：Facility B.

**Q**：What is the significance of Facility B?

**A**：It's a general population.

**Q**：As opposed to what, sir?

**A**：Security Housing Unit.

**Q**：Is there a transition of inmates from one facility like SHU, Security Housing Unit, to, say, general population?

**A**：Yes.

MR. DEEMER：Objection. I don't see the relevance.

THE COURT：Sustained.

**Q.** BY MR. CUMMINGS：Officer, what type of people what type of inmates are typically housed in Facility B?

MR. DEEMER：Again, objection. I don't see the relevance.

*Exercise 2*
*Cross-examination*

**Q.** BY MR. DEEMER：Officer Huston, who at that point unlocked the food port?

**A**：Officer Smith.

**Q**：And then was anything done with the food port prior to the door being opened?

**A**：You mean was there anythingit was opened prior to the door being

**Q**：But was it then closed again?

**A：** I could not say whether it was or not.

**Q：** Now, did any of the other officers at the time you were all at the doorand I take it there is eight or ten officers at the door; is that correct?

**A：** I have no idea if there was eight or ten. I am saying there was the four that I know of.

**Q：** But there were more than four. There were some other officers

**A：** I understand that there was, but I didn't have any identification and know who the officers are and how many others.

**Q：** Hey, I am not trying to trip you. All I am trying to figure out is there were four officers there that you know including yourself?

**A：** Yes.

**Q：** And there were some officers you didn't know?

**A：** Yes.

**Q：** You don't remember what the total number of the other officers were?

**A：** No.

**Q：** Could it have been as many as eight or ten?

**A：** I guess maybe, yes.

**Q：** Now, did any of the officers just prior to the time the cell door was opened put on some gloves?

**A：** I have no idea. I didn't put any on my myself, no.

**Q：** Do you recall any officers putting onpulling out the sidehandled batons, PRC 24 or something like that?

**A：** No, I don't recall that.

**Q：** Now, when the door was openedfirst of all, there is absolutely nothing aggressive about the defendant up until the time the door is opened; is that correct?

**A：** No, there wasn't anything aggressive about him until he dropped the trays.

**Q：** Okay. And when the door is opened Walker is standing in front of him?

**A：** Yes.

**Q：** And at that point the defendant is standing there and he has got two trays in his hands and he just drops the trays like that; is that correct?

**A：** Instantly.

**Q:** And brought his hands up toward his head?

**A:** He brought them up, yeah.

**Q:** How were they shaped when he brought them up towards his head?

**A:** In a clenched fist.

**Q:** And at that point you observed Walker push him?

**A:** I at that pointhe had struck Walker in the chest.

**Q:** With what?

**A:** With his fist.

**Q:** And then Walker pushed him back?

**A:** And Walker pushed him back into the cell.

**Q:** And then the melee ensues?

**A:** Yes.

**Q:** Now, you search inmates' cells frequently, don't you?

**A:** In my job once in a while I do.

**Q:** And when you search an inmate's cell, whether he is in General Population or in SHU, the first thing you do is get the inmate out of the cell; is that correct?

**MR. CUMMINGS:** Objection. Relevance.

**THE COURT:** Overruled. You may answer.

**THE WITNESS:** If you are going to search the cell, yes, you bring the inmate out andout of the cell.

第十单元

# 法庭交锋(英美法系)

**Unit 10 Courtroom Debate**
**(The Common-law System)**

# I. 专题知识 Legal Knowledge

## 一、预审 (Preliminary Hearing)

预审是在逮捕实施之后检察官提出控诉之前进行的一项诉讼程序，目的在于审查被告人是否符合起诉条件。在此程序中，控诉方需举证证明存在被逮捕人触犯被控之罪的"可能的理由"（probable cause）。如果法官认为存在可能的理由，则诉讼程序继续进行，由犯罪嫌疑人决定是否进行诉辩交易或由法官决定开庭审判事件，如果法官认为可能的理由不存在，则诉讼程序终结，犯罪嫌疑人获得释放。

预审必须在法官的主持下进行，并由法官作出裁决。在一般情况下，治安法官或地方法官主持预审。一些州法院还根据本州的法律制定了预审规则。

1. 预审的案件范围

原则上，并不是所有的刑事案件都会经历预审程序。《美国联邦刑事诉讼程序规则》第 5.1 条规定，如果被告人被指控犯有除轻罪（petty offence）之外的罪行，治安法官必须进行预审。但下列情形除外：①被告人放弃预审；②被告人已被大陪审团指控；③被告人被检察官根据第 7.1 条的规定立案控诉犯有重罪（felony）；④检察官立案控诉被告人犯有轻罪（misdemeanor）；⑤被告人被控犯有轻罪（misdemeanor）并同意在治安法院接受审判。

2. 预审的目的和程序

预审中，法官审查的重点不是犯罪嫌疑人是否有罪，而是检察官是否有充分的证据可以使犯罪嫌疑人接受司法审判。所以，预审的目的在于审查证据是否符合起诉的条件，即是否存在可能的理由。在审理中，可能的理由是法官作出裁决的唯一标准。

如果被告人已被关押，则预审一般在被告人初次聆听后 10 日内举行；如果被告人未被关押，则最晚在其初次聆讯后 20 日内举行。经过被告人同意并有合理的理由（good cause），法官可以一次或多次延长上述时间；如果被告人不同意，除非法官能证明有例外情况存在并出于公平考虑必须延长（extraordinary circumstances exits and justice requires the delay），否则不可随意延长上述期限。

预审实质上是法官听取控辩双方意见的过程。检察官可以召集证人出庭作证，并出示相关的证据材料，以说服法官，使案件进入审判程序；而被告人或其辩护律师通常仅对控诉方的证人进行交叉询问，并对控诉方出示的证据材料提出异议，以说服法官案件并不严重，应当驳回起诉，终结诉讼。

预审中，被告人可以聘请律师参加。在一般情况下，证人或警察在准备庭审时没有必要会见被告人的律师，所以在预审中听取控诉方证人的证言对被告人一方来讲是了解对方证人观点的绝好机会，如果案件需要进入审判程序，被告人可以做到胸有成竹。所以，被告人的律师一般不赞成被告人放弃预审以换取暂时的取保候审或降低保释金的优惠，理由就在于，通过预审结案的案件微乎其微，而大多数的案件在预审后都会进入审判程序，如果在审判之前放弃了解对方证人和证据的机会，那么庭审就不能充分做到知己知彼，得心应手。

预审中，如果被告人的辩护律师认为已经有充分的证据证明不存在可能的理由，在这种情况下可以不要求被告人本人出庭作证。因为如果被告人出庭作证，他对案件事实的描述和主要观点就会向对方暴露无遗，反而容易授人以柄，使控方在案件的审判阶段有针对性地进行庭审准备，提升被告一方的辩护难度。

预审的全部过程都必须被记录在案。法庭记录对当事人公开，在支付法定费用后，当事人可以取得副本。

3. 预审的放弃

预审是法官的职责，但是对于被告人来说不是强制性的。如果被告人同意放弃预审，则预审程序不再进行，案件直接进入审判程序。因此，被告人可以放弃预审，以承认起诉的效力。有时候，检察官也可以和被告人达成协议，如果被告人同意放弃预审，可以享有降低保释金的优惠条件等。所以，被告根据自身情况认为自己说服法院的可能性很小时，会宁可以支付保释金为条件获得暂时的自由，从而放弃接受预审的权利。一般来说，法院要求被告在作出决定前充分咨询自己的律师，以明确自己行为的法律后果。此外，法官还要求被告人签些弃权书，书面声明自己的弃权决定和对由此产生的法律后果的明知。

在被告人作出弃权声明后，法官将作出命令，指示案件下一步的处理程序，即进行审判，多提交大陪审团审查等。此外，该命令书还需对被告人是予以关押还是予以保释等作出决定。如果是予以关押，须写明关押的地点；如果是保释，则要确定保释金的数额等。

4. 预审的结果

预审是"审判前的审判（trial before the trial）"，并不是对被告人是否有罪的最终裁决，其仅对起诉是否有"可能的理由"进行审查。所以，如果法官经过审查认为被告人犯了被指控之罪，那么诉讼程序将继续进行，如果法官经过审查认为被告人没有犯被指控之罪，则将裁决驳回起诉，终结诉讼。

如果法官经审查认为诉讼存在可能的理由，诉讼程序将继续进行。法官一般会对被告人是否进行诉辩交易以及开庭审判时间等进一步予以确认，为下一步的审判做好准备。

## 二、律师的简要陈述

在法官宣布开庭后，民事案件原被告双方当事人的律师以及刑事案件控辩双方将作简要陈述，介绍当事人、案情以及主要观点等，并对对方观点进行简要驳斥，目的在于抓住陪审团首次接触案件的时机，在第一时间说服陪审团，使其相信本方的观点和意见。

由于陪审团对案件的第一印象会直接影响到其对案件事实的判断，所以律师把握好此机会，有说服力地在陪审员脑海中构建起预期的案件事实框架至关重要。此外，陪审团集中注意力听讲的时间较短暂，而律师又要利用此机会使陪审团对本方当事人产生深刻印象并相信自己的观点和证据，所以律师在陈述案情时应当注意把握如下几个方面的技巧：

第一，内容简短、精练，不展开陈述自己的观点或过多介绍证据。

第二，用叙事式的语气讲述案件的主要情况，强调当事人的主要证据，感动陪审团。

第三，在结尾部分强调己方的请求，要求陪审团在判决中支持本方观点。

第四，在陈述时可以离开自己的席位，最好站立在陪审团对面进行讲述，以便与陪审团有很好的交流，必要时可以两边走动，以照顾到所有陪审团成员，使之集中注意力。此外还要注意言辞和肢体语言的配合。

下面就 opening statement 的任务形式以及常用的处理方式进行简要的陈述：

1. 开场白的形式和任务

陪审团选拔完成，陪审团宣誓和陪审团坐定于陪审团席后，案件双方的律师可以对陪审团陈述"开场白"（opening statement）。开场白的目的在于让案件双方的律师概略陈述案件的事实，并且向陪审团介绍其主张或抗辩。系争案件里的证据并不会在陪审团面前以年代次序排列得一目了然的方式呈现，反而是依照证人作证的次序杂乱无章地呈现。因此，开场白是案件双方之律师对陪审团清楚地说明案件来龙去脉，而不能夹杂的任何辩论。

陪审团会被法官告知案件双方之律师的开场白并非证据，只是证据的指南。但是，研究显示，这个被视为证据指南的开场白非常重要。一项针对陪审团判决过程的研究显示：陪审团以建立案件的发生经过和将此发生经过与其生活中发生之类似故事或经验比照，以测试该发生经过之正确性的方式来判决案件。因为开场白是案件双方之律师以有条理的方式向陪审团各自陈述案件来龙去脉的机会，因此是说服陪审团的利器。

2. 律师对于开场白的处理方式

最好的开场白通常会按照年代次序排列的方式来陈述事实。不论以何种次序陈述，案件双方之律师的开场白内容均大致局限于陈述该律师提出的少数异议之一为"对方律师在辩论"（opposing counsel is arguing）。尽管如此，为了让陪审团明了案件双方之基本立场，双方之律师可向陪审团概略陈述其对证据的主张，而这可能会涉及对于适用法律的一些讨论。

# II. 词汇热身 Vocabulary Warm-up

**Directions**：*Give the English equivalents of the following Chinese expressions*：

| | | |
|---|---|---|
| clerk | waive | allegedly |
| bench | bail | hearsay |

incriminate                Destructive Convict        No true bill

prejudice                  Inadmissible               Physical evidence

                      determination              Preliminary examination

                      Recognizance               Pre-trial proceeding：

                      probation                  Pre-trial release conditions

                      Information                Reciprocal discovery

                      Initial appearance         Summons

                      Joinder Motion

# III. 课文口译 Text for Interpreting

## ◆ *Passage 1*

**Directions**：*Listen to the passage and interpret from English into Chinese at the end of each segment.*

（案情简介：在检察官也同意减刑的情况下，法官却对被告人"念念不忘"，到底是因为法官秉公执法，还是另有原因？）

**Clerk**：Docket 477—People versus Walter Mack. //

**Alan Shore**：Your Honor, while this case is marked for trial, in fact, the defendant would like to accept a plea. //

**Judge Clark Brown**：Is that so? //

**ADA Allison Hayes**：The people have offered reckless endangerment. In exchange, we'd recommend probation. //

**Judge Clark Brown**：That's a reduced charge. You're aware of that? //

**ADA Allison Hayes**：Yes, Your Honor. //

**Judge Clark Brown**：Up here. Both of you. Alan and ADA Hayes approach the bench. I don't like this. Your office gets behind, so you just let criminals walk? //

**Alan Shore**：It's reassuring to see that you haven't formed any conclusions about my client's guilt or innocence. //

**Judge Clark Brown**：You know what my mother always says? If it smells funny, I'm not eating it. //

**Alan Shore:** Exact opposite of my motto. //

**Judge Clark Brown:** This deal smells funny. //

**ADA Allison Hayes:** If I may, Your Honor, the object here is to enhance the quality of life for the tenants in Mr. Mack's building. And he is prepared to make considerable … //

**Judge Clark Brown:** No. The object here is to send a message to every landlord in Boston. Treat people like animals, we will cage you like one. //

**Alan Shore:** I don't mean to pry, Your Honor, but is everything okay at home? //

**Judge Clark Brown:** Step back. Both of you. Mr. Mack, I will accept your plea under one condition. You are to build a sign to be worn around your neck. Said sign to read "I am a slumlord." Because sir, that's what you are. //

**Walter Mack:** Judge, you don't know what I'm up against. The elevator in the Green Street building—some kids blew up the electrical system just for fun. I paint over their graffiti, it's back that day. I'm doing the best I can. Truly I am. //

**Judge Clark Brown:** You are to stand in front of your Green Street property wearing said sign for no less than four continuous hours. //

**Alan Shore:** Your Honor, I cannot allow my client to be subjected to an extra-judicial penalty whose only purpose is to humiliate. //

**Judge Clark Brown:** Get used to it, Mr. Shore. This is nothing new. From the top of my head, I can remember the case of a woman who didn't strap her daughter into a car seat. The judge made her write a mock obituary for the child. A drunken driving defendant was forced to put a warning sign on his car. A woman was ordered to place an ad in the paper admitting that she had bought drugs. Tell me, when did it become wrong to feel scorn for a criminal? //

**Alan Shore:** This sentence goes beyond scorn, Your Honor. And I have known my client for years. He is not a criminal. //

**Judge Clark Brown:** I'm not at all interested in your opinion, Mr. Shore. You don't want the deal, go to trial. But if you lose, your defendant will go to prison, and deservedly so. Talk it over. You have 60 seconds. //

**Alan Shore:** It's your call, Walter. //

**Walter Mack:** I'll do it. In four hours, this will all be over. //

◆ *Passage 2*

**Directions**：*Listen to the passage and interpret from English into Chinese at the end of each segment.*

（案情简介：一名患有侏儒症的男子一生碌碌无为，一个偶然的机会让他找到了杀人的快感和权力感。他的律师相信人性中善良的一面会重新回到这个弱小的男人身上，于是为他开罪。）

**Bailiff**：32611：Commonwealth versus Ferrion. Charge of murder in the first. //

**Alan Shore**：Alan Shore appearing for the defendant. We'll waive reading. I'd ask that my client be released on his own recognizance. //

**D. A. Bret Haber**：Opposed. The man is charged with homicide. Bail would certainly … //

**Alan Shore**：He has no record, your Honor. //

**D. A. Bret Haber**：He would be a threat to society. //

**Alan Shore**：Nonsense. He only kills mothers—allegedly—and he's fresh out of them. //

**Judge James Billmeyer**：Bail is set at one million dollars. Let's conference tomorrow at 9 am. We'll set up a trial schedule. //

**Alan Shore**：Wait one second, your Honor. It seems there's been a terrible mistake. My client never should have been arrested. //

**Judge James Billmeyer**：Because? //

**Alan Shore**：There's no evidence. According to the police report, there's been no determination of cause of death, no witnesses. //

**D. A. Bret Haber**：The victim identified the defendant as the killer. //

**Alan Shore**：That would be hearsay. //

**D. A. Bret Haber**：It was a dying declaration, and therefore, an exception to the hearsay rule. //

**Alan Shore**：For the dying declaration exception to apply, the declarant must know he or she is about to die when making the statement. Mrs. Ferrion was told by the doctor she was going to survive. She never thought for a second she was going to die. //

**D. A. Bret Haber**: Even so, your Honor, for her to incriminate her own son would be a declaration against her interest, which would also qualify as an exception to the hearsay rule. //

**Alan Shore**: I refer your Honor to Officer Coulier's interviews with the neighbors noted at the bottom of the page. Mr. Ferrion was reportedly verbally abused by his mother. She would blame him for anything that went wrong in her life. Well, here again, she was blaming him for the bump on her head. It was not a declaration against her interest, but just more of the same. The court cannot be satisfied as to its reliability. The hearsay rule very much applies. //

**Judge James Billmeyer**: Is this all you've got—the statement of the victim? //

**D. A. Bret Haber**: We'll get more. //

**Judge James Billmeyer**: Well, when you do, you can refile. Right now, you've got nothing. Victim's statement is inadmissible. The charges against Mr. Ferrion are dismissed without prejudice. //

◆ *Passage 3*

**Directions**: *Listen to the passage and interpret from English into Chinese at the end of each segment.*

（案情简介：本案中的代理人是个不受欢迎的商业巨鳄。他的律师采取了欲擒故纵的技巧，首先开门见山地将陪审团的疑虑和担忧摆上台面。找出了问题的症结所在。）

**Lomax**: Your Honor. We can break for lunch now or you can do a stop and start. If it's a choice, I'll go now. I won't be as long as Mr. Broygo. Ladies and gentlemen of the jury I know you've spent all morning listening to Mr. Broygo. I know you're hungry. What I need to tell you won't take very long at all. I don't like Alexander Cullen. I don't think he's a nice person. I don't expect you to like him. He's been a terrible husband to all three of his wives. He's been a destructive force in the lives of his stepchildren. He's cheated the city, his partners, his employees. He's paid hundreds of thousands of dollars in penalties and fines. I don't like him. I'm going to tell you some things during the course of this trial that are going to make you like him even less. But this isn't a popularity contest. It's a murder trial. And the single most important provable fact of this proceeding is that Alexander Cullen was somewhere else when these horrible crimes took place. Now, the state, the state is going all out here. They've got this whole team here throwing everything but the kitchen sink at this case. I want one thing from you. That's it. One thing. I want you to ask yourself: is not liking this man reason enough to convict him of murder? Enjoy your lunch. We'll talk again. //

## ◆ *Passage 4*

**Directions**: *Listen to the passage and interpret from English into Chinese at the end of each segment.*

（案情简介：本案的代理人是一个会巫术的巫医，他的律师在说理的基础上，采用了形象的对比和类比。使得说理更加真实可信，毫无疑问地征服了陪审团和法官。）

**Lomax**: That's a veal roast, Your Honor. USDA approved and stamped. Men kill animals and eat their flesh. Philippe Moyez killed a goat. He killed a goat. And he did it at home in a manner consistent with his religious beliefs. Now, Mr. Merto may find that bizarre. It's certainly not a religious practice performed by everyone. It's not as common as, say circumcision. It's not as common as the belief that wine transforms into blood. Some people handle poisonous snakes to prove their faith. Some people walk on fire. Phillipe Moyez killed a goat. And he did it while observing his constitutionally protected religious beliefs. Your Honor, this case is not about keeping goats or transporting goats or goat licensing. The city was less concerned with the care of the animals than the manner in which they were slaughtered. //

**Mr. Merto**: Objection! //

**Judge**: Enough, enough. I got it. Let's wrap it up. //

**Lomax**: Your Honor, the city timed this police action to catch my client exercising his constitutionally protected right to religious freedom. //

**Judge**: This is a law protecting kosher butchery. //

**Lomax**: Exactly, Your Honor. I'd like to move at this time for a verdict of dismissal. //

**Judge**: I happen to know a little bit about kashrut law, Mr. Lomax. //

**Lomax**: I'm aware of that, Your Honor. That's why I feel confident in requesting a dismissal. //

**Judge**: Mr. Merto? For God's sake, man //

# Ⅳ. 参考译文 Reference versions

## ◆ *Passage 1*

**书记员**：第 477 号诉讼案，集体控告沃特·麦克。//

**辩方律师**：阁下，虽然本案已经进入审判程序，但事实上，被告现在愿意认罪。//

**布朗法官**：是吗？//

**海耶斯检察官**：原告要求判处二级任意危害罪，作为认罪条件，我们建议缓期执行。//

**布朗法官**：这是减轻指控，你意识到了吗？//

**海耶斯检察官**：是的，阁下。//

**布朗法官**：你们两个都过来，我不希望这样，你们实力不行，就要放走罪犯吗？//

**辩方律师**：看到您尚未对我当事人清白与否作出定论，我还真是安心啊！//

**布朗法官**：你知道我妈妈常说的话吗？如果食物闻起来古怪，绝对不要吃。//

**辩方律师**：刚好跟我相反。//

**布朗法官**：这个案子很不正常。//

**海耶斯检察官**：阁下，请听我说，我们的目的只是提高麦克先生的房客们的生活质量，而麦克先生也愿意考虑 …… //

**布朗法官**：不，我们的目的是警告整个波士顿的房东们，如果你像对待动物一样对待人，你也会被关进笼子。//

**海耶斯检察官：**我不想打听您的隐私，阁下，但您家里一切安好吗？//

**布朗法官：**退下，你们两个。麦克先生，你的认罪条件是：你必须戴着一个上面写着"我是贫民窟的房东"的牌子，因为，你的确如此。//

**当事人：**法官，你不清楚我的立场。格林大街楼里的电梯电力系统被一些孩子为取乐而炸掉了，我刚把他们的喷图刷掉，当天又被画满。我已经尽力了，真的。//

**布朗法官：**你须在格林大街房产前面戴着那块牌子至少连续 4 个小时。//

**辩方律师：**阁下，我不能接受判决，这是逾越法律的，其目的仅仅是羞辱当事人。//

**布朗法官：**肖尔先生，你必须接受。这没什么新鲜的，我能举出很多先例：有一个女被告的案子，她没帮女儿系安全带，法官判她为女儿写一份假的讣告。一个酒后开车的被告被判处在车上挂警告牌。一个女被告被命令在报纸上登广告向公众宣告她吸毒。告诉我什么时候开始，蔑视罪犯变得不可接受了。//

**辩方律师：**阁下，您的判决不只是蔑视。我认识我的委托人好几年了，他绝不是罪犯。//

**布朗法官：**肖尔先生，我对你的看法不感兴趣。你不接受协议，那就审判吧。但一旦你输了，你的委托人将被判入狱。当然，他罪有应得。商量商量吧，一分钟后告诉我结论。//

**辩方律师：**沃特，你决定。//

**当事人：**接受，4 个小时以后一切就结束了。//

◆ *Passage 2*

**法警：**联邦 32611 号，控告费隆一级谋杀。//

**辩方律师：**我是阿兰·肖尔，辩方律师，开门见山地说，我请求允许当事人保释自己。//

**哈勃检察官：**反对，这个人被指控谋杀。保释应当……//

**辩方律师：**他没有前科，法官大人。//

**哈勃检察官：**他将对社会造成威胁。//

**辩方律师：**一派胡言！他只杀了自己的母亲，正如对方说的，而且还只是初犯。//

**法官：** 保释金 100 万，明天早上 9 点开会安排审讯计划。//

**辩方律师：** 等等，法官大人，似乎有个严重的错误，我的当事人不该被捕。//

**法官：** 因为？//

**辩方律师：** 没有证据，根据警方报告死因未定，也没有证人。//

**哈勃检察官：** 被害人证实被告就是凶手。//

**辩方律师：** 那是传闻。//

**哈勃检察官：** 被害人的遗言属于传闻证据否定法的例外，所以遗言要被采用。//

**辩方律师：** 但是，立遗言人在做表述时必须知道自己将要死去，而费隆太太被医生告知可以活下去，她没想到过自己会死。//

**哈勃检察官：** 即使如此，法官大人，指控自己儿子的罪行有悖于她的利益，这也符合传闻证据否定法的例外。//

**辩方律师：** 法官大人，请看靠利尔警官在此页底部记录的和周围邻居的谈话"据反映费隆先生经常被母亲羞辱"，她将生活中所有的不顺归咎于儿子，你看，有一次她将自己撞破脑袋算到了儿子头上，这不是有违她利益的陈述，只是和往常一样，法庭不能采信绝对适用传闻——证据否定。

**法官：** 你们只有这个受害者的陈述？//

**哈勃检察官：** 我们会找到更多的。//

**法官：** 那等你找到了再来吧，现在你什么也没有。被害人陈述不足采信，对费隆先生的控告驳回。//

◆ *Passage 3*

**罗麦斯：** 谢谢各位，你们要休息用餐，还是继续？可以的话，我要求继续。我不会耽搁各位太久。陪审团的女士、先生们，各位花了一上午听检察官起诉。我知道大家都饿了，所以我不想占用太久时间。其实我也不喜欢艾力·库伦。我认为他不是好人。我也不期望你们会喜欢他。他结了 3 次婚，不是个好丈夫。他对他的养子们任意动粗。他对全市市民、他的生意伙伴、他的员工都不老实。他所交的罚款有如天文数字，我不喜欢他。接下来，我让你们知道他的事，这会让你们更讨厌他。不过，这可不是最佳人气比赛，这是一件谋杀案的审判。最重要的事是，我们证明，艾力·库伦在血案发生当时是在别的地方。现在，司法当局虎视眈眈，他们正用尽一切方法，把莫须有的罪名往他身上推。我只要求各位一件事，如此而已。只有一件事，我希望各位问问自己，只因为讨厌这个人就足以判他犯了杀人罪吗？祝各位午餐愉快。下午见了。//

◆ *Passage 4*

**罗麦斯**：庭上，这是小牛肉，美国农业局认证许可，人类宰杀动物供食用，菲利浦·摩伊兹杀了一只羊，他杀了一只羊。而这件事是在他家中发生的，一切与他信仰的宗教仪式相符。莫道先生可能觉得诡异，当然，这项宗教仪式比较少见。它不像其他常见的宗教仪式，例如割礼，也不像一般的信仰，例如酒可以变成血。有人以舞弄毒蛇来证明信仰，有些人赤足过火，而菲利浦·摩伊兹则宰杀羔羊。他做的这件事只是行使获得宪法保障的权利——宗教信仰自由。庭上，这案子与饲养羔羊无关，也与羊肉运送宰杀许可无关。大家不去关怀动物保育问题，却在宰杀方式上大作文章。//

**道莫检察官**：抗议！//

**法官**：可以了，我都了解了，做总结吧。//

**罗麦斯**：庭上，警方对我客户实施逮捕，而他所行使的正是宪法保障的宗教信仰自由。这是法律保护的犹太教屠礼，完全正确，庭上，我在此请求对本案撤销控诉。//

**法官**：我对犹太教仪式也小有研究。//

**罗麦斯**：我也注意到了，庭上，所以我更有信心申请撤销控诉。//

**法官**：莫道检察官？看在上帝的份上。

# V．句子精炼 Sentences in Focus

**Directions**：*Interpret the following sentences into English*：

*Exercises 1*

**U. S. Attorney Joyner**：They're seeking damages for acts committed by a foreign government against a foreign citizenry. There's no jurisdiction here; no standing. And even if there were, any such lawsuit would be barred by sovereign immunity, which prohibits the U. S. government or its officials from being sued for foreign policy decisions.

**Judge Linda O'Keefe:** Miss Colson, I have to agree. How do I not toss this on its face?

**Lori Colson:** First, the United States government, through Congress, ratified the U. N. Convention against genocide. The government's current failure to stop the genocide in Sudan violates both U. S. law and policy.

**U. S. Attorney Joyner:** We have not failed. We have expended . . .

**Lori Colson:** You're arguing the merits, which I'm happy to do, but it means a trial. If a government begins a rescue operation which, in effect, stops other countries from pursuing that rescue, that government can be held liable for failing to complete that rescue.

**U. S. Attorney Joyner:** Never. Never has the United States government attempted any rescue mission in Sudan.

**Shirley Schmidt:** Your Honor, may I?

(Judge Linda O'Keefe nods)

**Shirley Schmidt:** We know this lawsuit is a bit of a stretch.

**Judge Linda O'Keefe:** Hmm. You understate it.

**Shirley Schmidt:** But the truth is, our country puts it out there. "We will root out terrorism wherever it thrives. " We elect our presidents on that theme. We go to war over it. Wherever oppression abounds, we get involved. It's almost become a motto. No one here denies an ethnic genocide is taking place in Sudan. Arab militia are wiping out the black population of Darfur. Am I boring you?

**Judge Linda O'Keefe:** Miss Schmidt. The court recognizes the atrocity. Why should the United States be held liable?

**Shirley Schmidt:** Well, if we're not going to do anything about it, maybe we should just say so. Lord knows, the world will understand. We've certainly got our hands full. But when our leaders do their bipartisan puffing, saying the genocide must end, other countries think we're going to do something. They then stay out of it, and, in the end, nothing gets done, while millions of people are being persecuted. Maybe as a compromise, we could just get the U. S. government to declare for the record, "Hey, not our problem. " That way, the world would be on notice—somebody else should play hero. I could try to sell that to my client.

**Judge Linda O'Keefe**: Mr. Joyner?

**U. S. Attorney Joyner**: The United States' response to an ethnic genocide is certainly not going to be, "Hey, not our problem. "

**Shirley Schmidt**: See? This is how other countries get confused.

(U. S. Courtroom)

**Judge Linda O'Keefe**: To be honest, I might have a hard time finding Sudan on a map. I certainly know

they've got big problems. Innocent people murdered every day, systemic rape, many of them children. It's the worst humanitarian crisis in the world.

**Shirley Schmidt**: Please don't say "but. "

**Judge Linda O'Keefe**: But, why does every crisis automatically fall to the United States to solve? We've got Iraq, Iran, the Democratic People's Republic of Korea—and these are people who might murder us. We're supposed to tend to a bunch of Africans killing each other? Why? Because we're Americans? The answer is ... yes. Because we're Americans. Because we're a nation—perhaps the nation—that's supposed to give a damn. What's going on is an organized extermination of an entire race of people. We're the country that's supposed to give a damn. Miss Schmidt, Miss Colson, your claim here most likely won't survive summary judgment. And maybe the American people don't care about what's happening over there, but for today, here, now—at least one federal court judge does. Defendant's motion to dismiss—denied. bangs gavel

## Exercises 2

**MR. CUMMINGS**: Thank you, Your Honor. Ladies and gentlemen, we are about to get under way and the purpose of my opening statement is basically to give you some idea of where I believe our witnesses are going to take us in testimony. Witnesses are the people who testify from the witness stand, nowhere else. In other words, as the judge told you, what the attorneys have to say is not evidence, and you notice neither side here have raised their hands to tell the truth and nothing but the truth. So your testimony comes from the witness stand.

As the prosecutor in the case I expect to call three, probably four witnesses. I may call more. I have an option of putting on rebuttal witnesses if I want to. You will see that if it happens. Eye witnesses are going to start out with Officer Huston who has worked at Pelican Bay State Prisonwho is what we call a percipient witness, which means he saw, he was present when the incident happened in 1992 at one of the branches at Pelican Bay State Prison. They call it B Facility. And I will have testimony about what B Facility means and what type of people are housed in B Facility.

The defendant, Mr. Johnson, was in his cell with his cell mate, a person by the name of Butler and that for whatever reason they refused to give up some trays, food trays. That on that date, March the 28th, 1992, Butler and inmate Johnson were in their cell. They had been fed in their cell, and, as I indicated before, for unknown reasons they were't going to give up their trays.

At that point in time several officers were summoned to go over to the cell and try to talk to them to give up their trays. And it's a mainline production, meaning they have to feed, get back the trays, and they have a lot of people to take care of. Officer Huston will testify that basically therewas a couple trays inside the cell and that he and other officers went into his cell along with some other people and talked to them about giving up the trays.

Officer Huston will tell youand I would suspect Officer Van Berg will tell you basically the same storythat Mr. Johnson had possession of the trays, he was holding on to them, and that in the door of the cell, the actual cell door, there was a little food port door. You can slide one tray at a time through there. And you can't slide two through and you can't slide one with a lot of garbage piled on top, just enough to slide one tray back and forth.

For whatever reason, inmate Johnson, the defendant in this case, was standing in the cell with the trays in his hand and he had had some discussion with the officers about a package. He wanted some package. And he was not going to relinquish those two trays. So basically what happened in the case, as Officer Huston and Van Berg and Walker will testify, is that a sergeant sent some of them over to discuss the matter with inmate Johnson and to try to persuade them basically verbally to give up the tray, "we have got to get on our route, our day's business".

He asked at that point in time to see a sergeant. And the officers will testify that what they told Johnson at that point in time was, "We'll get you a sergeant; we'll have a sergeant drop by and talk to you, but we can't do it right now. We have got our work to do. We have got to finish up what we are doing."

At that point Johnson was going to give up the trays. He was not verbally abusive. He was not physicallydidn't appear to be physically dangerous at that point. He was just standing there with his trays. So the officerand he wasn't too far back from the cell door. So one of the officers, the Officer Smith, signaled to the gentleman who controlsthe sectional officer who controls the doors electronically or hydraulically but they are controlled from a different locationgo ahead and open up the cell door.

So the cell door was opened a substantial distance, wide enough for somebody to charge out. And behind the door you have Johnson hanging on to the two trays piled with garbage. And basically at that point with Walker in front, Van Berg, Smith was there and Huston was there, their testimony is going to be that Johnson dropped the trays, kind of lowered his head a little bit and charged Officer Walker who was kind of at the head of this line where he can get the job done.

At that point in time the officers met him. The approximate location was the doorway to the cell. Stopped him at the door as he tried to approach them rapidly. He was swinging his fists, clenched right fist, that the officers basically pushed him back into the cell. The cells are not that large. Got him on top of a table and subdued him. One officer had handcuffs on one side of him and Mr. Johnson still was swinging, being combative. He was still trying to injure people and they were trying to subdue him. So four or five officers at this point, trying to subdue him and get him cuffed up, handcuffed.

During the course of that melee two officers were injured. One ended up with a broken boneI think it was a bone chip in his thumband was off work a period of time, suffered some injuries. Another officer went down to Sutter Coast Hospital with a shin injury, received a small laceration on his shin.

These are the two counts of battery that I am going to ask you to consider. The people will put on a final witness, probably an officer by the name of Henderson who will testify about a 969B package. It's a package of documents from the prison certified to verify that that person was lawfully in custody at Pelican Bay State Prison at the time. I do have to prove that he was in custody at the time. And it basically establishes the fact that he was in our prison system as well, which is another element that I have to prove.

I would expect at this point in time that would be my case in chief. Depending on how andwhat the defense puts on, I may call rebuttal witnesses, probably officers or actually two lieutenants, Foster and Kurtz. I will call those two as rebuttal. Thank you.

# 最后陈述及评议判决（英美法系）

## Unit 11 The Last Statement and Verdict (The Common-law System)

# I．专题知识 Legal Knowledge

在法官向陪审团指示完毕后，庭审将进入最后陈述阶段。最后陈述是当事人在庭审中向陪审团表明本方观点和立场并反驳对方的最后一次机会。

## 一、最后陈述的程序

最后陈述程序仍然在法官的主持下进行。首先，法官就最后陈述的程序向陪审团作出说明，然后由民事案件的原被告或刑事案件的控辩双方分别进行陈述。法官一般作如下介绍：

**Court**：Are both sides ready?

**Plaintiff's lawyer**：Ready，your Honor.

**Defendant's lawyer**：Ready，your Honor.

**Court**：Member of the jury, we are now going to hear the closing arguments of the lawyer. The closing arguments are the lawyer's opportunity to argue to you why you should return a verdict in their favor. The rules are as follows. Plaintiff (or People) argues first, then defendant. After the defendant is done, plaintiff (or People) gets to make a short rebuttal argument. In other words, because plaintiff (or People) has the burden of proof, plaintiff (or People) gets to argue first and last. Plaintiff (or People), please proceed.

## 二、最后陈述的技巧

最后陈述是律师对本方观点的总结，也是说服陪审团支持自己主张的最后一次机会。掌握陈述的技巧非常重要。总的来讲，作最后陈述时需要注意以下几点：

（1）开场简洁，直奔主题。比如，刑事案件被告律师可以这样表述：

"Once again, an innocent man has been framed, and there's nothing funny about it. And it's got to stop now."

民事案件被告律师可以这样表述：

"Taking responsibility for your own actions. We said at the beginning that this was a case about someone refusing to take responsibility for hid own actions, and now we know why, don't we?"

（2）论证有力，观点鲜明。最后陈述绝不是对本方辩论观点的总结，而是一次全面论理的过程。律师需要精心准备，从证据到论理，环环相扣、有理有据、旗帜鲜明地完整表述本方观点赖以成立的事实理由和法律依据。在论理过程中，可以有针对性地挖掘对方证据的薄弱环节，削弱对方的证明力和陪审团对其证据的信任度。为了加强本方的说理性和说服力，在必要的时候，还可以将律师的口头陈述和法庭对现代化多媒体设备的运用结合起来，加强论理的生动性。

（3）提高效率，速战速决。由于庭审已接近尾声，陪审团的注意力开始分散。长篇大论的陈述很难使陪审团聚精会神。所以，用最短的时间高效率地完成最后陈述是明智之举。当然，为使陪审团的注意力始终集中在律师身上，律师此时最好站在陪审团的正前方作陈述。

### 三、评议和判决

在最后陈述结束后，陪审团就会退庭回到陪审室（jury room）进行评议。陪审团的评议过程是保密的，任何人不允许介入。整个评议过程始终由法警（sheriff/bailiff）在外面保护。

陪审团的评议过程程序一般由陪审员自由决定。评议的主要依据就是法官口头或书面的陪审团指示，评议考虑的唯一问题就是证据问题。陪审团综合考虑双方当事人证据的效力，衡量承担举证责任一方当事人举出的证据是否达到证明标准，在此基础上作出判决（verdict）。陪审团可以经法官允许将证明材料（exhibit）带回陪审室研究，也可以根据法庭的指示参阅自己的笔记。如果在评审过程中遇到问题，要向法官询问，可以书面记载并经由法警交给法官。法官在征求双方律师的情况下作出回复。陪审团在作出判决后，陪审团主席（foreperson，由陪审员选举产生）可以通过法警示意法官判决已经作出。这样，所有庭审参与人员恢复到庭，陪审团也恢复到庭。法官向陪审团询问判决是否作出，如果已经作出，则陪审团主席回答"yes"，并经由法警将判决递交法官。法官在对判决进行形式审判之后，交由书记员最后宣读判决结果。判决宣读完毕后，法官会询问双方当事人是否还需要征求陪审员对判决的意见，一般来讲，败诉一方会要求在此征询陪审团意见。书记员会向每一位陪审员询问法庭宣读的判决是否系其一致同意的判决，如果得到的回答是"yes"，或放在施行多数决的法院回答"yes"的占到多数，则判决生效，陪审团审判结束，法官对陪审团作最后指示，解散陪审团。否则，法官只能命令重新评议。

陪审团的判决必须是一致的（可以是全体一致或多数决同意，具体规则各州规定不一）。如果不能达成一致的意见，法官一般会征求陪审团的意见，能否再次倾听双方的意见并重新进行评议。如果陪审团同意，则法官安排再次评议，如果陪审团拒绝，则法官宣布解散陪审团，并择期重新选择陪审团审理条件。

## 四、审后动议（post-motions）与上诉（appeal）

在判决作出后，双方当事人可能提出一些动议，或者要求法官重新审理案件，或者要求法官在刑事案件的量刑上予以适当减轻，或者要求法官在民事案件的损害赔偿数额上降低陪审团确定的标准等。法官在闭庭之前，要宣布审理这些动议的预定日期，届时由双方当事人和律师到庭进行审理并作出裁决，在法官对审后动议审理完毕后，出具裁判书（judgment）。判决书的出具意味着一审审理程序的终结。如果当事人对此判决书不服，可以在法律规定的上诉期限内向上一级法院提出上诉。

# II. 词汇热身 Vocabulary Warm-up

**Directions**：*Give out the Chinese equivalents of the following English idioms*：

| | | |
|---|---|---|
| attorney | counsel | conscience |
| felony priors | coerce | unanimous |
| witness | discretion | statement of reasons |
| adored | Equal Protection Clause | stipulation |
| preliminary | amendment | supervised release |
| reasonable doubt | civil rights violation | guilty verdict |
| defendant | mandatory | grand jury |
| confess | innocent | grand jury foreperson |
| consistent | premeditated | indictment |
| conviction | accused | judgement |
| delusional | verdict | |

# III. 课文口译 Text for Interpreting

◆ *Passage 1*

**Directions**：*Listen to the passage and interpret from English into Chinese at the end of each segment.*

[案情简介：这是一场关于合理存疑（reasonable doubt）的刑事辩论，案情是对辩论律师当事人（client）的盗窃指控。"盗窃"事实不可辩驳，但是辩论律师引用了一个她小时候发生的轶事征服了陪审团，使得她的当事人免于处罚]

**D. A. Huff**：A man with felony priors for robbery and burglary. But this time, he stole the wallet by mistake. Sure. //

**Sally Heep**：One day, I was in my kitchen. I think I was about 15. And in came Fred, my big chocolate Lab. And in his mouth was a dead rabbit. The neighbor's pet rabbit. And I thought "This is it for Fred." If they find out he killed their adored pet, Animal Control would be down, and …So, I took the rabbit. Washed him off in the sink. Pulled out the blow dryer. Got him all white and fluffy looking. And I snuck over to my neighbor's backyard and I put him back in his cage, hoping they'd think he died of natural causes. That night my parents came into my room. The neighbor's pet rabbit had died three days ago, they told me. They buried him in the woods. And some wacko evidently dug him up, washed him off, and put him back in the cage. But I remember thinking to myself the truth is not only stranger than fiction, but often less believable. And that's what we have here, ladies and gentlemen. The logical version, I suppose, is that my client stole that wallet. The less believable, but quite possibly true account is that he mistook it for his own. Nobody, not one of us, can be sure it didn't happen exactly the way Ramone Valesquez said it did. That's reasonable doubt. //

## ◆ *Passage 2*

**Directions**：*Listen to the passage and interpret from English into Chinese at the end of each segment.*

（案情简介：一个已经自己供认罪行的犯罪嫌疑人，一个有过吸毒前科的瘾君子，一个被咄咄逼人的检察官指控罪行将受审的"罪犯"，却被辩方律师洛里临时准备的总结陈词解救）

**ADA William Preston**：You heard from witness Frank Simmons who saw an S. U. V. speed by him a mile from the scene around the time of the murder. With a license plate beginning with 3−L−6. Mr. Litch's S. U. V. has a license plate beginning with 3−L−6. And when the police entered the defendant's apartment, what did he do? He didn't ask "What's this about?" He didn't say, "Hey, what's going on?" He knew exactly why they were there, and he immediately began his escape. And then in the hospital, he confessed. It wasn't a delusional confession. He described a fact pattern that was completely consistent with the crime. The defendant admitted that he was afraid of yet another drug conviction that would land him a life sentence. He panicked, pulled out a gun, and fired. Now, his lawyers suggest he was, perhaps, delusional when he confessed or that he simply lied to protect the real killer. A friend or a loved one. Desperate suggestions for a desperate client. It's insulting to this court, to you, and especially to that woman and her two children. Warren Litch murdered her husband. Warren Litch killed their father. He admitted to the police that he did so. Let's not waste any more time. //

**Lori Colson**: Edwin? It's your turn. //

**Edwin Poole**: I fell asleep last night and forgot to prepare a closing. I meant to tell you. //

**Lori Colson**: You don't have a closing? //

**Edwin Poole**: No. Do you? //

**Judge Peter Harding**: Counsel? //

**Lori Colson**: Edwin, you've got nothing? //

**Edwin Poole**: When I was a little boy, my father said to me—I can still hear his voice— //

**Lori Colson**: I believe he said "ladies first". I don't know about you, but if I hear that someone confessed to a crime, then I just assume he's guilty. But if I hear the confession is coerced, then…For example, you could have a man bleeding out with a stomach wound, put him in a room with police and clergy who keep insisting to him that he did something and he might actually come to believe it. And gee, what if it was a friend or a loved one who was driving Warren's car that night? That would explain why Warren was trying to flee, wouldn't it? He likely knew the police were coming to mistakenly arrest him. Did the police investigate any of this? My God, we all assume Warren Litch is guilty. But what if he isn't? Now, let's turn to the other evidence. Wait. There is no other evidence. No gun, no witnesses, no fibers, no forensics. All they have is that coerced confession. Now, you might think he did it. And if you're determined, you can even still assume it, I suppose. But if you're to uphold the law and demand proof beyond all reasonable doubt, and if we don't demand that, do we really want to send a message to the police? "Hey, forget the evidence. Just bring us that confession." //

◆ *Passage 3*

**Directions**：*Listen to the passage and interpret from English into Chinese at the end of each segment.*

（案情简介：这是一宗种族歧视案，黑人女孩托米凭借精妙绝伦的表演赢得了大家的认可，却被制片人拒之门外，被剥夺了扮演剧情中孤儿的机会。）

**Sarah Toomy**：. . . when I'm stuck with a day that's gray and lonely; I just stick out my chin and grin and say—tomorrow, tomorrow, I love ya tomorrow, you're always a day away. //

**Judge Rita Sharpley**：Thank you. That was . . . //

**Sarah Toomy**：Tomorrow, tomorrow, I'll love tomorrow. You're always a day away. //

**Alan Shore**：That was great! //

**Judge Rita Sharpley**：Sarah, that was magnificent. But the other little girl was quite good, too. And given the discretion that has to be allowed to producers in these situations. //

**Alan Shore**：Your Honor, we have something called the Equal Protection Clause, we have something called the 14th Amendment—I believe it's actually required reading for judges. I could be wrong there. //

**Reverend Al Sharpton**：Could I be heard, your Honor? I heard about this matter. I would like to address this court on what I consider. //

**Judge Rita Sharpley**：I'm sorry, Reverend, but you have no standing here. //

**Reverend Al Sharpton**：I have standing as an American citizen speaking up on a civil rights violation. //

**Judge Rita Sharpley**：Reverend Sharpton, I will ask you to step down. //

**Reverend Al Sharpton**：I have standing as Bobby Kennedy had standing. on the steps of the courthouse in Alabama! //

**Judge Rita Sharpley**：No one is denying this little girl an education, sir. She just can't play Annie. //

**Reverend Al Sharpton**：You may think this is a small matter. But this is no small matter. This child is being denied the right to play an American icon because she doesn't match the description. Those descriptions were crafted 50 years ago! We're supposed to be in a different day! //

**Judge Rita Sharpley**: Reverend . . . //

**Reverend Al Sharpton**: You talk about racial equality, how we're making progress. The problem with that progress is always a day away. Tomorrow, tomorrow—you love that—because it's always a day away. I'm here to stick out my chin today! Today! Give us an African-American Spider Man! Give us a black that can run faster than a speeding bullet and leap over tall buildings in a single bound! Not tomorrow—today! Today! The sun needs to come out today! Not tomorrow, your Honor! God Almighty! Give the American people a black Orphan Annie. It's just not good enough to say she doesn't look the part. //

**Reverend Al Sharpton**: That's what you call a rabbit, son. //

## ◆ *Passage 4*

**Directions**: *Listen to the passage and interpret from English into Chinese at the end of each segment.*

（案情简介：这是一件关于医疗事故的案件，原告方代理律师抓住了对方律师的一个颇具争议的形容词，发表了一篇发人深省的结案陈词）

**Attorney Braxton Mason**: It's bad enough that patients are running to the courts suing their doctors for all their ills. Now we have one suing for his imagined ills. This case represents the height in frivolous litigation. What's next? Seeking damages for a bad dream? I hope not. //

**Alan Shore**: "Frivolous." Is that what he said? "Frivolous"? Astonishing. This man, who suffers, day in and day out, from migraines so excruciating he cannot work, can't endure 10 minutes at his computer - a trained software engineer. And here he is subjecting himself to depositions, to examinations, the laborious, mind numbing blather of attorneys. All for what? "Frivolity"? For six months Bill Morgan reached out to his doctor, week after week, each time invoiced for thousands and thousands of dollars in sum. And then each time dismissed, patted on the head and sent on his way. Had Mr. Morgan actually received the right medical care, or even been directed to a doctor who could specifically give him that care, psychiatric or otherwise, his current state would most likely have been alleviated. But the defendant couldn't be bothered to care. As Dr. Rayburn told you himself, he treated Bill Morgan like a mascot. Opposing counsel regards him as a nuisance. He's a human being. He's a human being. We teach our children that everyone is entitled to respect and dignity. How pathetic it is when adults can't abide such a basic lesson in humanity. How unconscionable. //

## ◆ *Passage 5*

**Directions**：*Listen to the passage and interpret from English into Chinese at the end of each segment.*

[案件陈述：本案讲述的是美国的陪审团制度，一个青年因为涉嫌谋杀他的父亲而被逮捕，证据确凿，在面对这样一份指控的时候，陪审团竟然合理存疑（reasonable doubt），显示了司法程序公正以及陪审团制度的清晰架构。以下是法官对陪审团的指示部分]

**Judge**：You did a wonderful job. Wonderful! You've listened to a long and complex case, murder in the first degree. Premeditated murder is the most serious charge tried in our criminal courts. You've listened to the testimony. You've had the law interpreted to you. It is now your duty to sit down and separate the facts from the fancy. One man is dead. Another man's life is at stake. If there's a reasonable doubt as to the guilt of the accused a reasonable doubt, then you must bring me a verdict of not guilty. If there's no reasonable doubt, you must in good conscience find the accused guilty. However you decide, your verdict must be unanimous. If you find the accused guilty, the bench will not consider any mercy. The death sentence is mandatory in this case. You are faced with a grave responsibility. Thank you, gentlemen. The jurors are excused. //

## ◆ *Passage 6*

**Directions**：*Listen to the passage and interpret from English into Chinese at the* *end of each segment.*

[案件陈述：在陪审团讨论的过程中，所有的陪审员都必须参与讨论，并且要达成一致的结论。然而，12 个陪审员各有特点，每个人都有自己的价值观和道德标准，每个人的世界观、价值观迥异，要达成一致的结论谈何容易。这使第一次讨论遭遇了分歧。11 比 1 的结果仍然无法通过，因为必须全体一致（unanimous）才可以。12 个陪审员，按照顺序依次编号为 1~12]

**1**：And, well, we can vote on it right now. //

**4**：I think a preliminary vote is customary. Yeah, let's vote. //

**7**：Who knows, maybe we can all get out of here. Okay, then. Of course you know that we have a first-degree murder charge... and if we vote the accused guilty, we've got to send him to the chair. //

**3**：That's mandatory. //

**10**：We know that. //

**1**：Yeah. Anyone doesn't want to vote? //

**7**：It's all right with me. //

**1**：Remember that this has to be 12 to nothing, either way. That's the law. Okay, are we ready? Now, all those voting guilty, please raise your hands. One, two, three, four, five, six, seven, eight, nine, ten, eleven. Okay, that's eleven guilty. Who's voting not guilty? One. Right. Eleven, guilty. One, not guilty. //

**1**：Well, now we know where we are. //

**10**：Boy, oh, boy, there's always one. //

**7**：So, what do we do now? //

**8**：I guess we talk. //

**3**：Boy, oh, boy. You really think he's innocent? //

**8**：I don't know. //

**3**：You sat in court with the rest of us. You could see the kid's a dangerous killer. //

**8**：He's 18 years old. //

**3**：Well, that's old enough. He stabbed his own father in the chest. They proved it a dozen ways in court. Would you like me to list them? //

**8**：No. //

**7**：Then what do you want? //

**8**：I just want to talk.

**7**：Talk about what? Eleven say, "guilty". Nobody has to think about it but you. //

**10**：I want to ask you. Do you believe his story? //

**8**：I don't know if I do. Maybe I don't. //

**7**：So how come you vote not guilty? //

**8**：With eleven votes for guilty, it's not easy to raise my hand... and send a boy to die without talking about it. //

# Ⅳ. 参考译文 Reference versions

## ◆ *Passage 1*

**哈弗检察官**：一个有抢劫和入室行窃前科的人，这次却因为误会而被指控偷钱包！//

**萨利·希普**：有一天我在厨房，大约是 15 岁的时候，佛瑞德走了过来——我可可豆色的大拉布拉多犬，嘴里叼着一只死兔子——邻居的宠物。我以为是佛瑞德闯的祸。如果被知道它杀了他们的宠物，管制就会来人把它……所以我拿起兔子在水槽里冲洗干净，用吹风机吹干，让它白白的，毛茸茸的。然后，我偷偷溜进邻居的后院把它放回笼里。希望他们觉得兔子是自然死亡，那天晚上我父母来到我房间，他们告诉我邻居的兔子三天前死了，他们把它埋在树丛里，居然有个疯子把兔子挖出来洗干净又放回笼子里去了。我当时就觉得真相可以比虚构更离奇，更让人难以置信。女士们、先生们，这正如我们现在遇到的，我认为，合理的解释是，我的委托人的确拿了钱包，虽然难以置信却极有可能是他误认为钱包是自己的。在座各位没有人能百分之百肯定事实与巴斯克斯所说的不同——理当存疑。//

## ◆ *Passage 2*

**普雷斯顿检察官**：你们已经听过弗兰克·西蒙斯的证词了，大约就在凶案发生时，他在离案发现场 1 英里处看见了一辆 SUV 飞快地驶离，车牌是以"3L6"开头的，而里奇先生的 SUV 牌照也是以"3L6"开头。而当警察闯入被告的公寓时他是什么反应？他没有问这是怎么回事，没有问，你们要干吗。他很清楚为什么警察会出现，然后他决定马上逃跑，接下来在医院里，他认罪了。不是因为错觉才招供，他详细描述了他所犯下的罪行，被告承认他当时是因为害怕再次被定贩毒罪，从而被判终身监禁。他慌了，掏出枪，开火！而现在他的辩护律师说：也许他在供认时，产生了错觉。或者他只是想保护一个朋友、一个爱人而撒谎顶罪。绝望之人的垂死狡辩！这侮辱了法庭，还有你们，尤其是侮辱了那位女士和她的 2 个孩子。沃伦·里奇谋杀了她的丈夫，沃伦·里奇杀害了他们的父亲，他已经向警察供认了罪行。没必要再浪费时间了！//

　　**辩方律师**：埃德温，该你了。//

　　**埃德温·普尔**：我昨晚睡着了，忘了准备结案陈词，我本来想告诉你的。//

　　**辩方律师**：你没有结案陈词？//

　　**埃德温·普尔**：没有，你有吗？//

　　**哈丁法官**：辩方？//

　　**辩方律师**：埃德温，你什么都没准备？//

　　**埃德温·普尔**：当我还是个孩子时，我父亲对我说过——我现在依然记得他肯定是说——//

　　**辩方律师**：女士优先。我不知道你们怎么看，但是如果我听说某人承认犯罪了，我会认为他是真的有罪。但是，如果我知道他是被迫的，那么……比如说一个腹部伤口流血不止的人被一屋子的警察和牧师坚持指认他做了某件事，也许他就会信以为真。如果他的好友或亲属刚好那天晚上开了沃伦的车，那就能解释为什么沃伦会想要逃了。不是吗？他能预感到警察会错误地逮捕他，警察调查过这些吗？上帝，我们全都认为沃伦·里奇有罪，但是如果他没有呢？现在我们再来看看其他证据，等等，没有其他证据，没有枪、没有目击证人、没有纤维、没有法医鉴定，有的只是一份被迫作出的供词。你们可能认为是他做的，甚至认为这是理所当然的，但是你应该相信法律要求用证据以排除所有合理疑点。当我们放弃这种要求时，我们真的希望对警察说："嘿，去它的证据，只要口供就好！"//

### ◆ *Passage 3*

**萨拉·托米：**……当我被困在灰色和孤独的一天；我只是伸出下巴，微笑着说，明天，明天，我爱你，你总是在今天之后。

**夏普雷法官：**谢谢，这是……

**萨拉·托米：**明天，明天，我爱明天，你总是在今天之后。

**辩方律师：**太棒了！

**夏普雷法官：**萨拉非常精彩，但是另一个小女孩也非常好。鉴于此种情况，制作人拥有自由选择的权利。

**辩方律师：**法官阁下，我们有平等权利保障条款，有第十四修正案，我确信法官阁下都曾经阅读，也许我是错的。

**夏普顿牧师：**请允许我发言，法官阁下。听说此事我十分乐意在此表达我的观点。

**夏普雷法官：**很抱歉，神父，您没有立场……

**夏普顿牧师：**我以一个美国公民的身份在此评论公民权利的侵犯。

**夏普雷法官：**神父，请你退下。

**夏普顿牧师：**我站在此地，正如波比·肯尼迪站在阿拉巴马州法院的台阶上。

**夏普雷法官：**先生，没人否认她的受教育权，她只是不能扮演安妮。

**夏普顿牧师：**也许您认为这是小事，但它不是。这个孩子被拒绝了成为美国偶像的权利，仅仅因为她不符合漫画形象。那些作品已经过去了 50 年，今日的世界应有所不同。

**夏普雷法官：**神父……

**夏普顿牧师：**您说种族平等……取得了怎样的进展，但这种进展总是在说未来如何。明天，明天，你们喜欢它，因为它总是在今天之后。我要在今天疾呼，就在此时此刻：给予我们黑皮肤的蜘蛛侠吧！给我们一个比子弹还要快，穿梭在高楼顶端的黑人英雄吧！不是明天，而是今天！今天，太阳要在今天升起，不是明天，法官阁下。全能的主啊，请赐予美国一个黑皮肤的孤儿安妮吧！说她不像角色，这个理由是站不住脚的。

**夏普顿牧师：**这才是那只兔子，孩子。

### ◆ *Passage 4*

**梅森律师：** 糟糕的是，病人们跑到法庭，因为自己生病而状告医生，更何况这次是幻想中的病，这是场毫无意义的诉讼，接下来会是什么？因为噩梦追讨损失？希望不会。//

**辩方律师：** "毫无意义"？他是这么说的吗？"毫无意义"？令人震惊。这个男人，日夜受着折磨，剧烈的偏头痛，让他无法工作。身为一个软件工程师，在电脑前甚至无法坚持 10 分钟，他遭受辞退，接受检查，忍受律师们让人脑子发麻的唠叨。这些都为了什么？"毫无意义"？6 个月来，比尔·摩根每周都向医生求助，每次都被收费超过千元。却每次都被打发，只是拍拍头送他走，摩根先生得到过实质性的医治吗？或者被指导去找一个能给他正确医治的医生，精神科或其他的可以减轻他的疼痛吗？但被告甚至不愿麻烦自己这么做。正如雷鹏博士自己说的，他把比尔·摩根当成个吉祥物，辩方把他当成个讨厌的麻烦。他是人类，他是个人啊！我们教导孩子们：人生来就应有尊严、被尊重。可悲的是，成年人们却无法遵循人性这最基本的一点，多么荒谬！//

### ◆ *Passage 5*

**法官：** 你们做得很好，非常好。漫长复杂的审理程序已经结束，这是一宗一级谋杀案。预谋杀人在刑事诉讼中是刑责最重的罪名。你们都已经听过证词，也明了法律条文的规定，现在你们必须坐下来好好地厘清这宗案子的真伪。在本案中已有一人身亡，另一个人的生死掌握在你们手上，如果你们能提出合理的怀疑无法确认被告是否有罪，基于这个合理的怀疑，你们必须作出无罪的判决。如果你们找不出合理的怀疑，你们必须基于良知判决被告有罪。然而，你们的决定必须一致，如果你们裁定被告有罪，本庭将会对他施以严厉的惩罚，最高的刑罚会是死刑，这是一项沉重的责任。谢谢各位！后备陪审员可以离去。//

### ◆ *Passage 6*

**1：** 当然，我们可以立刻进行表决。//

**4：** 我想依照惯例，我们得先进行假投票。//

**7**：谁知道呢？或许我们可以立刻离开这里。好吧，大家都知道，这是一宗一级谋杀案……如果我们裁决被告有罪，那便等于是送他坐上电椅。//

**3**：那是必然的结果。//

**10**：我们知道。//

**1**：好了，有人反对进行表决吗？//

**7**：我没意见。//

**1**：记住，不论如何，我们都得达成共识，那是规定。大家都准备好了吗？认为他"有罪"的人请举手，一、二、三、四、五、六、七、八、九、十、十一，十一个人认为他有罪。认为他"无罪"的人请举手，一票，好吧。十一票有罪，一票无罪。//

**1**：至少现在我们有结论了。//

**10**：天啊，总是会出现唱反调的人。//

**7**：我们现在该怎么办呢？//

**8**：我猜我们得好好讨论一下。//

**3**：天啊，你真的觉得他是无辜的？//

**8**：我不知道。//

**3**：你跟我们一样坐在法庭里，你应该可以看得出来，那孩子是个危险的杀手！//

**8**：他才 18 岁。//

**3**：他已经够大了，他拿刀子往他父亲的胸口戳去，把他给杀了。在法庭上他们不断证明了这一点，你要我一一跟你说明吗？//

**8**：不必了。//

**7**：你到底想怎么样？//

**8**：我只是想谈一谈。//

**7**：你想谈什么？十一票"有罪"，除了你，大家都达成了共识。//

**10**：我想问你，你真的相信他的说辞？//

**8**：我不知道，或许我不相信。//

**7**：你为什么会认为他"无罪"？//

**8**：十一个人都认为他"有罪"，我真的很难举起手……送这个孩子坐电椅，完全不去讨论这件事。//

# V. 句子精炼 Sentences in Focus

**Directions**: *Interpret the following sentences into Chinese*:

*Exercise 1*

**THE COURT**: The jury has returned to the courtroom. Both attorneys and defendant are present. It is the defense case, Mr. Deemer.

**MR. DEEMER**: Thank you. Ladies and gentlemen of the jury, it's my opportunity at this time to outline to you basically where I expect the defense case is going to go. And again, you never know what witnesses are going to testify to sometimes so I may end up being surprised. But essentially what I believe took place is this. Is that the defendant was notified that a package had arrivedthat he was aware of the fact somehow or other that a package had been sent to him by his family. A substantial period of time goes by.

The first thing that happens is that apparently the wrong Johnson is taken down to get the package. To get the package the inmates in General Population have to go to what they call R and R, which I understand stands for release and receiving or receiving and release or something of that sort. I wonder if there is some sort of analogy with R and R in the service.

So apparently around the 12th of March the wrong Johnson goes down to R and R to get the package. The next dayand probably most of you remember this; it was the 13th of Marchthe electricity goes off and there was some delays. Now, the officer that's in charge of doing the R and R routine and escorting inmates out to get the package had to go on vacation. So he leaves a note in the sergeant's office or in the office in this unit which the defendant watches this note written and gets stuck up on one of those little postem slips to go down and get the package.

This officer goes on vacation and this drags on and drags on. The defendant says "I want to see a lieutenant or a sergeant I can get my package. " That never happens. Finally on the 28th he withholds the tray, which I agree is disobedient. He is asked to give up the tray.

Now, essentially everything that you have heard up until the time that the defendant drops the trays is consistent with the defendant's recollection except one or two things. Number one, the defendant does not recall the tray slot being opened and is standing there waiting for the tray slot to be opened in order to slide the trays through the slot.

The second thing is that he has this recollection of Officer Walker placing gloves on just before the doors open. And the third thing is that the defendant has been incarcerated as you have heard since around 1983 or '85 and he knows Officer Walker, knows who Officer Walker is. Officer Walker came up here from Folsom and he knows what Walker's reputation is. At least among the inmates Officer Walker has a reputation for pounding on inmates.

So there he is standing with the trays in his hand. Walker is on the other side. He can obviously identify him because it says Walker on the name tag. And the door opens and instead of the tray slot opening, the door opens and he figures he is going to get pounded. He drops the trays, drops his head, puts his hands up over his head, and as the officers testified to the melee ensues.

The defense testified that to his knowledge he never, ever came in contact with Officer Huston or Officer Van Berg, which is really curious because so far they have- and I doubt that it will come back to this, but neither of them testify as to any contact by them between them and the defendant in terms of force. And the only officer he comes in contact with is this Officer Walker until after he is escorted out of the cell, at which place some additional incidents take place. But it wasn't any of the officers that got battered at that time.

There are two other inmates, possibly three other inmate witnesses. One of them is the defendant's cell mate, whose recollection of the incident is somewhat different from the officers and who I believe in essence is going to testify that Officer Walker came in, just piled through the door and the defendant ended up getting beaten. The other inmate is an inmate who is in an adjacent cell that could see the crowd of what they believed is eight or ten officers outside the door and see this incident take place. There isone of these two inmates, I'm not sure which, was with the defendant I believe at some point in time prior to this incident and observed Walker engaging in some, shall we call it, aggressive conduct towards another inmate outside a kitchen area and then some comments made by either Walker or Walker and Van Berg afterwards. And which goes to basically what he thinks is going to happen when the door opened.

### Exercise 2

**THE COURT**: Let the record reflect the defendant and both attorneys and the jury are present in court. Mr. Baker, has jury reached a verdict?

**MR. BAKER**: Yes, sir.

**THE COURT**: Hand the verdict to the bailiff, please.

**THE CLERK**: " Superior Court of the State of California, County of Del Norte, People of the State of California versus James Johnson. We the jury impaneled in the aboveentitled matter find the defendant, James Johnson, guilty of battery on a correctional officer in violation of Section 4501. 5 of the Penal Code, Officer Huston, Count 1.

We the jury empaneled in the aboveentitled matter find the defendant, James Johnson, guilty on Count 2, battery on correctional officer in violation of Section 4501. 5 of the Penal Code, Officer Van Berg. Now, what I got to have you understand is this, is that I'm not trying to establish that Walker is a bad guy or is an aggressive officer in this case. The key thing is this, if you have reason to believe that you are going to be assaulted you can do something to defend yourself. And in essence I believe what the testimony is going to show is that the defendant had this belief that when this door opens he dropsI mean he is standing there totally not aggressive, dropped the trays, okay, ducks his head and does the most normal thing that all of us would do under those circumstances, puts his hands over his head to avoid getting beat.

# 第十二单元 诉讼外争端解决

## Unit 12 Alternative Dispute Resolution

# I. 专题知识 Legal Knowledge

诉讼是解决争议的有效方式，但并不是解决争议的唯一方式。通过非诉讼方式（ADR）解决争议同样可以实现公平合理，且 ADR 具有花费低廉、耗时少等优点。

ADR 为"Alternative Dispute Resolution"的英文简称，中文可直译为选择性争议解决方式，又称为"诉讼外纠纷解决机制""替代性纠纷解决机制"，是诉讼外或非诉讼解决争议的各种方法的统称。这一概念起源于美国，而后在欧洲大陆各国、日本、韩国、澳大利亚等国亦广为盛行。目前，ADR 已普遍为人们所接受和使用，作为替代诉讼解决国际民商事争议的方法，其合法性和先进性毋庸置疑。日本、德国、澳大利亚都根据各自的实际构建了相应的 ADR。我国在历史上是 ADR 的先进国，目前法律制度中也存在各种非诉讼纠纷解决机制。

## 一、ADR 的特点和优越性

（1）灵活性。几乎所有的 ADR 方法都允许当事人选择调解人、中立人、仲裁员和"法官"（如聘请法官）。并且，在大多数 ADR 方法中，双方当事人可以协商决定处理纠纷的实体法和程序。所选调解人、中立人、仲裁员的费用相对较低，程序又相当灵活，所费时间和金钱少。

（2）一般不公开进行，其结果无须汇编成册，对商事和婚姻家庭纠纷的当事人来说有一种安全感。

（3）方法强调当事人的妥协和让步，特别是经济纠纷的当事人，有利于继续保持友好关系，保留以后合作的可能。

（4）给予人们更多选择机会，为解决纠纷提供多种思维，促进纠纷及时解决，同时也减轻法院的负担，缓和法院案件冗积"消化能力"不足的矛盾。

## 二、ADR 的种类

常见的 ADR 主要有以下几种：

1. 调解（Mediation）

调解是指第三者应争议双方当事人的请求，通过尽量协调双方的分歧，而不是作出有约束力的决定的方式解决当事人之间争议的方法。调解可以说是 ADR 中最为常见和最重要的一种形式，是所有其他形式的 ADR 的基础。与法庭审判相比，调解花费低廉、耗时少，当事人心理压力较小。

2. 模拟诉讼形式的调解（又称微型审理"Mini-trial"）

微型审理并非我们通常所说的一般意义上的法庭审理，它实质上是一种模拟诉讼的调解方式。通常由当事人双方各指派一名高级行政长官组成专门小组，并共同推选一名首席调解员。各方当事人所指定的行政长官一般只代表各方当事人的利益。轮流以口头或书面方式提出自己的意见，如同法院公开审理一样，只不过形式更简单。

3. 仲裁/调解（Mediation-Arbitration，"Med-Arb"）

这是介于调解和仲裁之间的一种解决争议的模式。在这种模式中，当事人事先同意在调解失败时，调解员将继续担任仲裁员。

## 三、各国有关 ADR 的实践

1. 美国

在美国，ADR 作为诉讼外解决争议的方法发展迅速，尤其是在加利福尼亚州，ADR 被广泛用于处理离婚案件、邻里小事、医疗事故、环境争议、产品责任，直至复杂的涉及多方当事人的数以亿美元计。另外，设在华盛顿州和佛罗里达州的争议解决中心的"多门径法庭"是运用选择性争议解决方式解决争议的典型。在华盛顿，当某些民事案件被提交给法院时，首先由有关的专家会晤起诉人，并根据案情和当事人的愿望，帮助当事人选择最合适的手段（例如调解、仲裁，甚至审判），以解决争议。佛罗里达州比其他州拥有更为广泛的"调解和仲裁计划"。根据该州的一项法律，法官将案件分流，指导当事人去进行调解或仲裁。调解是佛罗里达州最普遍采用的选择性争议解决方式。

2. 澳大利亚

澳大利亚也是一个盛行 ADR 的国家。在澳大利亚，早在 1892 年，昆士兰州就已有了《法院调解法案》（现在仍有效）。在新南威尔士州也有《贸易争议调解和仲裁法》。但直至 20 世纪 80 年代，调解这种程序才开始被用于解决公司之间的纠纷。目前，调解是最重要的 ADR 形式。微型审理也广为运用。特别是非常重要的采矿和合营企业合同及保险合同常常包含调解条款。1991 年，澳大利亚联邦政府通过了《法院（调解和仲裁）法》。根据该项法律，法院可以命令当事人进行强制性调解（compulsory mediation）。它实际上是在由法院任命的特别代表的主持下进行的强制性磋商。

3. 英国

在英国，ADR 受到了很大的怀疑。它主要存在于司法中，如诉讼中的调解。仲裁本身也在 ADR 范畴之内。虽然在英国，ADR 尚未制度化，甚至连诉讼中的调解也未像美国那样制度化，但许多职业协会对 ADR 存有浓厚的兴趣，如仲裁员特许协会、争议解决中心、英国专家协会、建筑仲裁员协会等都尽可能提供调解服务。

4. 法国和其他大陆法国家

在法国和其他大陆法国家，除了少数例外情况，ADR 并没有像美国、澳大利亚那样制度化或规范化。当然，国际商会仲裁院及其他一些仲裁机构（如英国的仲裁机构）已经制定了调解规则。瑞士苏黎世商会已经制订了使微型审理制度化的规则。荷兰仲裁院也正在准备在其仲裁规则中加入有关微型审理的规则。

# Ⅱ. 词汇热身 Vocabulary Warm-up

**Directions**：*Give the English equivalents of the following Chinese expressions*：

| | | |
|---|---|---|
| 香港发展局 | 《建业图新》报告书 | 承包商 |
| 香港建造业议会 | 广泛覆盖/涵盖了 | 金融海啸 |
| 概括 | 解决索赔和纠纷 | （工程）保证金 |
| 香港特区政府特首 | 现金周转 | 临时支付 |

超过……最高达到          具有成本效益的          争端解决顾问
"按工程进度"的付款        预防胜于治疗            土木工程
方式                     ·  新工程合同             任期
隧道掘进机                仲裁                   香港国际仲裁中心
高时效

**Directions**：*Give the Chinese equivalents of the following English expressions*：

| | |
|---|---|
| Victoria | "soft touch" approach |
| Magistrates' Court | cost penalties |
| VCAT | Access to Justice Task force report |
| Attorney-General | a whole-of-government approach |
| Litigation | The Hon Chief Justice |
| Associate Judges | Professor Sander |
| Biota pharmaceuticals case | ground-breaking |
| Opes Prime litigation | Varieties of Dispute Processing |
| pre-action protocols | Roscoe Pound Conference |
| backfire | The Causes of Popular Dissatisfaction with |
| synergy | the Administration of Justice |
| asbestos | multi-door courthouses |
| plaintiff | incentives |
| mediation | key stakeholders |
| to vindicate the Court of Appeal | be bogged down |
| the Civil Justice Council | Mediator |
| "non adversarial justice" | intractable disputes |
| Chief Counsel Litigation | the Native Title Amendment Bill |
| AGS | the Access to Justice |
| "ADR and the Commonwealth" | Amendment Bill |
| NADRAC | National Mediator Accreditation System |

# III. 课文口译 Text for Interpreting

## ◆ *Passage 1*

**Directions**：*Listen to the passage and interpret from Chinese into English at the end of each segment.*

（以下为香港发展局时任局长林郑月娥 2009 年 10 月 12 日于替代性争端解决论坛的发言）

下午好，女士们，先生们，//

我很高兴大家来到由香港发展局主办、香港建造业议会（CIC）承办的替代性争端解决方式（ADR）论坛。我也很高兴看到这么多香港建造业的领导成员能拨冗出席。我相信今天的论坛将为我们提供一个极好的机会来提升彼此的知识储备，交换彼此对 ADR 的意见，并探讨我们能如何以最好的方式推行这些意见，从而为香港的建造业作出贡献。//

我先做一个简单的回顾。2000 年 4 月，香港特区行政长官委任唐英年先生担任建造业检讨委员会（CIRC）的主席，以全面检讨建造业的状况，并提出改善措施的建议。2001 年 1 月，该委员会完成了这项任务，并向行政长官提交了一份题为《建业图新》的报告书。该报告书概述了 109 项改善措施，广泛涵盖了建筑的活动范畴，以提高建筑业的质量并确保其成本效益。在过去的几年中，这些建议的执行取得了良好的进展，特别是法定 CIC 的建立及前建造业训练局与 CIC 的成功合并。我借此机会感谢 CIC 以及所有参与协助我们取得现有成就的各方。//

今天的论坛是为了解决另一个报告重点提出的一套建议，即在建造行业内，采用积极的方法解决索赔和纠纷、培训争端解决的项目团队以及采取积极合作的方式解决争端。我很高兴 CIC 能与发展局携手举办这个论坛，以推动这些建议的执行。//

由于缔约双方之间的纠纷不可避免地因金钱而起或与之有关，因此我想先向各位报告发展局最近针对这个问题所采取的一些措施。//

对于承建商而言，现金周转尤为重要。发展局已注意到承建商在经济衰退时期所面临的困难。在去年，金融海啸来袭不久，我们就及时出台了一系

列措施，以减轻我们的公共工程承建商所面临的困难。我总结一下迄今为止我们所取得的进展：//

第一，在所有不包含临时支付规定的现有合约中，设立以上安排。若没有这一点，报酬只有在工程竣工时才会被支付。截至 2009 年 8 月底，一共有 162 个合同受惠。在不久的将来，还将有两个合同也会受惠。现已结算了 2.58 亿美元，在接下来的 3 年至 4 年，还将会结算 1.05 亿美元。//

第二，维护期过去一半后，发还一半的工程保证金，维护期通常是 12 个月。截至 2009 年 8 月底，已有 87 份合同受惠。在不久的将来，还有 29 份合同会受惠。现已发还了 4700 万美元，在接下来的 1 年到 2 年，还将发还 4300 万美元。//

第三，对于在工程订单完成时，临时支付的最高金额低于工程的估计价值 90% 的定期合同，支付的金额水平提高到 90%。截至 2009 年 8 月底，已有 54 份合同受惠。不久的将来，还有 2 份合同会受惠。现已支付了 1.53 亿美元，在接下来 3 年至 4 年，还将支付 3600 万美元。

第四，对于已完成 3 年的工程的合同，工务部门将努力尽早使这些账户实现融资。截至 2009 年 8 月底，已有 36 份合同受惠，并融资了 9000 万美元。//

第五，对于那些使用"按工程进度付款"方式的合同，当材料或建筑设备时，如隧道掘进机，被运至工程现场时，定金可以预付。截至 2009 年 8 月底，已有 4 个合同受惠。现已预付了 7.06 亿美，在未来一年到两年半，还将预付 6.34 亿美元。不久的将来，还有 5 个合同会受惠。//

从总体来看，这 5 项措施已覆盖了 376 份合同，涉及约 20.7 亿美元的合同付款，其中 12.5 亿美元已经支付，8 亿美元将根据工程进度支付。发展局将会于 2009 年年底回顾上述措施的成效。//

让我们回到今天的主题"争端"，随着政府开始进行大型公共基础设施的建设，这个问题也受到越来越多的重视。这些项目如要做到及时交付且把预算控制在范围内，需要建造业各方的通力合作。毫无疑问，作为雇主，发展局和我们的工务部门将继续发挥关键作用。然而，我们虽然出于良好的意图和目的但偶尔还是会有业务关系上的纠纷，建造业也不例外。//

在香港，解决建筑纠纷的传统方式有时会以诉讼对抗的方式结束。诉讼的过程是昂贵的、漫长的，并且会使所有当事方承受与他们负担能力不相称

的财力和时间。如果可以在一开始就避免纠纷，这将大大地提高时间效率和成本效益。//

如同许多其他问题一样，预防胜于治疗。所以处理争端的最好方式就是一开始就不让它发生。CIRC 的报告书建议采用更广泛的伙伴合作方式，并把伙伴合作方式与一种新形式的合同融合在一起。事实上，早在 1997 年，在公共工程合同中就已引入了非合同制伙伴合作关系。对于合同制伙伴合作关系，工务科正在试验用新工程合同（NEC），这是英国土木工程学会于 1993 年发起推行的一种合同制伙伴合作形式。首个试行 NEC 的政府合同在 2009 年 8 月得到了授权，而在未来几年内，将会有更多的合同获得授权试行。//

在香港，20 世纪 80 年代前，仲裁是解决公共工程合同争端的唯一手段。直到 20 世纪 90 年代初，政府才在公共工程合同的一般条件中引入调解。在机场核心计划工程中，政府把审判裁决作为替代性争端解决方式的一种添加到合同之中。早在 1991 年初，公共部门就已推行雇用争端解决顾问（DRA）以减少合同纠纷的概念。建筑署自 1991 年 12 月以来，在 66 份建设工程合同中采用了 DRA 制度，后来在 2005 年时，该制度扩展到民用工程，共 17 个土建工程合同被选为试行 DRA。//

基于 2007 年的中期检查及工务部门之间于 2009 年 4 月进行的经验交流会，DRA 制度被认为能最大限度地减少争端，因此政府建议更广泛地使用 DRA。经过咨询香港建造商会，我们已经决定，即将实施的 15 个合同（相当于 2009 年中期至 2010 年初即将展开的主要合同的一半数量）以及现有的 2 个合同，将以补充协议的方式，采用 DRA。为了加快合同的完成进程，我们也扩大了 DRA 的保有周期，把维修周期也囊括进来。//

要广泛应用 DRA，自然需要更多经验丰富的顾问。为确保能够供应足够的优质 DRA，以应对未来的潜在需求，我们与香港国际仲裁中心于 2009 年 6 月进行了讨论，并邀请他们协助对有潜力的 DRA 进行培训，以促进和鼓励有潜力的 DRA 候选人的参与。在这方面，我想感谢香港国际仲裁中心的郑若骅女士和苏嘉贤先生的热情和支持。//

我们还审查了 DRA 的现行制度，并决定扩大现有的评审小组，集思广益，以争取吸引更多的建筑专家参与到这个制度中来。//

我毫不怀疑，纠纷的解决方式会不断发展，而且建设部门必须与时俱进，甚至最好能引领未来的趋势。政府鼓励在公共工程合同中更广泛地应用伙伴合作方式和 DRA 制度，从而在纠纷真正发生之前，促进意见分歧的解决。一旦出现纠纷，政府希望能迅速解决，从而在最短的时间内保证承建商能得到合理的支付。为了支持这项工作，我很高兴看到 CIC 即将发表一份关于争端解决的方针。据我了解，该方针将提供多种不同的 ADR，供公共和私营部门的雇主和承包商选择，以满足不同情况下可能出现的纠纷。我对 CIC 推行此项非常有意义的行动表示高度的赞扬。//

我鼓励每一位与会者积极交流，分享彼此实施 ADR 的技术和经验，开阔你的思想，思考这些经验技术是否适合用于解决纠纷，或是能从一开始就防范纠纷的发生。

谢谢。//

## ◆ *Passage 2*

**Directions**：*Listen to the passage and interpret from Chinese into English at the end of each segment.*

（The following is a speech entitled "Utilizing ADR：the evolving landscape" by the Hon Robert McClelland, Attorney-General for Australia, in Canberra on Feb. 15, 2009）

Mr Tom Howe QC, Chief Counsel Litigation, Australian Government Solicitor Simon Daley, Ladies and gentlemen, //

It is a pleasure to be here at the first Government Law Group event for the year and to speak to you about alternative dispute resolution (ADR) in the federal justice system. It is also my pleasure to launch the AGS/LEADR training program "ADR and the Commonwealth". //

The National Alternative Dispute Resolution Advisory Council's (NADRAC) recent inquiry into the use of ADR in the civil justice system found that while ADR has "expanded into a large, highly diverse and innovative field, it is still significantly under-utilized in many areas". //

The Federal Government is considering a range of initiatives for promoting greater use of ADR in the civil justice system. As the biggest single litigator in the federal justice system, the Commonwealth and its agencies play an important leadership role in increasing the use of ADR in Australia. Today I want to talk to you about how Commonwealth agencies can fulfill this role. //

ADR has many benefits when utilized within the context of litigation, as well as an alternative to litigation. It often ensures earlier and speedier resolution of disputes, and offers parties more privacy, confidentiality and cost saving benefits. Resolving disputes through ADR also allows parties to have an element of control on the process and a say in the outcome. As a result, they are more likely to feel satisfied and empowered. //

Even if a dispute is not resolved in an ADR process, the process itself can help draw out facts, identify issues and explore new options. This means that even if litigation is ultimately commenced, its duration, cost and potential distress upon parties can be reduced. //

These are just some of the benefits of ADR—and for these reasons, the Australian Government strongly encourages the greater use of ADR. Indeed, ADR plays an important role in ensuring better access to justice in the federal civil justice system. //

ADR should not be seen as a "soft touch" approach to resolving disputes. For example, cost penalties can be imposed for failing to take an opportunity to resolve a dispute such as failing to entertain a reasonable offer of settlement. As many of you may be aware, the Government passed amendments last year to the Federal Court Act 1976 to ensure that ADR is taken seriously by parties, lawyers and judges. //

Access to justice is not just about access to a court or a lawyer. It is about providing practical, affordable and easily understood information and options to assist people to avoid or resolve their disputes. //

This point is made in the Access to Justice Taskforce report, a Strategic Framework for Access to Justice in the Federal Civil Justice System. Its central recommendation is a Strategic Framework for Access to Justice to guide the consideration of future civil justice reforms. //

The Strategic Framework has been adopted by the Government and is based on the principles of: Accessibility, Appropriateness, Equity, Efficiency and Effectiveness. The Framework emphasizes a number of themes including early intervention, ensuring costs are proportionate, and providing pathways to fair and equitable outcomes whether it be through better access to information, resolution with the assistance of a Court or ADR. //

Consistent with the Framework, the Government is pursuing several measures to boost the use of ADR in the civil justice system. In November last year, the Access to Justice (Civil Litigation Reforms) Amendment Bill passed the Parliament and created a new overarching obligation on the Federal Court that requires the Court, litigants and legal practitioners to facilitate the just resolution of disputes according to law and as quickly, inexpensively and efficiently as possible. //

This provision will enable judges to employ a number of case management powers, including: referring parties to ADR; requiring parties to narrow the issues in dispute; limiting the length of submissions or the number of witnesses; or setting time limits for the completion of part of a proceeding. Over time I believe these changes will encourage a cultural shift in the approach taken to resolving disputes. //

In 2008 I asked NADRAC to look into strategies to ensure greater use of ADR in civil proceedings. In September last year NADRAC delivered its report, entitled The Resolve to Resolve—Embracing ADR to Improve Access to Justice in the Federal Jurisdiction, which contains 39 recommendations including proposed legislative amendments and policy initiatives for the legal profession, courts and tribunals, government agencies and the public. Several of the recommendations relate to increasing both public and professional awareness of ADR as well as ways for Governments to engage in greater use of ADR. //

As the biggest single litigator in the federal civil justice system, the Commonwealth and its agencies are well placed to play a leadership role in moving from a culture of litigation to a culture of dispute resolution. Commonwealth agencies are required by the Legal Services Directions to act as "model litigants" which means acting with complete propriety, fairness and to the highest professional standard. This obligation, despite its title, applies not just to the conduct of court-based litigation, but to all ADR processes. //

Further, agencies are required to consider ADR before initiating legal proceedings and to keep the costs of litigation to a minimum, using appropriate methods such as ADR. Agencies are also required to participate "fully and effectively" in ADR processes. //

In its 2009 report, NADRAC recommended that the Legal Service Directions be amended to require agencies to develop and regularly review dispute management plans that require appropriate use of ADR. Accordingly, I have asked NADRAC to prepare a model dispute management plan that could be used by agencies to comply with their obligations under the Directions. As part of this reference, NADRAC conducted a roundtable with lawyers and decision makers from Commonwealth agencies last week. //

A dispute management plan is not just a litigation plan—it is a practical approach to resolving disputes involving communication, openness to other views, negotiation and reasonableness. These factors are the essence of ADR—and should be part of the professional toolkit of any lawyer. //

Government agencies are obliged to ensure that Commonwealth resources are expended lawfully and are protected from unjust claims. This obligation should not prevent Commonwealth agencies from doing all that they can to resolve Government disputes without necessarily having to go to court. Government lawyers will play a key role in effecting the cultural shift from litigation as the only tool to resolve disputes to much greater use and incorporation of ADR. Government lawyers need to consider ADR and obligations contained in the Directions as part of their wider, whole-of-government approach to the provision of Commonwealth legal services. //

The feedback that I have received from lawyers, courts and tribunals has been that too frequently legal officers that attend ADR are not sufficiently on top of the issues and/or do not have the authority to negotiate and settle a matter. In my view, ADR is as much a management issue as a legal practice. This means that effective ADR requires management to empower the participating legal officers to negotiate effectively and as early in the proceedings as possible.

It is important that they view themselves as lawyers for the Commonwealth, not just their agency. The use of ADR as part of a whole-of-government approach will ensure the effective and efficient resolution of disputes involving the Commonwealth. //

The Office of Legal Services Coordination can assist government lawyers with queries they may have regarding the procurement and provision of legal services, and their awareness of and compliance with the Legal Service Directions. In considering how to better inform and encourage government lawyers to use ADR, I recognize that appropriate training and education are crucial. Education about ADR processes is essential in equipping the profession with adequate understanding and relevant skills, and in improving ADR culture. //

Both the Access to Justice Taskforce and NADRAC made specific recommendations about improving legal education which the Government will be progressing. Given the growing importance of ADR in the resolution of Commonwealth disputes, there is a need for agency staff to better understand how different processes can be used. //

I commend AGS and LEADR for taking the initiative to develop the "ADR and the Commonwealth" training program for Commonwealth agencies. I have no doubt that participants will find the program worthwhile and beneficial to their work. I would also like to again thank NADRAC for their ongoing work in promoting ADR as a key part of the federal civil justice system. It is now my great pleasure to launch the "ADR and the Commonwealth" program. //

Thank you. //

# IV. 参考译文 Reference versions

## ◆ *Passage 1*

(The following is the speech by Mrs. Carrie Lam, the Secretary for Development Bureau, HKSAR at the Alternative Dispute Resolution Forum on Oct 12, 2009)

Good afternoon, ladies and gentlemen, //

It gives me great pleasure to welcome you all to this forum on Alternative Dispute Resolution (ADR) organized by Development Bureau, with the support of the Construction Industry Council. I am also pleased to see so many leading members of the Hong Kong construction industry who are able to make your time here. I am sure the forum today will provide an excellent opportunity for us to update each other and exchange views on the ADR processes and to explore how best we could take them forward for the benefit of Hong Kong's construction industry. //

To recap, in April 2000, the Chief Executive of the HKSAR appointed a Construction Industry Review Committee (CIRC) chaired by Mr. Henry Tang to review comprehensively the state of the construction industry and to recommend improvement measures. In January 2001, the committee completed this task and submitted a report entitled "Construct for Excellence" to the Chief Executive. The report outlined a total of 109 improvement measures covering a wide spectrum of construction activities with a view to raising the quality and ensuring cost – effectiveness of the industry. Over the past few years, good progress has been made in implementation of those recommendations, notably with the establishment of a statutory CIC and the successful merging of the former Construction Industry Training Authority with CIC. I take this opportunity to thank the CIC and all involved in taking us thus far. //

Today's forum is to address another set of key recommendations in the report, that is, adopting a proactive approach in resolving claims and disputes, training of project teams on dispute resolution and using proactive and collaborative dispute resolution methods in settling disputes in the construction industry. I am glad that CIC has, in partnership with Development Bureau, organized this forum with a view to furthering the implementation of these recommendations. //

As disputes between contracting parties inevitably arise from or are related to money matters, may I start by updating the audience on the recent measures Development Bureau has taken on this front. //

Cash-flows are particularly important to a contractor. The Development Bureau is mindful of the difficulties faced by contractors during the economic downturn. Shortly after last year's financial tsunami, we promptly promulgated a package of measures to alleviate the difficulties faced by our public works contractors. Let me summarize progress made to date: //

To institute in all existing contracts which do not contain an Interim Payment provision such anarrangement. Without this, payment will be made only upon completion of the works. Up to the end of August 2009, a total of 162 contracts have benefitted. Two more contracts will be included in the near future. A total of $258 million was settled and $105 million will be settled over the next three to four years. //

To release early a portion of the Retention Money after a lapse of half of the maintenance period, which is normally 12 months. Up to the end of August 2009, a total of 87 contracts have benefitted. 29 more contracts will be included in the near future. A total of $47 million was settled and $43 million will be settled over the next one to two years. //

For term contracts in which the maximum amount of interim payment is capped below 90% of the estimated value of the works upon completion of a works order, the payment level is now raised to 90%. Up to the end of August 2009, a total of 54 contracts have benefitted. Two more contracts will be included in the near future. A total of $153 million was settled and $36 million will be settled over the next three to four years. //

For those contracts with works completed over three years, Works Departments will strive tofinalise the accounts as early as possible. Up to the end of August 2009, a total of 36 contracts have benefitted and $90 million was settled. //

For those contracts using "milestone payment" method, advanced payment is made when materials or construction plant, e. g. Tunnelling Boring Machine, are delivered to the site. Up to the end of August 2009, four contracts have benefitted. A total of $706 million was settled and $634 million will be settled in the next one to 2. 5 years. Five more contracts will be included in the near future. //

In aggregate terms, the five measures have covered a total of 376 contracts, involving contract payments of about $2. 07 billion, out of which $1. 25 billion had been paid and $800 million will be paid in accordance with the works progress. The Development Bureau will review the effectiveness of the above measures by the end of 2009. //

Coming back to the topic of "Disputes" today, this matter is gaining significance as the Government is embarking on a major public infrastructure programme. The delivery of these projects on time and within budget would depend on the collaboration of every party in the industry. No doubt, as the Employer, the Development Bureau and our Works Departments will continue to play a key role. Despite all good intents and purposes, disputes occur from time to time in business relationships. The construction industry is of no exception. //

In Hong Kong, the conventional way of resolving construction disputes sometimes would end up with adversarial litigation. This process is costly, lengthy and will impose disproportionate time and financial burdens on all parties involved. It will be far more time−efficient and cost−effective if disputes could be avoided in the first place. //

As with many other problems, prevention is better than cure. So the best way to handle disputes is not to let it happen in the first place. The CIRC Report recommended wider adoption of a partnering approach and the integration of a partnering approach into a new form of contract. In fact, non − contractual partnering was introduced in public works contracts back in 1997. For contractual partnering, Works Branch is piloting contractual partnering using New Engineering Contract (NEC), which is a contractual partnering form of contract launched in 1993 by the Institution of Civil Engineers in UK. The first trial government contract using NEC was recently awarded in August 2009 and more trial contracts will be let out in the years to come. //

In Hong Kong, before 1980s, arbitration was the only means for dispute resolution in public works contracts. Since early 1990s, Government introduced mediation to the General Conditions of Contracts in public works. In the Airport Core Programme projects, Government has added adjudication as an alternative dispute resolution means. The concept of employing Dispute Resolution Advisors (DRA) in minimizing contractual disputes was practiced by the public sector in early 1991. The Architectural Services Department adopted the DRA system in 66 building works contracts since December, This was subsequently extended to civil engineering works in 2005 when a total of 17 civil engineering works contracts have been selected for the trial use of DRA. //

Based on an interim review in 2007 and an experience sharing session conducted amongst Works Departments in April 2009, the DRA system is considered helpful in minimizing disputes and thus the wider use of DRA is recommended. Having consulted Hong Kong Construction Association, we have decided that an addition of 15 upcoming contracts, which is equivalent to about 50% of all upcoming major contracts to commence between mid-2009 and early 2010, and two existing contracts, by means of supplementary agreements, will adopt DRA. With a view to expediting contract finalization, we have also extended the tenure of DRA to cover the Maintenance Period. //

The wider adoption of DRA naturally calls for a greater supply of experienced advisors. To ensure a sufficient supply of good quality DRAs to meet the possible future demand, we discussed with the Hong Kong International Arbitration Centre in June 2009 and invited them to help organize training courses for potential DRAs to promote and encourage enlisting of potential candidates. In this regard, I would like to thank Teresa Cheng and Gary Soo for their enthusiasm and support. //

We have also reviewed the current system in enlisting DRA, and decided to expand the current assessment panel and to devise means to attract more able construction experts to enlist in the system. //

I have no doubt that dispute resolution is an evolving subject and the construction sector must move with times, or better still, ahead of the trend. Government encourages a wider use of the partnering approach and DRA system in public works contracts, with an aim to encourage the resolution of all differences in opinion before formal disputes arise. Once disputes arise, Government is keen to see them being resolved in a speedy manner so that justified payments to contractors can be secured in the shortest time possible. To support this work, I am glad that the CIC Committee on Subcontracting is about to issue a guideline on dispute resolution. As I understand, the guideline will provide a host of different ADR methods for employers and contractors in the public and private sectors to choose from in order to cater for different scenarios where disputes may arise. I pay tribute to the CIC for taking forward this highly worthwhile initiative. //

I encourage every participant at this forum to share experience in implementing the various ADR techniques and be open to consider whether these techniques will be suitable in resolving dispute cases or even to prevent them from arising in the first place.

Thank you. //

◆ *Passage 2*

（以下是 2009 年 2 月 15 日，澳大利亚司法部部长罗伯特·麦克利兰在堪培拉发表的一篇题为《ADR 的运用——不断变化的风景》的演讲）

王室法律顾问汤姆·豪先生，首席诉讼律师、澳大利亚政府代表律师西蒙·戴利先生，女士们，先生们：//

我很高兴能够出席此次首届政府法律小组的年度活动，向各位发表我对替代性纠纷解决方式（ADR）在联邦司法系统中的看法。同时，我也高兴能在此启动 AGS／LEADR 的培训计划 "ADR 与澳大利亚联邦"。//

国家替代争议解决咨询理事会（NADRAC）最近对 ADR 在民事司法系统中的使用情况进行了调查，并通过调查发现，ADR 的运用 "已扩展到大规模、高度多样化且创新的领域，但在许多领域使用仍明显不足"。//

联邦政府正在考虑开展一系列活动来促进 ADR 在民事司法系统更进一步的运用。作为联邦司法系统中最大的独立诉讼律师，澳大利亚联邦政府及其机构在促进 ADR 的使用上发挥着重要的领导作用。今天，我想和各位谈谈如何使联邦机构发挥这一作用。//

在诉讼框架下使用时，ADR 有许多好处，同时也可以作为替代诉讼的另一种纠纷解决方式。ADR 往往能确保更早、更迅速地解决争端，并为当事人提供更好的隐私权和保密性且能节省成本。通过 ADR 解决争端还可以使各方当事人对过程有一定程度的控制，并对结果有一定的发言权，从而使各方当事人对结果感到更满意，感到更有自主权。//

即使纠纷没有在 ADR 的过程中得到解决，这个过程本身也可以帮助提炼出事实，找出问题所在，并探索新的解决方式。这意味着，即使最终不得不诉诸诉讼，诉讼所持续的时间、耗费各方当事人的金钱和潜在的困难都可以大大减少。//

这些仅是 ADR 的一部分好处而已——而且正因如此，澳大利亚政府大力鼓励更多地使用 ADR。事实上，ADR 能在联邦民事司法系统中发挥重要作用，确保司法正义的伸张。//

ADR 不应该被视作 "儿戏" 的争端解决方式。例如，若不能抓住机会解决争端，拒绝接受合理的和解要求，有关当事人可能会被处以罚款。在座的各位中有不少人或许已注意到，政府在去年通过了《1976 年联邦法院令》的修正案，以确保当事人、律师和法官认真对待 ADR。//

伸张司法正义并不只是指诉诸法院或律师。这关乎提供实用的、可负担得起且容易理解的信息和选项，以帮助人们避免或解决他们的纠纷。//

伸张司法正义特别工作组的报告阐述了这一观点。该报告书是在联邦民事司法系统伸张司法正义的战略框架。它的核心建议是为伸张司法正义建立一个战略框架，以指导未来民事司法制度改革的因素。//

该战略框架已通过政府审核，且立足于以下原则：可达性、适当性、公平性、效率和效益。该框架强调了多个主旨，包括早期干预、确保成本相称并通过提供更好的获取信息的途径或是通过法院或 ADR 的协助，以获取公平和公正的结果。//

在遵守该框架的前提下，政府正在采取多项措施，以提高 ADR 在民事司法系统中的使用。去年 11 月，《伸张司法正义（民事诉讼改革）条例修正案》获得议会通过，并为联邦法院创建了一个新的首要任务，即要求法院、当事人和法律界人士依照法律，尽可能快速、低价、高效地促进纠纷的公正解决。//

这项规定将使法官行使多个案件管理权力，其中包括：建议当事人使用 ADR、要求当事双方缩小争议问题的范围、限制意见书长度或证人数目或对部分程序设定完成的时限。随着时间的推移，我相信，这些变化将鼓励争端解决在方式上发生文化的转变。//

2008 年，我要求 NADRAC 研究战略，以确保在民事诉讼中更多地使用 ADR。去年 9 月，NADRAC 发表了一份报告，题为"决心解决——鼓励使用 ADR 以改善联邦司法管辖中司法正义的伸张"，其中包含 39 项建议，包括法例修订的建议和对法律界、法院和法庭、政府机构和公众的政策措施。若干项建议涉及提高公众和法律界对 ADR 的意识，以及促进澳大利亚政府更多地使用 ADR 的方法。//

作为联邦民事司法制度中最大的独立诉讼律师，澳大利亚联邦及其机构处于有利地位，发挥着领导性的作用，使公众从诉诸诉讼向解决争端的文化意识转化。根据《法律服务方向》的要求，联邦机构必须以"模范诉讼人"为准则。这意味着联邦法院的行为必须符合完全恰当、公平和最高专业水平的标准。这一义务，虽然名称有所限制，但其不仅适用于以法院为基础的诉讼

行为，而且向也适用于所有 ADR 过程。//

　　此外，根据要求，联邦机构在提出诉讼前，须优先考虑 ADR，并使用适当的方法，如 ADR，把诉讼的成本降到最低。联邦机构还必须"充分且有效地"参与到 ADR 过程中。//

　　在其 2009 年的报告中，NADRAC 建议对《法律服务方向》加以修订，要求各机构制定并定期审查需要适当使用 ADR 的纠纷管理计划。因此，我已要求 NADRAC 准备一份可以让联邦机构用于遵守其在《法律服务方向》中义务的模拟纠纷管理计划。作为这份参考的一部分，上周 NADRAC 与来自澳大利亚联邦机构的律师和决策者进行了圆桌会谈。//

　　争端管理计划不仅仅是一个诉讼的计划——这是一个实用的纠纷解决方式，涵盖了交流、听取他人意见、谈判及合理性。上述这些因素是 ADR 的精髓——同时也是每一位律师都应该掌握的专业技能。//

　　政府机构有责任确保澳大利亚联邦的开支花费符合法律，并保护其免受不公正的索赔。这项义务不应该妨碍联邦机构在不必要诉诸法庭的情况下，尽其所能地解决和政府有关的争端。政府律师将发挥关键作用，改变人们对争端解决的固定看法，即从视诉讼为解决争端的唯一手段，转变到更为广泛地使用并融合 ADR。政府律师需要考虑《法律服务方向》中所涵盖的 ADR 和义务，并将其作为相对澳大利亚联邦法律服务规定的更广泛、更全面的政府手段。//

　　我从律师、法院、审判团收到的反馈意见频繁表明，参与 ADR 的法律人员无法充分掌握问题所在且/或没有权力进行谈判和解决争端。我认为，ADR 既是管理问题，又是法律实践。这意味着，有效的 ADR 需要管理层授权法律人员进行有效的谈判，并尽可能在诉讼程序的早期进行。//

　　重要的是，他们认为自己是澳大利亚联邦的律师，不只是隶属他们的机构。把 ADR 作为政府整体手段的一部分来使用，能确保涉及联邦政府的争端得到实效和高效的解决。//

　　法律事务协调办公室可以协助政府律师，回答他们对于法律服务的采购和提供，以及对于遵守《法律服务方向》的疑问。在考虑如何更好地宣传和鼓励政府律师使用 ADR 时，我认识到，关键在于适当的培训和教育。有关 ADR 过程的教育是必不可少的，它能使政府律师对 ADR 具备足够的了解和相关的专业技能，并提升 ADR 的普及率。//

无论是伸张司法正义特别工作组还是 NADRAC 都给出了具体的建议，改善法律教育，以促进政府工作的进步。鉴于 ADR 在解决联邦政府争端中的作用日益重要，机构工作人员有必要更好地了解不同的 ADR 过程该如何使用。//

在此，我对 AGS 和 LEADR 主动为联邦机构发展"ADR 和澳大利亚联邦"的培训计划表示赞扬。我毫不怀疑，参与此项活动的有关人员将体会到该培训计划给他们工作所带来的意义和好处。我还要再次感谢 NADRAC 对促进 ADR 成为联邦民事司法制度的重要组成部分的不懈努力。在此，我非常高兴地启动"ADR 和澳大利亚联邦"计划。//

谢谢。//

# V. 句子精炼 Sentences in Focus

**Directions**：*Interpret the following sentences alternatively into English or Chinese*：

1. 今天的论坛是为了解决另一个报告中重点提出了一套建议，即在建造行业内，采用积极的方法解决索赔和纠纷、培训争端解决的项目团队以及采取积极合作的方式解决争端。

2. 截至 2009 年 8 月底，一共有 162 个合同受惠。在不久的将来，还将有两个合同也会受惠。现已结算了 2.58 亿美元，在接下来的 3 年至 4 年，还将会结算 1.05 亿美元。

3. 从总体来看，这 5 项措施已覆盖了 376 份合同，涉及约 20.7 亿美元的合同付款，其中 12.5 亿美元已经支付，8 亿美元将根据工程进度支付的。发展局将会于 2009 年年底回顾上述措施的成效。

4. 在香港，解决建筑纠纷的传统方式有时会以诉讼对抗结束。诉讼的过程是昂贵的、漫长的，并且会使所有当事方承受与他们负担能力不相称的财力和时间。如果可以在一开始就避免纠纷，这将大大地提高时间效率和成本效益。

5. 为确保能够供应足够的优质 DRA，以应对未来的潜在需求，我们与香港国际仲裁中心于 2009 年 6 月进行了讨论，并邀请他们协助对有潜力的 DRA 进行培训，以促进和鼓励有潜力的 DRA 候选人的参与。

6. 我毫不怀疑，纠纷的解决方式会不断发展，而且建设部门必须与时俱进，甚至最好能引领未来的趋势。政府鼓励在公共工程合同中更广泛地应用伙伴合作方式和 DRA 制度，从而在纠纷真正发生之前，促进意见分歧的解决。

7. 我鼓励每一位与会者积极交流，分享彼此实施 ADR 的技术和经验，开阔你的思想，思考这些经验技术是否适合用于解决纠纷，或是能从一开始就防范纠纷的发生。

8. It is a pleasure to be here at the first Government Law Group event for the year and to speak to you about alternative dispute resolution ( ADR ) in the federal justice system. It is also my pleasure to launch the AGS/LEADR training program "ADR and the Commonwealth".

9. ADR has many benefits when utilized within the context of litigation, as well as an alternative to litigation. It often ensures earlier and speedier resolution of disputes, and offers parties more privacy, confidentiality and cost saving benefits. Resolving disputes through ADR also allows parties to have an element of control on the process and a say in the outcome.

10. Access to justice is not just about access to a court or a lawyer. It is about providing practical, affordable and easily understood information and options to assist people to avoid or resolve their disputes.

11. This provision will enable judges to employ a number of case management powers, including: referring parties to ADR; requiring parties to narrow the issues in dispute; limiting the length of submissions or the number of witnesses; or setting time limits for the completion of part of a proceeding.

12. Commonwealth agencies are required by the Legal Services Directions to act as "model litigants" which means acting with complete propriety, fairness and to the highest professional standard.

13. Government lawyers will play a key role in effecting the cultural shift from litigation as the only tool to resolve disputes to much greater use and incorporation of ADR. Government lawyers need to consider ADR and obligations contained in the Directions as part of their wider, whole-of-government approach to the provision of Commonwealth legal services.

14. The feedback that I have received from lawyers, courts and tribunals has been that too frequently legal officers that attend ADR are not sufficiently on top of the issues and/or do not have the authority to negotiate and settle a matter.

15. The Office of Legal Services Coordination can assist government lawyers with queries they may have regarding the procurement and provision of legal services, and their awareness ofand compliance with the Legal Service Directions.

# 调解与仲裁

## Unit 13 Mediation & Arbitration

# I . 专题知识 Legal Knowledge

仲裁，作为争议解决方式，其历史悠久，早在公元前 6 世纪的古希腊即已存在。依仲裁是否具有涉外因素，分国内仲裁和国际仲裁。实践中，大多数国家均对国际仲裁给予较国内仲裁更多的自由，体现为更多的当事人自治和较少的司法干预。

广义的国际仲裁包括国际仲裁（狭义）和国际商事仲裁。国际仲裁被用于解决国家之间的国际争端，为国际法上的一种法律制度。国际商事仲裁则主要被用于解决具有涉外因素的民商事纠纷，主要包括国际经济贸易仲裁、海事仲裁和跨国商事仲裁。三者的受案范围不同，其中，海事仲裁被应用于解决国内、国际海事争议；跨国商事仲裁被用于解决国家与外国国民之间的商事争议。比较而言，解决国际经贸纠纷的国际经济贸易仲裁在实践中应用广、影响大。

## 一、国际商事仲裁的形成背景

从国际范围来看，仲裁正式成为解决争议的法律制度始于中世纪。瑞典1887 年制定了第一部《仲裁法令》。19 世纪初，世界上许多其他国家为适应国内和国际经贸发展，纷纷开展仲裁专门立法工作。随着国际经贸的日益活跃，19 世纪末 20 世纪初，作为一种解决国际贸易纠纷的常用解决方式，仲裁获得了国际社会的普遍认可和应用。20 世纪后，国际贸易发展迅速，国际商事纠纷也日益增多。当事人力求经济、迅速地解决纠纷。仲裁制度的优势日益凸显，为人们广泛关注。许多国家修改了原有仲裁法或进行仲裁立法活动，并设立了各自的常设仲裁机构。各国仲裁立法和仲裁实践的冲突问题也日益突出。这给国际贸易发展带来了阻碍。为解决法律冲突问题，国际社会开始统一国际仲裁法的立法活动，并取得了巨大成果。到目前为止，国际上已有许多关于国际仲裁制度的协定、条约和公约。

## 二、国际商事仲裁制度的创立

国际商事仲裁制度的确立始于区域性国际公约的订立。1889 年的《蒙得维的亚公约》即是第一部这类公约。它规定了参与订约的南美国家承认和执行外国仲裁裁决的条件和程序。1923 年在国际联盟的支持下，《仲裁条款议定书》（即《日内瓦议定书》）订立。

该议定书为第一个真正意义的国际仲裁公约。1927 年，《日内瓦外国仲裁裁决执行公约》签订。这两部日内瓦公约虽有局限性，却在寻求仲裁裁决的国际执行问题上进行了初步而有益的尝试。

20 世纪的后几十年中，协调和统一国际仲裁法已渐成潮流。1958 年联合国通过了《承认及执行外国仲裁裁决公约》（即《纽约公约》）。现已有 100 多个国家加入了该公约。

该公约是迄今为止国际商事仲裁方面最重要的多边国际条约。以该条约为基础建立起来的仲裁协议及仲裁裁决的承认和执行制度已成为现代国际商事仲裁制度的基石。1965 年，在世界银行主持下，《关于解决各国和其他国家国民之间投资争端的公约》（即《华盛顿公约》）签订。该公约规定以仲裁方式解决各国与他国私人投资者之间的投资争议。1966 年，以该公约为基础，解决投资争端国际中心（ICSID）成立。1976 年《联合国国际贸易法委员会仲裁规则》在联合国第 31 次大会上通过。1985 年联合国国际贸易法委员会制定了《国际商事仲裁示范法》。该示范文本对规范国际商事仲裁的做法起了积极的推动作用。目前，已有许多国家以该法为蓝本制定或修改了其仲裁法。这有力地促进了各国国际商事仲裁立法的现代化和统一性。

目前，国际社会统一国际仲裁法的努力已产生了丰硕成果。许多国家原有的仲裁法上的一些差异已经消失，在商事仲裁的一些领域已成统一之势，如对外国仲裁裁决的承认和执行、对仲裁裁决的司法追诉等方面。

## 三、现代国际商事仲裁制度的新发展

随着国际经济一体化的进程，仲裁被广泛地应用于国际经贸争议的解决。

这得益于国际社会的不懈努力，国际商事仲裁制度日益完善和成熟，并出现了一些新发展。其一，当事人意思自治原则得以充分体现。当事人享有更多的法律选择自由和高度的自治权。其二，仲裁的灵活性和多样性增强。例如，仲裁制度在适用法律方面不再局限于传统的仲裁法，体现灵活性的最密切联系原则被广泛应用。其三，机构仲裁成为国际商事仲裁的主要形式。其四，国际商事仲裁法治化、国际化和一体化。许多国家制定了仲裁法，在赋予法院一定程度的支持和监督仲裁的权力的同时，减少司法干涉，增强了仲裁的法律效力和社会公信力。在国际经济一体化的大背景下，国际社会的不懈合作及努力、日益增多的有关仲裁的国际条约及规则使得国际商事仲裁形成了国际化和一体化的趋势。

现代国际商事仲裁制度的新发展是世界经济一体化的必然结果，也是与当前法律统一和国际化的发展趋势保持一致的。可以肯定的是，在未来的国际经贸合作和发展中，随着国际商事仲裁制度的完善和成熟，这一制度必将获得更广泛的承认和应用，从而更好地实现该制度的创设目的——经济、有效地解决国际经贸纠纷，促进国际经贸的交流和发展。

## II. 词汇热身 Vocabulary Warm-up

**Directions:** *Give the English equivalents of the following Chinese expressions:*

| | | |
|---|---|---|
| 香港律政司司长 | 展开"调解为先"的 | 符合资格要求 |
| 大律师公 | 承诺 试点项目 | 《内地与香港关于建立 |
| 香港律师会 | 事务律师 | 更紧密经贸关系的安 |
| 比……有优势 | 出庭律师 | 排》 |
| 给……配备人员 | 有限责任合伙制 | 《关于内地与香港特别 |
| 关键所在 | 《2009 年法律执业者 | 行政区法院相互认可和 |
| 司法的独立性 | （修订）条例草案》 | 执行民商事案件判决的 |
| 保持警觉 | （律师在法庭上的）发 | 安排》 |
| 刑事检控专员 | 言权 | （条例）生效 |
| 仲裁制度 | 高等法院 | 夫妇分居令 |
| 成为……仲裁枢纽 | 终审法院 | 《婚姻法律程序与财产 |
| 跨部门工作小组 | 二读 | 条例》 |
| 《调解实务指示》 | 实施草案 | 有（司法）权做 |
| 《香港调解守则》 | 立法年度 | 受理申请 |

经济援助            融资               在……的前提下

法律界             《联合国反酷刑公约》     固步自封

金融行动特别工作组     《行政安排与当值律师

打击洗钱和恐怖主义     服务的备忘录》

**Directions**：*Give the Chinese equivalents of the following English expressions*：

tailored to

impartial

adjudication award

*Convention on the Recognition and Enforcement of Foreign Arbitral Awards*

*New York Convention*

UNCITRAL

*UNCITRAL Model Law on International Commercial Arbitration*

*Explanatory Note*

at the forefront of

President Martti Ahtisaari

inaugural conference

Asian Mediation Association（AMA）

Delhi Mediation Centre

a holistic and sophisticated dispute resolution centre

issue of the writ

disposal of the trial

underpin

resort to litigation

an arbitration venue of choice

ICC International Court of Arbitration

GenevaZurich clauses

to gain ground internationally

Maxwell Chambers

state-of-the-art facilities

acrimony

a protracted litigation

Ethos

last gap Subordinate Courts

Community Mediation Centre（CMC）

in the global context

culmination

since inception

capacity-building

# Ⅲ．课文口译 Texts for Interpreting

**Directions**：*Listen to the passage and interpret from English into Chinese at the end of each segment.*

President Martti Ahtisaari，Chief Justice，Judges，Excellencies，Distinguished guests，Ladies and gentlemen，

Thank you for inviting me to this inaugural conference of the Asian Mediation

Association (AMA) . //

The members of the AMA—the Delhi Mediation Centre, Hong Kong Mediation Centre, Indonesian Mediation Center, Malaysian Mediation Centre, Philippine Mediation Center and Singapore Mediation Centre—have come together to promote mediation in an effective way. The AMA brings together institutions which have deep knowledge of the cultures they serve to discuss challenges encountered in this field and share the best practices available with each other. This is crucial to building mediation thought leadership in this part of the world, and is a highly commendable initiative. //

Mediation is a crucial facet of our efforts to build a holistic and sophisticated dispute resolution centre. Any dispute resolution system should have at least three key pillars: dispute resolution through the Courts, arbitration and mediation. We have focused a lot on making suredispute resolution through our Courts is effective and efficient. //

A dispute can be heard in Singapore from the time of issue of the writ to the disposal of the trial within 18 months. Any appeal can be disposed of within three to four months thereafter. International organisations today rank Singapore's Judiciary highly. Singapore's strong reputation for the rule of law is underpinned by a strong and independent judiciary. And under the leadership of our Honourable Chief Justice, our Judiciary will continue to be a highly regarded institution. //

But, litigation is not without its drawbacks. Compared to alternative dispute resolution methods, litigation can be costlier, more public, more time-consuming and often creates irreparable damage to the relationships amongst the parties involved. A significant number of parties do not actually need to resort to litigation. Society will benefit if strong and comprehensive alternate dispute resolution processes are made readily accessible. //

The two alternates arearbitration and mediation. //

In recent years, Singapore's convenient location, good legal system and neutrality have made us an arbitration venue of choice in the region. //

We have created an environment that is not only conducive, but also attractive for arbitration hearings to be held in Singapore. A 2007 report published by the ICC

International Court of Arbitration ranked Singapore as the top city in Asia for ICC arbitrations and one of the five most popular ICC arbitration venues since 2000, alongside Paris, London, Geneva and Zurich. Parties' rights to arbitrate have been strongly upheld, and our Courts do not intervene too readily in arbitrations. Parties are free to engage lawyers of any nationality and use any governing law, and not just Singapore−qualified lawyers or Singapore law. Parties now have access to top international arbitral institutions in Singapore, such as the American Arbitration Association and the Permanent. //

We also have our very own Singapore International Arbitration Centre, whose clauses and reputation are gaining ground internationally. Its recent board appointments of world − renowned arbitrators not only brings with them international expertise, but undoubtedly positions it to be one of the leading arbitration centres in Asia and the world. Last but not least, we have established the Maxwell Chambers, which will house a first−class venue for international hearings equipped with state−of−the−art facilities for arbitration. We have been anticipating the opening of the Maxwell Chambers for some time now and this will be taking place very soon in a matter of months. //

But arbitration is only one pillar of the alternate dispute resolution system. While Singapore develops as an important arbitral centre, we also recognise that mediation must also be strongly supported and is the other pillar of alternate dispute resolution. The processes of civil litigation and arbitration have a strong economic focus − more so of course for arbitration then litigation. Mediation with its strong social focus complements litigation and arbitration. In that way, mediation performs a critical role. //

Mediation increases access to justice by mitigating the costs and risks involved in litigation and arbitration. Particularly for the man in the street, without the deep pockets of a large corporation, mediation is an important way of accessing justice. And for corporations involved in large disputes, mediation is still a sensible route to take, to see if litigation or arbitration can be avoided. //

A sensible and firm mediator can often help reduce a messy dispute, saving the parties much money and the acrimony and a protracted litigation or arbitration. Mediation not only offers betteraccess to justice, it also improves the process of justice. This is essential as justice is not only about the results achieved. Being private, non-confrontational and non-intimidating, mediation is ideal for a society like ours, where there is an underlying ethos of maintaining harmony. The flexibility that mediation offers also affords opportunities for imaginative solutions to be formulated. For example, I understand that in a case mediated at the Singapore Mediation Centre, the "last gap" (or final difference) between the parties was closed by way of a donation to a charity in the parties' joint names. //

Mediation has flourished in Singapore since the early 1990s. Our Judiciary introduced court-based mediation in 1994 through the institution of Court Dispute Resolution in the Subordinate Courts. In 1996, the Honourable the Chief Justice, then the Attorney-General, in a far sighted move, suggested the establishing of a commercial mediation centre to encourage a more harmonious approach to settling differences. This led to the setting up of the Singapore Mediation Centre (SMC) a year later in 1997. To encourage the use of mediation in resolving community and social disputes, the first Community Mediation Centre (CMC) was set up by the Ministry of Law in 1998. //

Today, the SMC is Singapore's flagship mediation centre. It has set our mediation scene in the global context through its numerous avenues of cooperation with international partners. For instance, SMC co-founded the International Mediation Institute, a non-profit foundation incorporated in the Netherlands. This was the culmination of a pioneering effort to standardise and promote an international competency standard for mediators. The SMC has also continually made efforts in capacity-building for its international partners. To date, it has provided negotiation and mediation training for more than 900 overseas participants from more than 80 different countries worldwide. Twice or thrice a year, SMC will also host 20 to 30 participants from all around the world in conflict resolution workshops as part of the Singapore Cooperation Programme. //

SMC's commercial emphasis is completed at the community level by the CMC, which focuses on community and neighbourly disputes, ensuring a robust social fabric. We now have three CMCs providing mediation services to Singaporeans living in various parts of the island. //

In addition to mediation at these institutions, mediation is also being conducted at tribunals and Government departments and agencies. There are also numerous mediation services provided by professional, industry, trade and consumer bodies for practically every significant area of dispute. //

Some numbers would give us a sense of how far mediation has come since the 1990s. Between June 1994 and March 2009, the Subordinate Courts mediated some 188,000 cases. These include civil matters, maintenance, small claims and other family-related disputes. The average settlement rate is 90 per cent. //

There is also encouraging feedback from users of mediation. The SMC has been administering an ongoing survey to parties and lawyers at the end of each mediation session at the Centre. Of the 1,911 parties who responded to the survey from 1997 to the end of March 2009, 81 per cent indicated that they had saved costs. Eight-five per cent reported that they had saved time. The response from lawyers is equally positive. Out of 1,590 lawyers who responded over the same period, 82 per cent noted that their clients were likely to have saved costs. Eighty-one per cent thought that they and their clients were likely to have saved time. Costs and time savings were reported even in cases that were not settled or partially settled. What I think is most heartening, however, is this: 93 per cent of the parties and 98 per cent of the lawyers said that they would recommend the use of mediation to others in similar situations. //

Within the community, the CMC has come a long way since its inception. The Centres have handled a total of more than 4,100 cases in the last 10 years. From the 120 cases the first CMC processed in 1998, the three CMCs handled almost 700 cases in 2008. //

Mediation has proven to be a vital part of our legal system. The Government will continue to strongly support the use of mediation and encourage efforts to develop the field of mediation through research, studies and training. //

The members of the AMA are well-placed to promote the appropriate use of mediation both in the board rooms and the communities at home. Together, this will bring about greater harmony and prosperity to the region. //

But we should not stop there. There are different levels of development in the capacity for mediation across various countries in the region. I would also like to urge the AMA and other mediation players within and even outside Asia to broaden your efforts to help each other with capacity-building. Our societies can only be enriched by efforts to spread the spirit of peace and to share mediation as a method of making peace. //

Let me conclude by congratulating the AMA for putting this Conference together and the SMC for hosting it. //

My best wishes for all bonds of friendship and co-operation. Thank you. //

# Ⅳ. 参考译文 Reference Versions

马尔蒂·阿赫蒂萨里总统、终审法院首席法官、法官们、阁下们、尊敬的各位来宾、女士们、先生们：

感谢诸位邀请我到这个亚洲调解协会（AMA）的就职招待会。//

AMA 的成员们——印度德里调解中心、中国香港调解中心、印度尼西亚调解中心、马来西亚调解中心、菲律宾调解中心和新加坡调解中心——共同携手以实效的方式推广调解的应用。AMA 使那些对其所服务的文化有着深入了解的机构齐聚一堂，共同探讨它们在调解这个领域所遭遇的挑战，并互相分享彼此最佳的实践经验。通过领导才干来建设调解，对于这一部分的世界而言是非常重要的，而且也是一个值得高度赞扬的倡议。//

调解是我们努力建设全面且缜密的纠纷调解中心的一个重要方面。任何争端解决机制都应至少有三个主要支柱：通过法庭的争端解决、仲裁和调解。而我们一直致力于确保通过法庭的争端解决这一方式的实效性和高效率。//

在新加坡，从令状发出到处理审讯的 18 个月内可以举行争端的听审。此后的 3 个月至 4 个月内，任何上诉都可得到处理。如今，国际组织纷纷对新加坡的司法机构给予高度评价。新加坡强大和独立的司法体制为其良好的法治声誉打下了坚实的基础。而且，在我们的首席大法官的领导下，我们的司法体系将继续得到外界的高度评价。//

但是，我们的诉讼程序并非完全没有缺点。相比于替代性争端解决方式（ADR），诉讼更昂贵、更无隐私可言、更费时，并且往往对有关各方之间的关系造成无法弥补的损害。相当多的当事人实际上没有必要诉诸诉讼。如果我们能使用有力且全面的替代性争端解决方式，在程序上更加便民，那将大大地造福社会。//

替代性的解决方式主要有两种：仲裁和调解。//

近年来，新加坡便利的地理位置，及其良好的法律制度和中立性，使其成了亚洲地区的仲裁审判地之选。//

我们已经创造了一个不仅有利且还能吸引仲裁听证会在新加坡举行的环境。国际商会（ICC）国际仲裁法院于2007年发布的报告把新加坡列为亚洲国际商会仲裁的首选城市，及2000年以来5个最流行的国际商会仲裁场所之一，与巴黎、伦敦、日内瓦和苏黎世并列。我们一直坚持当事人有获得仲裁的权利，并且我们的法院不会轻易干预仲裁的进行。当事各方可以自由聘请任何国籍的律师和使用任何有关的法律，而不仅仅是符合资格的新加坡律师或新加坡的法律。现在在新加坡，人们可以接触到顶尖的国际仲裁机构，如美国仲裁协会和常设仲裁法庭。//

我们也有自己的新加坡国际仲裁中心，其法律条款和声誉在国际上的地位也在不断提高。最近，新加坡国际仲裁中心董事会任命了数位世界知名的仲裁员，除了带来了国际化的专业知识，也使其当之无愧地成了亚洲和世界首屈一指的仲裁中心。最后还有很重要的一点，那就是我们已经建成了麦士威议事厅。麦士威议事厅配备了国际一流的仲裁设施，将会成为举行国际听证会的首选场所。我们一直在期待麦士威议事厅的正式启用，而我们的这个期待将在数月之内实现。//

但是，仲裁只是替代性争端解决系统的支柱之一。而随着新加坡发展成为重要的仲裁中心，我们也认识到调解也是替代争端解决的另一个支柱，我们必须为调解提供大力的支持。民事诉讼程序和仲裁有很强大的经济关注性。当然，对仲裁的关注要比对诉讼的关注多。有着强大社会关注性的调解与诉讼和仲裁相辅相成。这样一来，调解发挥了其关键的作用。//

通过减轻诉讼和仲裁所涉及的成本和风险，调解增加了伸张正义的渠道。尤其是对于没有大财团在背后撑腰的普通民众而言，调解是伸张正义的重要途径。而对于牵扯大型纠纷的企业而言，调解也不失为一个明智的选择，从而避免诉讼或仲裁。//

一位睿智且坚定的调解员往往可以帮助缓解错综复杂的争端纠纷，为当事人节省钱财，免于难堪的对峙和旷日持久的诉讼或仲裁。调解不仅为伸张正义提供了更好的方式，同时也完善了司法程序。这是必要的，因为司法不仅只是为了取得成果。调解具有隐私性、非对抗性和非恐吓性，非常适合像我们这样把维持和谐作为根本精神的社会。调解的灵活性同时还为富有想象力的解决方案提供了形成的机会。例如，据我所知，新加坡调解中心的一个调解案子，当事双方"最后的差距"（或最终的差异）是通过由双方联名捐赠给慈善事业的方式结案的。//

自20世纪90年代初起，调解开始在新加坡蓬勃发展。我们的司法机构在1994年通过初级法院的法庭纠纷解决机构引入了以法庭为基础的调解制度。1996年，我们的首席大法官及后来的总检察长提出了一个有远见的举措，即建议成立一个商业调解中心，以促进通过更和谐的方式来解决分歧。这使得一年之后，即1997年，成立了新加坡调解中心（SMC）。为了鼓励民众使用调解来解决社区和社会的纠纷，法律部于1998年成立了第一个社区调解中心（CMC）。//

今天，SMC是新加坡的龙头调解中心。通过与国际伙伴以多样化的方式合作，SMC使新加坡的调解中心成功地与国际接轨。例如，SMC共同创办的国际调解研究所，是一个于荷兰注册成立的非营利基金会。这使得规范和完善调解员国际竞争力的标准达到了巅峰。在能力建设方面，SMC亦不断地为其国际伙伴努力。迄今为止，它提供了来自80多个不同国家的谈判和调解培训世界各地的900多名外国与会者。作为新加坡合作计划的一部分，SMC每年会举行2次至3次冲突解决研讨会，邀请20个至30个来自世界各地的组织集思广益。//

SMC的商业重点由社区级别的CMC来完成，主要集中于解决社区和邻里的争端，以确保社会结构健全。我们现在有三所CMC为生活于新加坡各地的民众提供调解服务。

调解除了在这些机构，也在法庭及政府部门和机构执行。还有几乎每一类争端的重要领域的专业人士及工业、贸易和消费者组织，也提供了数不胜数的调解服务。//

通过以下这些数字，我们可以看到，自20世纪90年代来调解得到了长足的发展。1994年6月至2009年3月，初级法院调解了近18.8万宗案子，包括民事案件、赡养费、小额索赔及其他与家庭有关的纠纷，平均和解率高

达 90%。//

一些使用过调解的当事人也给出了令人鼓舞的反馈。一直以来，在每一个调解阶段结束后，SMC 都会对调解各方和律师进行反馈调查。从 1997 年到 2009 年 3 月，在 1911 名调查参与者中，81% 表示调解帮助他们节省了费用，85% 则表示节省了时间。律师们也同样给出了积极的反馈。在同一时期给出反馈的 1590 名律师中，82% 指出他们的当事人节省了成本。81% 则认为，他们和他们的当事人都节省了时间。即使在尚未解决或部分解决的案件中，有关方面就已经给出了节省了金钱和时间的回馈。然而，我认为最令人振奋的是，93% 的当事人和 98% 的律师表示，他们会向其他情况类似的当事人推荐使用调解。//

而在社区内，CMC 自成立以来得到了长足的发展。该中心在过去 10 年已受理了超过 4100 宗案件。与 1998 年第一所 CMC 受理了 120 宗案子相比，2008 年 3 所 CMC 受理近 700 宗案子。//

调解已被证明是我们的法律制度的重要组成部分。政府会继续大力支持使用调解，并鼓励通过调查研究和培训，努力发展调解的领域。//

AMA 的成员，不管在董事会还是国内的社区中，在促进调解的合理使用方面都做得十分到位。总而言之，这将给亚洲地区带来进一步的和谐与繁荣。//

但是，我们切不可就此自满而止步不前。亚洲地区各国的调解在发展潜力上还处于不同的水平。我还要敦促 AMA 及其他在亚洲甚至亚洲之外的调解组织，进一步扩大努力，帮助彼此加强调解能力的建设。只有凭着努力传播和平的精神，并把调解作为缔造和平的手段共享互助，我们的社会才能富强。//

最后，我在此祝贺 AMA 和 CMC 成功组织举办了此次会议。//

我谨在此对诸位的友谊和合作送上最诚挚的祝福。谢谢。//

# V. 句子精炼 Sentences in Focus

**Directions**：*Interpret the following sentences alternatively into English or Chinese*：

1. The members of the AMA—the Delhi Mediation Centre, Hong Kong Mediation Centre, Indonesian Mediation Center, Malaysian Mediation Centre, Philippine Mediation Center and Singapore Mediation Centre—have come together to promote mediation in an effective way.

2. Any dispute resolution system should have at least three key pillars: dispute resolution through the Courts, arbitration and mediation. We have focused a lot on making sure dispute resolution through our Courts is effective and efficient.

3. Compared to alternative dispute resolution methods, litigation can be costlier, more public, more time-consuming and often creates irreparable damage to the relationships amongst the parties involved.

4. A 2007 report published by the ICC International Court of Arbitration ranked Singapore as the top city in Asia for ICC arbitrations and one of the five most popular ICC arbitration venues since 2000, alongside Paris, London, Geneva and Zurich.

5. Last but not least, we have established the Maxwell Chambers, which will house a first-class venue for international hearings equipped with state-of-the-art facilities for arbitration.

6. Being private, non-confrontational and non-intimidating, mediation is ideal for a society like ours, where there is an underlying ethos of maintaining harmony.

7. To date, SMC has provided negotiation and mediation training for more than 900 overseas participants from more than 80 different countries worldwide. Twice or thrice a year, SMC will also host 20 to 30 participants from all around the world in conflict resolution workshops as part of the Singapore Cooperation Programme.

8. Mediation has proven to be a vital part of our legal system. The Government will continue to strongly support the use of mediation and encourage efforts to develop the field of mediation through research, studies and training.

第十四单元 司法体制改革

**Unit 14  Judicial Reforms**

# Ⅰ. 专题知识 Legal Knowledge

　　改革开放以来，伴随着经济体制的转型和社会的变迁，我国的司法制度进行了多项改革。特别是中共十七大明确了司法改革的目标要求，提出了权力的优化配置和司法行为规范化的具体路径，推动司法体制内部和外部两方面的改革向纵深发展。而司法改革包含着从观念到制度、从理论到实践各方面的变革与创新。基于社会、经济、政治发展的现实需求，在世界司法改革潮流和国际人权公约的推动下，我国的司法改革正朝着加强司法过程中的人权保障，追求司法公正，讲求司法的效率性、经济性这几个方面不断努力。我国司法体制改革的趋势如下所述。

　　（1）适应国情发展。根据党的十七大报告精神，司法体制改革作为政治体制改革的组成部分，事关整个社会的大局；深化司法体制改革，必须与人民民主的扩大以及经济、社会的发展程度相适应。司法体制改革是社会主义司法制度自我完善和发展的需要，也是解决人民群众日益增长的司法需求与司法能力不相适应的矛盾的需要。深化司法体制改革必须契合社会主义初级阶段的基本国情，这也决定了司法体制改革是一个长期的、动态的过程。

　　（2）回应社会需要。随着社会主义民主法治建设的发展，人民群众对司法公正、效率以及权威的期望和要求越来越高。我国正处于向依法治国的转型时期，改革最先在经济领域取得成效并且逐步延伸和渗透到社会生活的每一个角落。通过社会主义法治搭建的诉求表达平台和冲突解决机制，国家可以有效引导各种利益主体以理性、合法的方式，在表达利益诉求的基础上，使社会中的矛盾和冲突得以解决，努力构建社会主义和谐社会。

（3）司法独立的相对意义。在我国，司法独立的含义主要是相对于行政机关的行政活动而言的，即司法机关在行使司法权时不受行政机关、社会团体和个人的干涉。但是，我国司法机关独立行使司法权时并不排斥、否定国家权力机关的监督以及社会监督。目前，坚持司法独立就必须建立一套真正独立于行政机关和各级地方政府的司法系统，改变目前地方司法机关在人、财、物等方面过度依赖地方政府的倾向，将各级地方司法机关的人事权、财权由目前的地方管理转变为由最高司法机关统一集中管理。尤为重要的是，坚持司法独立必须与党的领导、司法监督统一起来。总之，中国司法制度改革的长远目标是建立与市场经济、民主法治建设相适应的现代司法制度。在改革的过程中要注意正确处理党的领导、司法监督与司法独立问题，要坚持党的领导与审判独立相统一，司法独立与司法受制相统一。

（4）落实司法民主，增进司法透明。建立健全民意沟通表达机制。加强与人大代表、政协委员的联络沟通，完善与各民主党派、工商联、无党派人士的沟通协调机制，确定专门机构和人员负责联络工作。研究建立人民法院网络民意表达和民意调查制度，完善社会舆情汇集工作机制，妥善解决司法工作中涉及民生的热点问题，完善司法公开制度。最高人民法院于 2009 年底发布了《关于司法公开的六项规定》，从立案公开、庭审公开、执行公开、听证公开、文书公开、审务公开六个方面切实保护公众的知情监督权和当事人的诉讼权，实现了透明公开、阳光司法。

（5）加强队伍建设，强化司法监督。改革法官遴选制度，保证法官的良好素质。认真贯彻《法官法》，严格法官职业准入，保证法官具有较高的素质；逐步实现从律师、专家、学者中选拔法官，上级法院从下级法院选拔法官。建立分类管理制度，提高法官司法能力。实现法官、法官助理、书记员、执行员、司法警察、司法行政人员分类管理，形成身份明确、职责清楚、管理规范、保障到位的分类管理格局；加强教育培训，提高法官正确适用法律、善做群众工作、化解社会矛盾的能力。改革和完善人民法院接受外部制约与监督机制。通过专题报告工作、司法解释备案、接受执法检查等形式，主动接受权力机关监督。建立特约监督员制度，加强党外人士监督制度建设，成立人民监督工作办公室，完善联络工作组织保障。健全新闻发言人例会制度，完善记者旁听开庭机制等，从多方面加强与新闻媒体的沟通联络，为舆论监督提供方便。改革检察长列席审判委员会制度，依法接受监督。

# II. 词汇热身 Vocabulary Warm-up

**Directions:** *Give the English equivalents of the following Chinese expressions:*

| | | |
|---|---|---|
| 司法制度 | 律师执业 | 优惠照顾政策 |
| 改革试点 | 律师收费制度 | 法律援助 |
| 新型监狱体制 | 司法考试 | 司法鉴定 |
| 社区矫正 | 社会主义法治理念 | |

**Directions:** *Give the Chinese equivalents of the following English expressions:*

| | | |
|---|---|---|
| adjudicating | tribunal | Britannica |
| discharging | corner on | misalignment |
| litigation | luncheon speech | grapple with sweepstake |
| collegiate | guild system | differentiate |
| downturn | vulnerability | empower |
| legislature | keynote | leverage |
| teething | address bottom line | sophistication |
| mediation | orthogonal | vestige |
| enactment | decentralized | |

法庭口译词汇对照表（按单元分）

## ◆ *Unit 1*

| 依法治国 | to rule/govern the state affairs according to law |
|---|---|
| 法律援助 | legal aid |
| 弱势群体 | vulnerable groups |
| 人民调解 | people's mediation |
| 便民措施 | convenience measures |
| 拖欠工资 | arrears of wages |
| 普法规划 | the planning of law popularization |
| 互谅互让 | mutual understanding |
| 改造罪犯 | rehabilitation of offenders |
| 法律顾问 | legal counsel |
| 公证员 | notary |
| 和谐社会 | harmonious society |
| 润滑剂 | a lubricant for sth |
| 依法执政 | to exercise state power according to law |
| 公职律师 | government lawyers |
| 应运而生 | to come with the tide of fashion |
| chief judge | 首席法官 |
| chambers | （特指）法官办公室 |
| judiciary | 司法制度；司法机关；法官（总称） |
| appeal court | 上诉法院 |

续表

| appellate | 与上诉相关的 |
|---|---|
| vandalism | 故意破坏公物的行为（罪） |
| adjudicative | 判决的，裁定的 |
| multiple murder | 多重谋杀（罪） |
| levelheaded | 头脑冷静的，清醒的 |
| anguishing | 苦恼的 |
| juvenile delinquent | 少年犯 |
| squander | 浪费，挥霍 |
| out of hand | 立刻，马上 |
| -consuming | 消耗……的，如 time-consuming（耗时的） |

## ◆ *Unit 2*

| 立法听证会 | the legislative hearing |
|---|---|
| 个人所得税 | personal income tax |
| 起征点 | the threshold of tax |
| 舶来品 | import |
| 拆迁 | demolition |
| 知情权 | the right to learn the truth about... |
| 见义勇为 | gallantly rising to the occasion |
| 立法机关 | the legislature |
| 专门委员会 | the special committee |
| 座谈会 | to hold forums |
| 公用设施 | public facilities |
| contentious | 具有争议性的 |
| hearing procedure | 听证程序 |
| to spell out | 清楚地说明 |
| statute | 法规，法令；成文法 |

| to overturn | 推翻 |
| --- | --- |
| testimony | （书面或口头的）证词（尤指发誓后作出的） |
| legislative | 与立法相关的；立法权 |
| record | （书面）记录 |
| publication | 出版（物）；发表 |
| ordinance | 法令，条例（尤指由市政府发出的） |
| transcript | 文字记录；笔录；抄本 |
| to testify | （尤指出庭）作证 |
| rebuttal | 据反证；反驳 |
| deliberation | 审议 |
| warrant | （法院授权的）令状 |
| apolitical | 不关心政治的，不涉及政治立场的 |
| proceedings | 诉讼（程序） |
| disturbance | 扰乱 |

## ◆ *Unit 3*

| 庭审直播 | live broadcast of trials |
| --- | --- |
| 裁判文书 | judgement writ |
| 人民陪审员 | People's Juror；the citizen jury system |
| 错判错杀 | to make wrong ruling and execution |
| 抗诉 | to challenge the ruling |
| 《人权白皮书》 | The White Paper on the Human Rights Situation in China |
| 疑罪从无 | The accused is assumed as innocent if there are any suspicious points about the case. ［注：疑罪从无是现代刑法"有利被告"思想的体现，是"无罪推定"（presumption of innocence）原则的具体内容之一］ |
| 模拟审判 | mock trail |
| 首席大法官 | Chief Judge；Chief Justice |

| 国家赔偿 | national compensation |
|---|---|
| 精神赔偿 | the compensation for mental harm |
| 共同犯罪 | a joint crime/offence |
| 明星代言 | stars or celebrities advertising |
| 医疗器械 | medical devices |
| 突发事件 | the outbreak of emergency |
| 非法行医 | illegal medical practice |
| 定罪量刑 | to make conviction or sentence |

## ◆ *Unit 4*

| 法治建设 | rule of law |
|---|---|
| 国家法律制度成熟的标志 | the symbol of a politically civilized society |
| 全国人大及其常委 | he National People's Congress (NPC) and its Standing Committee |
| 享有立法权 | be vested with the power of legislation |
| 非诉讼程序法 | extra-judicial procedure |
| 法律规范 | legal norms |
| 中国特色社会主义法律体系 | a Chinese-style socialist legal system |
| 有法可依，依法治国 | to provide the legal guaranty for governing the country according to law |
| 人民当家作主 | the power of people to run the country as the masters |
| 共同的行为准则 | the common code of conduct |
| 起支架作用的法律 | laws that are supportive in the legal system |
| 推进政府职能转变 | to carry forward functional transformation of the government |
| 管理创新 | administrative innovation |
| 依法行政 | administration according to law |

续表

| 提请……审议法律议案 | to make legislative proposals to... for deliberation |
|---|---|
| 向社会公开征求意见 | to solicit opinions from the general public |
| 取消……（法令） | to rescind |
| 行政执法责任制度 | an accountability system for administrative law-enforcement |
| 行政复议制度 | administrative reconsideration system |
| 上位法 | upper-level laws |
| "红头文件" | official documents |
| 深入人心 | to take root in people's heart |
| 中国人民银行行长 | Governor of the People's Bank of China（PBC） |
| 国务院发展研究中心 | Development Research Center of the State Council |
| 金融研究所 | Financial Research Institute |
| 金融管制 | financial supervision |
| 市场自律 | market self-displine |
| 有市场就会有风险 | where there is market，there is risk |
| 经济体制转轨 | the transition of the economic system |
| 金融体制的不适应 | the rigidity of financial system |
| 金融机构退出 | market exit of financial institutions |
| 存款保险 | deposit insurance |
| 金融控股公司 | financial holding companies |
| 资产证券化 | asset securitization |
| 委托理财 | entrusted wealth management |
| 破产法 | the Insolvency Law |
| The Bar Council of the Hong Kong Bar Association | 香港大律师公会 |
| Chief Justice | （终审法院）首席法官 |
| Secretary for Justice | （香港）律政司司长 |
| "off piste" | 跑出跑道，比喻话题扯远了 |

| Legal Aid Scheme | 法律援助计划 |
|---|---|
| access to Justice | 取得司法（正义）的渠道 |
| non-Permanent Judge | 非常任法官 |
| Kafkaesque doorkeeper | 卡夫卡式的守门人［注：出自卡夫卡的长篇小说《诉讼》中神父为男主角说的寓言故事"在法的门前"］ |
| prohibitive | 令人望而却步 |
| Billable hours | 可收费时数 |
| pro bono | ［拉］为慈善机构和穷人提供的免费（法律）专业服务 |
| public expense | 公帑 |
| life and limb | 出生入死的；关乎生命危险的 |
| Convention Against Torture（CAT） | 《联合国禁止酷刑公约》 |
| Earthly Branches | 地支 |
| Animal zodiac | 十二生肖 |
| in no small measure to | 对……而言是无可估量的 |
| separation of powers | 分权体制 |
| tenure | 任期 |
| On the bench | 担任法官（的职位） |
| Continuous Profession Development（CPD）points | 持续专业发展的学分 |

◆ *Unit 5*

| 具有里程碑意义的 | landmark |
|---|---|
| 两百周年 | bicentenary |
| 《法国民法典》 | French Civil Code |
| 香港城市大学 | City University of Hong Kong |
| 盛事 | proud events |

续表

| | |
|---|---|
| 从大局/宏观层面思考 | to look at the big picture |
| 大中华地区 | Greater China |
| 民法法系制度 | the civil law system |
| 大陆法系制度（即民法法系） | the continental law system |
| 普通法法系制度 | the common law system |
| 英美法系制度（即普通法系） | the Anglo-American law system |
| 屹立不倒 | stand tall |
| 欧洲大陆 | continental Europe |
| 综合性法典 | comprehensive codes |
| 澳门特别行政区 | Macau SAR |
| 在英国管治时期 | under British administration |
| 香港特别行政区 | Hong Kong SAR |
| 动荡的/风云变幻的年代 | to experience turbulent times |
| 可见一斑 | sth. is reflected in... |
| 苏维埃模式的法律制度 | a Soviet-style legal system |
| 沿用下来的法律原则 | conventional legal principles |
| 废除 | to denounce |
| 反右运动 | Anti-Rightist Campaign |
| 荡然无存 | all gone; nothing left |
| 取而代之 | to reign in place of |
| 动荡和纷乱 | chaos and disorder |
| 保障人民民主 | to safeguard people's democracy |
| 加强法制 | to strengthen the legal system |
| 为……奠下根基 | to underpin |

| 傲人的经济增长 | incredible economic growth |
|---|---|
| 中国入世 | China's accession to the WTO |
| （香港、澳门）回归中国大陆 | Reunification |
| 司法管辖区 | legal jurisdictions |
| 美国路易斯安那州 | Louisiana |
| 加拿大魁北克省 | Quebec |
| 履行欧盟所订下的众多义务 | give effect to the multitude of EU obligations |
| 越来越多人认同 | a growing consensus on |
| 加强沟通 | keep up our dialogue |
| inaugural lecture | 就职演说 |
| the Bar | 大律师公会 |
| the then director-general of Criminal Justice IT | （CJIT）时任刑事司法 IT 处处长 |
| CPS （Crown Prosecution Service） | 皇家检察署 |
| the Lord Chancellor's Department | 大法官部 |
| investment on the margins | 无谓的投资 |
| a back office system called CREST | 名为 CREST 的后勤办公室系统 |
| Crown Courts | 英国刑事法院（英国最高法院的组成部分） |
| computerized bulk claims centre | 电脑批量索赔处理中心系统 |
| Northampton | 北安普敦（英国英格兰南部城市） |

| legal aid | 法律援助（指对无钱聘请律师或进行诉讼者给予的经济援助） |
|---|---|
| MP（Member of Parliament） | 议员（尤指下院的） |
| the House of Commons | 下议院 |
| civil justice | 民事司法 |
| Lord Woolf | 伍尔夫勋爵（前英国上议院普通上诉法官、前高等法院院长，英国法制史上推动民事司法改革的第一先驱，著有《伍尔夫报告》，又名《接近司法》报告） |
| Woolf Day | 伍尔夫勋爵纪念日 |
| to cause an uproar | 引起轩然大波 |
| to remain unscathed | 毫发无损；安然无恙；可比喻关键问题没有得到解决 |
| pilot schemes | 试点计划 |
| Digital audio recording | 数码录音（DAR）系统 |
| electronic presentation of evidence | 证据呈现电子化（EPE）系统 |
| bungalow | 平房 |
| the civil and family courts | 民事和家庭法院 |
| on pragmatic grounds | 以实务的理由 |
| to spearhead | 当……的先锋、为……扫清道路 |
| CBE（Commander of the British Empire） | 大英帝国司令勋章 |
| OBE（Officer of the Order of the British Empire） | 大英帝国勋章 |
| Money Claims Online system | 金钱索赔在线系统 |
| the Home Office | 英国内政部 |
| judicial liaison | 司法（单位之间的）联系 |

| criminal proceedings | 刑事诉讼 |
|---|---|
| to plead guilty | 承认有罪 |
| Blackfriars | （伦敦）布莱克佛里阿斯 |
| a VAT fraud trial | 增值税欺诈案的审讯 |
| the Treasury | 财政部 |
| Tasmania | （位于澳大利亚东南部岛屿）塔斯马尼亚岛 |
| "whispering witness" technology | "耳语证人"技术 |
| to take the initiative | 主动去…… |
| wireless amplification | 无线扩音（器） |
| one-off experiment | 一次性实验 |
| Manchester | 曼彻斯特 |
| the preliminary stages of a criminal trial | 刑事审判的初步阶段 |
| magistrates' courts | 裁判法院 |
| police escorts | 警察护送/押运（犯人） |
| the Court Service | 法院服务处 |
| to pay a heart felt tribute to | 对……表示衷心的感谢 |
| coherent chronological order | 连贯的时间顺序 |
| on circuit as a High Court judge | 以高等法院法官的身份作巡回审判 |
| to grind to a halt | （被迫）停止运作 |
| high staff turnover | 员工流失率高 |
| to enthuse about/over sth. | 对……极度喜爱或热心 |
| to pull the plug | 停止对……（的资助） |
| to disband | 解散 |

| long snake close to the top of the Snakes and Ladders Board | 比喻即将达成或非常接近目标 |
|---|---|
| "jam tomorrow" | "明天的果酱"，比喻永远不会兑现的承诺 |
| to adjourn the trial | 休庭；暂停审判 |
| provide a panacea to all ills | 治百病的灵丹妙药 |
| in arrears | 拖欠债款 |
| the sky fell on St Swithin's Day | 晴天霹雳 |
| Bangor University | 班戈大学 |
| Magna Carta | 英国大宪章 |

## ◆ *Unit 6*

| 案由 | brief |
|---|---|
| 律师见证书 | Lawyer's written attestation/authentication |
| 委托辩护 | to brief/entrust sb. to defend for sb. |
| 答辩状 | pleading；a bill of defense |
| 本诉 | action in chief |
| 共同诉讼人 | coplantiff |
| 传票 | subpoena；summons |
| 变通管辖 | to accommodate jurisdiction to… |
| 基层人民法院 | the People's Court at basic level |

## ◆ *Unit 7*

| 审判长 | Chief Judge |
|---|---|
| 法警 | bailiff |
| 刑事诉讼法 | Criminal Procedure Law |

| | |
|---|---|
| 合议庭 | the Collegiate Panel |
| 书记员 | stenographer |
| 公诉人 | public prosecutor |
| 举证 | to adduce evidence |
| 物证 | material evidence |
| 书证 | documentary evidence |
| 法庭辩论 | court debate |
| 无申报通道 | Nothing-to-declare channel |
| 海关缉私局 | Anti-smuggling Bureau of Customs |
| 旅检处 | Passenger Inspection Division |
| 扣押物品清单 | the list of detained articles and documents |
| 看守所 | Detention house |
| 盐酸海洛因 | Heroin hydrochloride |
| 亚的斯亚贝巴（埃塞俄比亚首都） | Addis Ababa |
| 走私毒品 | to smuggle drugs |
| 行为犯 | the behaviour crime |
| 从轻判处 | toappeal for a lighter punishment |
| 从犯 | accessory |
| 现在休庭 | Now the court session adjourns. |
| Domicile | 住址 |
| had no objection about | 对……不反对 |
| Statement of Defense | 辩护声明 |
| People's Procuratorate | 人民检察院 |
| the accused | 被告 |
| Bill of Indictment | 起诉状 |
| public prosecution | 公诉 |

续表

| | |
|---|---|
| the Collegiate Bench | 合议庭 |
| the Clerk | 法院办事员 |
| the Public Prosecutor | 公诉人 |
| adducing evidence | 引证，举证 |
| luggage declaration form | 行李申报表格 |
| intentional crime | 故意犯罪 |
| adjudication | 判决；宣告 |

## ◆ *Unit 8*

| | |
|---|---|
| 人民检察院 | People's Procuratorate |
| 认定事实 | determine facts |
| 刑事诉讼 | criminal proceedings |
| 上诉案件 | appellant case |
| 一审案件 | cases of trials of first instance |
| 原告 | plantiff |
| 驳回反诉 | dismiss a counterclaim |
| 休庭 | The court is adjourned. |
| 宣判 | to pronounce a judgement/sentence; to adjudge |
| 答辩 | to defence; to plea |
| 高级人民法院 | The People's High Court |
| 二审案件 | cases of trials of second instance |
| 答辩陈述书 | The Statement of Defence |
| 二审 | trials of second instance |
| 辩护律师（辩护人） | counsel; the defence |
| 辩论阶段 | stage of court debate |
| 驳回上诉 | reject the appeal |
| 维持原判 | sustain |

| | |
|---|---|
| 驳回请求 | overrule |
| 上诉人 | appellant |
| 答辩状 | Statement of Defense |
| 刑事审判庭第一庭 | The First Court of Criminal Tribunal |
| 合议庭 | the Collegiate Panel |
| 审判长 | Chief Judge |
| 代理审判员 | acting Judge |
| 速录员 | stenographer |
| 指派 | to assign |
| 指定 | to appoint |
| 有利害关系 | have conflict interests of the case |
| 回避 | be challenged |
| 要求回避 | to challenge for cause |
| 传唤（证人） | to summon；to subpoena |
| 控辩双方 | both the prosecuting party and the defence party |
| 原件，原物 | the original |
| 副本 | duplicate |
| 复印件 | a copy of |
| 委托 | to brief；to entrust |
| 支持公诉 | to support the public prosecution |
| 法庭调查 | court investigation |
| 法庭辩论 | court debate |
| 被告人最后陈述 | the final statement of the accused |
| 讯问完毕 | Interrogation is over. |
| dismiss a counterclaim | 驳回反诉 |
| reject a counterclaim | 拒绝反诉 |
| deny/dismiss a motion | 驳回动议 |

续表

| Higher People's Court | 高级人民法院 |
|---|---|
| reject/dismiss the appeal | 驳回/拒绝上诉 |
| sustain the original judgment/ruling | 维持原判 |
| appellant | 上诉人；上诉相关的 |
| adjourn the court | 休庭 |
| pronounce judgment | 宣读判决 |
| determination | （国际法庭）作出裁断/断定 |
| case of trial of first instance | 一审案件 |
| plaintiff | 原告 |
| determine facts | 认定事实 |
| appellate case | 上诉案件 |
| case of trial of second instance | 二审案件 |
| petition for appeal | 上诉申请书 |
| keep in records | 记录在案 |
| deliberation | 审议 |
| The court is in session. | 开庭 |
| The court is in recess. | 暂时休庭 |
| The court is in adjournment. | 休庭 |
| We are adjourned. | 休庭 |
| criminal detention | 罪犯拘留处 |
| detain | 拘留，扣押 |
| arrest | 逮捕 |

## ◆ *Unit 9*

| | |
|---|---|
| Acquittal | 宣告无罪，无罪开释 |
| Challenge for cause | 有正当的理由反对（某陪审员出庭）；请求……回避 |
| Closing argument | 结案陈词 |
| Cross-examination | （交叉）盘问证人 |
| Guilty plea | 认罪答辩［注：指在英美法系中，被告承认有关罪行的每一项控诉。这种情况一般出现在开庭审理之前，检察官与辩护律师互相协商后，达成了辩诉交易（plea bargain），以检察官撤销指控或降格指控为条件，换取被告人的认罪答辩。一般而言，控辩双方达成协议后，法官就不会对该案进行实质性审判，而是根据辩诉交易的内容作出判决。］ |
| Alford plea | 也叫"Alford Guilty plea"，定义同"认罪答辩"。该名称源自美国 1970 年 Henry Alford 被控一级谋杀罪一案。 |
| Jury selection | 挑选陪审团成员 |
| leading question | 诱导性询问；暗示性讯问 |
| Motion for judgment of acquittal | 请求判定无罪 |
| Objection | 反对 |
| Overrule | 驳回 |
| Parole | 假释 |
| Peremptory challenge | 不陈述理由而要求（陪审员）回避；无因回避 |
| Plea agreement | 认罪求情协议 |
| Presumption of innocence | 无罪推定 |
| Subpoena | 传票 |
| Sustain | 维持原判 |
| Voir dire | 对陪审员或证人进行预备审查，以决定他们的能力是否胜任 |

◆ *Unit 10*

| clerk | 法院办事员 |
|---|---|
| bench | 法官担任职务 |
| waive | 放弃……的权利；免除…… |
| bail | 保释 |
| allegedly | 依其申诉；据称 |
| hearsay | 道听途说 |
| incriminate | 使负罪；使有罪 |
| prejudice | 偏见 |
| Destructive Convict | 有严重危害的罪犯 |
| Inadmissible | （尤指法庭上）不可采纳的，不承认的 |
| determination | 裁断 |
| Recognizance | 保释金 |
| probation | 缓刑 |
| Information | 控告 |
| Initial appearance | 初次出庭 |
| Joinder Motion | 联合诉讼的动议 |
| No true bill | 不予起诉；不予受理（注：true bill，大陪审团批准的正式起诉状） |
| Physical evidence | 物证 |
| Preliminary examination | 初步调查 |
| Pre-trial proceeding | 预审程序 |
| Pre-trial release conditions | 预审释放条件 |
| Reciprocal discovery | （控辩双方）互相开示证据 |
| Summons | 传票 |

## ◆ *Unit 11*

| attorney | 律师 |
|---|---|
| felony priors | 有重罪前科 |
| witness | 证人 |
| adored | 非常喜爱的 |
| preliminary | 初步的；预备性质的 |
| reasonable doubt | 合理性怀疑 |
| defendant | 被告 |
| consistent | 一致 |
| conviction | 定罪 |
| counsel | 律师 |
| confess | 供认；坦白 |
| coerce | 胁迫；强制 |
| delusional | 妄想的 |
| discretion | 酌情决定权；裁量权 |
| Equal Protection Clause | 平等权保障条款 |
| amendment | 修正案 |
| civil rights violation | 公民权受到侵害 |
| mandatory | （法律）强制性的 |
| innocent | 无罪的 |
| premeditated | 有预谋的 |
| accused | 被告 |
| verdict | 裁决；判决 |
| conscience | 良心，道德心 |
| unanimous | 一致的 |
| statement of reasons | 理由说明 |
| stipulation | 规定；条款 |

| | |
|---|---|
| supervised release | 监控释放（注：监督释放是最富有创新精神的项目，是指对不能个人具保释放的犯人依其意愿采用的有严密组织进行监督、咨询和治疗的一种非监禁刑措施，而且该措施能使罪犯从中受益。） |
| guilty verdict | 判定有罪 |
| grand jury | 大陪审团 |
| grand jury foreperson | 大陪审团的主席（发言人/首席陪审员） |
| indictment | 控告；起诉状 |

## ◆ *Unit 12*

| | |
|---|---|
| 香港发展局 | Development Bureau |
| 香港建造业议会 | the Construction Industry Council |
| 概括 | to recap |
| 香港特区政府特首 | the Chief Executive of the HKSAR |
| 《建业图新》报告书 | "Construct for Excellence" report |
| 广泛覆盖/涵盖了 | to cover a wide spectrum of . . . |
| 解决索赔和纠纷 | to resolve claims and disputes |
| 现金周转 | cash-flows |
| 承包商 | Contractor |
| 金融海啸 | financial tsunami |
| （工程）保证金 | Retention Money |
| 临时支付 | interim payment |
| 超过……最高达到 | to cap（with）… |
| "按工程进度"的付款方式 | "milestone payment" method |
| 隧道掘进机 | Tunnelling Boring Machine |
| 高时效 | time-efficient |

| 具有成本效益的 | cost-effective |
|---|---|
| 预防胜于治疗 | prevention is better than cure |
| 新工程合同 | New Engineering Contract（NEC） |
| 仲裁 | arbitration |
| 争端解决顾问 | Dispute Resolution Advisors（DRA） |
| 土木工程 | civil engineering works |
| 任期 | tenure |
| 香港国际仲裁中心 | Hong Kong International Arbitration Centre |
| Victoria | 澳大利亚维多利亚州 |
| Magistrates' Court | 裁判法院 |
| VCAT | 维多利亚州民事及行政仲裁委员会 |
| Attorney-General | 总检察长 |
| Litigation | 诉讼 |
| Associate Judges | 陪审法官 |
| Biota pharmaceuticals case | Biota 制药公司诉讼案 |
| Opes Prime litigation | 澳大利亚证券经纪机构一案 |
| pre-action protocols | 诉讼前协议 |
| backfire | 适得其反 |
| synergy | 协同效应 |
| asbestos | 石棉 |
| plaintiff | 原告 |
| mediation | 调解 |
| to vindicate | 澄清；证明……无辜 |
| the Court of Appeal | 上诉法院 |
| the Civil Justice Council | 民事司法委员会 |
| "non adversarial justice" | "非对抗性司法" |
| Chief Counsel Litigation | 首席诉讼律师 |

| | |
|---|---|
| "ADR and the Commonwealth" | "ADR 与澳大利亚联邦" |
| NADRAC | 国家替代争议解决咨询理事会（The National Alternative Dispute Resolution Advisory Council） |
| "soft touch" approach | "儿戏"的方式 |
| cost penalties | 罚款 |
| *Access to Justice Taskforce* report | 《伸张司法正义特别工作组》报告 |
| a whole-of-government approach | 全面的政府手段 |
| The Hon Chief Justice | 尊敬的首席法官阁下（Hon 为 Honerable 的缩写） |
| Professor Sander | 哈佛法学院的弗兰克·桑德教授 |
| ground-breaking | 具有开创性的 |
| *Varieties of Dispute Processing* | 《争端解决之多样化》 |
| Roscoe Pound Conference | 纪念罗斯科·庞德的会议 |
| *The Causes of Popular Dissatisfaction with the Administration of Justice* | 《对司法行政部门普遍不满的原因》（美国社会法学派代表性权威罗斯科·庞德的著作） |
| multi-door courthouses | 多门径法庭 |
| incentives | 激励措施 |
| key stakeholders | 主要利益相关者 |
| be bogged down | （案件）深陷泥沼 |
| Mediator | 调解员 |
| intractable disputes | 极为棘手的争端 |
| the Native Title Amendment Bill | 《土著人权利修正议案》 |
| the Access to Justice | 伸张司法正义之途径 |

续表

| Amendment Bill | 修正议案 |
|---|---|
| National Mediator Accreditation System | （澳大利亚）全国调解员资格认证制度 |

## ◆ *Unit 13*

| 香港律政司司长 | the Secretary for Justice |
|---|---|
| 香港大律师公会 | the Bar Association |
| 比……有优势 | have an edge over/on |
| 给……配备人员 | be manned by |
| 关键所在 | lynchpin |
| 司法的独立性 | judicial independence |
| 保持警觉 | to be vigilant |
| 刑事检控专员 | Director of Public Prosecutions（DPP） |
| 仲裁制度 | arbitration regime |
| 成为……仲裁枢纽 | to serve as a regional hub for international arbitration |
| 跨部门工作小组 | cross-sector Working Group on Mediation |
| 《关于调解的实务指示》 | Practice Direction on mediation |
| 《香港调解守则》 | the Hong Kong Mediation Code |
| 展开"调解为先"的承诺 | to launch the "Mediate First" Pledge |
| 试点项目 | a pilot project |
| 事务律师 | solicitor |
| 出庭律师 | barrister |
| 有限责任合伙制 | limited liability partnerships（LLPs） |
| 《2009 法律执业者（修订）条例草案》 | The Legal Practitioners（Amendment）Bill 2009 |

续表

| （律师在法庭上的）发言权 | rights of audience |
|---|---|
| 高等法院 | the High Court |
| 终审法院 | Court of Final Appeal |
| 二读 | second reading |
| 实施草案 | to enact a bill |
| 立法年度 | legislative session |
| 符合资格要求 | to satisfy the eligibility requirements |
| 《内地与香港关于建立更紧密经贸关系的安排》 | the Closer Economic Partnership Arrangement（CEPA） |
| 《内地与香港民事和商业判决交互强制执行的安排》 | the Mainland on Reciprocal Enforcement of Judgments in Civil and Commercial Matters |
| （条例）生效 | to come into effect |
| 夫妇分居令 | the matrimonial order |
| 《婚姻法律程序与财产条例》 | the Matrimonial Proceedings and Property Ordinance |
| 有（司法）权做 | to have jurisdiction to do sth. |
| 受理申请 | to entertain applications |
| 经济援助 | financial relief |
| 法律界 | legal fraternity |
| 金融行动特别工作组 | Financial Action Task Force（FATF） |
| 打击洗钱和恐怖主义融资 | to combat money laundering and terrorism financing |
| 《联合国禁止酷刑公约》 | the UN Convention Against Torture without compromising the "One Country, Two Systems" principle |
| 《行政安排与当值律师服务的备忘录》 | Memorandum of Administrative Arrangements with the Duty Lawyer Service |

续表

| 在……的前提下 | on the premise that... |
|---|---|
| 固步自封 | to be inertia |
| tailored to | （为某目的）做某事物或适应某事物 |
| impartial adjudication | 公正裁决 |
| award | 判决；裁定 |
| Convention on the Recognition and Enforcement of Foreign Arbitral Awards | 《关于承认及执行外国仲裁裁决》 |
| New York Convention | 纽约公约 |
| UNCITRAL | 联合国国际贸易法委员会（贸易法委员会） |
| UNCITRAL Model Law on International Commercial Arbitration | 《联合国国际贸易法委员会国际商事仲裁示范法》 |
| Explanatory Note | 《示范法注释》 |
| at the forefront of | 在最前沿 |
| President Martti Ahtisaari | （芬兰前总统）马尔蒂·阿赫蒂萨里，2008 年诺贝尔和平奖获得者 |
| inaugural conference | 就职招待会 |
| Asian Mediation Association（AMA） | 亚洲调解协会 |
| Delhi Mediation Centr4 | 印度调解中心 |
| a holistic and sophisticated dispute resolution centre | 一个全面且缜密的纠纷调解中心 |
| issue of the writ | 发出手令 |
| disposal of the trial | 处理审讯 |
| underpin | 支撑、巩固 |
| resort to litigation | 诉诸诉讼 |

续表

| an arbitration venue of choice | 仲裁之都 |
|---|---|
| ICC International Court of Arbitration | 国际商会（ICC）国际仲裁法院 |
| Geneva | 日内瓦 |
| Zurich | 苏黎世 |
| clauses | 法律条款 |
| to gain ground internationally | 国际地位得到提高 |
| Maxwell Chambers | 麦士威议事厅 |
| state-of-the-art facilities | 国际一流的设备 |
| acrimony | （争论）剑拔弩张 |
| a protracted litigation | 被延长的诉讼 |
| Ethos | （集体、社团、文化的）气质、道德观、思想或信仰 |
| last gap | 最后的隔阂 |
| Subordinate Courts | 初级/下级法院 |
| Community Mediation Centre（CMC） | 社区调解中心 |
| in the global context | 在国际上 |
| culmination | 巅峰；顶点 |
| since inception | 自成立以来 |
| capacity-building | 能力建设 |

◆ *Unit 14*

| 司法制度 | Judicial system；Judiciary |
|---|---|
| 改革试点 | pilot reform |
| 新型监狱体制 | a new prison system |

续表

| 社区矫正 | community correction |
|---|---|
| 律师执业 | the licensing system for lawyers |
| 律师收费制度 | the lawyer fee system |
| 司法考试 | judicial examination |
| 社会主义法治理念 | the socialist concept of law |
| 优惠照顾政策 | (to adopt) a favor policy on... |
| 法律援助 | legal aid |
| 司法鉴定 | judicial appraisal |
| adjudicating | 判决，裁定 |
| discharging | 获释；解除（权利、义务等） |
| litigation | 诉讼 |
| collegiate | 合议 |
| downturn | 衰退；低迷时期 |
| legislature | 立法机关 |
| teething (problems/troubles) | 比喻创业初期遇到的小问题 |
| mediation | 调解 |
| enactment | （法律法规等的）制定 |
| tribunal | 法院；审理团；特别法庭 |
| corner on | 胁迫；威胁 |
| luncheon speech | 午餐会致辞 |
| guild system | 行会制度 |
| vulnerability | 弱点；易受攻击（的方面） |
| keynote | 主基调 |
| address bottom line | 提出底线 |
| orthogonal | 垂直的，直角的 |
| decentralized | 权力下放 |
| Britannica | 大不列颠 |

| misalignment | 不重合；误差方向 |
|---|---|
| grapple with sweepstake | 独占彩票或赌博的奖金 |
| differentiate | 区分；鉴别 |
| empower | 授权，准许，使之有……的权力 |
| leverage | 杠杆作用；杠杆式借贷；位置上享有优势 |

# 参考文献

S. Berk-Seligson, *The Bilingual Courtroom*, The University of Chicago Press, 1990.

Alicia B. Edwards, *The Practice of Court Interpreting*, John Benjamins Publishing Company, 1995.

Holly Mikkelson, *Introduction to Court Interpreting*, St. Jerome Publishing, 2000.

Franz Pöchhacker, *Introducing Interpreting Studies*, London: Routeldge, 2004.

Mark Shuttleworth, Moira Cowie, *Dictionary of Translation*, Shanghai, Shanghai Foreign Language Education Press, 2004.

杜碧玉主编：《法律口译教程》，对外经济贸易大学出版社 2006 年版。

李克兴、张新红：《法律文本与法律翻译》，中国对外翻译出版公司 2006 年版。

纪坡民："'英美法系'和'大陆法系'"，载《中国税务》2008 年第 1 期。

靖鸣、刘锐："记者招待会的功能和作用"，载《改革与战略》2004 第 2 期。

齐树洁："我国司法体制改革的回顾与展望"，载《毛泽东邓小平理论研究》2009 年第 4 期。

宋靖："完善我国立法听证会的立法构想"，载《福建政法管理干部学院学报》2007 年第 1 期。

沈四宝："现代国际仲裁制度"，载《人民日报》2001 年 8 月 3 日。

王保安、关晨霞："中国公职律师制度研究"，载《中国司法》2008 年第 7 期。

王芳："'法治'演进与我国法理学发展"，载《法制与社会》2010 年第 22 期。

王煊林、贾陈亮："我国立法听证制度的现状及完善"，载《河南公安高等专科学校学报》2007 年第 1 期。

杨映娜："试论公职律师制度的建立与完善"，载《中山大学学报论丛》2005 年第 4 期。

袁泉、郭玉军："ADR——西方盛行的解决民商事争议的热门制度"，载《法学评论》1999 年第 1 期。

赵军峰："法庭言语行为与言语策略"，载《广东外语外贸大学学报》2007 年第 2 期。

赵军峰："言语行为与法庭口译"，载杜金榜主编：《中国法律语言学展望》，对外经济贸易大学出版社 2007 年版。

赵军峰、陈珊："中西法庭口译研究回顾与展望"，载《中国科技翻译》2008 第 3 期。

赵军峰、张锦："作为机构守门人的法庭口译员角色研究"，载《中国翻译》2011 年第 1 期。

最高人民法院："深化司法体制改革　保障社会公平正义"，载《求是》2010 第 8 期。

# 后 记

本书的完成得益于身边无法细数的诸多师友。首先，非常感谢中国银行北京高级研修院赵春堂院长、李秀华副院长、徐葆乐副院长、刘庆萍资深经理等领导同事对我的真切关怀与无私帮助。感谢本人曾任教的中国政法大学外国语学院历任领导与同仁对我的支持鼓励，尤其感谢本书主编赵军峰教授一直以来对本人的提携、关心、鞭策和帮助！本书的出版还得益于中国政法大学出版社资深编辑丁春晖老师高效细致的工作。

法律翻译类教材尤其是法律口译教材编写背后的艰辛人所共知。本书所涉及之中国司法制度、英美法律制度及其相关术语的翻译颇费周章，即使经过反复推敲、力求优中选优，但仍恐词不达意。加之编者才疏学浅，鲁鱼亥豕之谬恐难幸免，希望广大读者不吝赐教，电子邮箱：fadawgy@163.com。

本书分工如下：

张新红：总审校

罗雯琪：第一单元、第二单元、第四单元

王超：第三单元、第十三单元、第十四单元

赵军峰：第五单元、第十二单元

张鲁平、管雯：第六单元、第七单元、第八单元

张鲁平、胡晓凡：第九单元、第十单元、第十一单元

赵军峰全书统稿

本书编写过程中得到了好友张伟律师的鼎力支持，感谢他提供的大量一手资料及对法律术语翻译的专业解答！

感谢好友中信建投证券投资银行业务管理委员会高级副总裁宋杨先生对于本书编写付出的宝贵时间和精力！

感谢好友中国证券投资者保护基金有限责任公司高级经理罗丹老师通读本书并站在专业译员视角提出的独到见解！

　　感谢资深法律译员刘芳女士百忙之中为本教材提供了宝贵素材并解答专业问题！

　　感谢的名单还可以列很长，但限于篇幅有限及编者的记忆偏差，肯定存在挂一漏万，在此并致谢忱！衷心感谢曾经在白云山下、云溪河畔为本人的成长付出无限辛劳，默默给予无私帮助的杜金榜教授、张新红教授、袁传有教授、徐章宏教授、葛云锋教授、韩征瑞教授以及广外枫林学社的师友们！

　　感谢家人的陪伴和支持，殷殷之情切切之意，思之念之。

编者于百望山下<br>2023 年 7 月